Raising a Nation

Raising a Nation

10 Reasons Every American Has a Stake in Child Care for All

ELLIOT HASPEL

Oxford University Press is a department of the University of Oxford.
It furthers the University's objective of excellence in research, scholarship,
and education by publishing worldwide. Oxford is a registered trade mark of
Oxford University Press in the UK and in certain other countries.

Published in the United States of America by Oxford University Press
198 Madison Avenue, New York, NY 10016, United States of America.

© Oxford University Press 2025

All rights reserved. No part of this publication may be reproduced, stored in a retrieval system, transmitted, used for text and data mining, or used for training artificial intelligence, in any form or by any means, without the prior permission in writing of Oxford University Press, or as expressly permitted by law, by license or under terms agreed with the appropriate reprographics rights organization. Inquiries concerning reproduction outside the scope of the above should be sent to the Rights Department, Oxford University Press, at the address above.

You must not circulate this work in any other form
and you must impose this same condition on any acquirer.

Library of Congress Cataloging-in-Publication Data
Names: Haspel, Elliot author
Title: Raising a nation : 10 reasons every American has a stake in child care for all /
by Elliot Haspel.
Description: New York : Oxford University Press, [2025] |
Includes bibliographical references and index.
Identifiers: LCCN 2025002788 (print) | LCCN 2025002789 (ebook) |
ISBN 9780197799291 hardback |ISBN 9780197799314 epub | ISBN 9780197799321 epub
Subjects: LCSH: Child care—Government policy—United States |
Child care—Social aspects—United States |Family policy—United States | United States—Social policy
Classification: LCC HQ778.63 .H377 2025 (print) | LCC HQ778.63 (ebook) |
DDC 362.71/20973—dc23/eng/20250331
LC record available at https://lccn.loc.gov/2025002788
LC ebook record available at https://lccn.loc.gov/2025002789

DOI: 10.1093/oso/9780197799291.001.0001

Pod

The manufacturer's authorised representative in the EU for product safety is
Oxford University Press España S.A., Parque Empresarial San Fernando de Henares,
Avenida de Castilla, 2 – 28830 Madrid (www.oup.es/en).

For the caregivers, in all your wild diversity.

Contents

Introduction: What We Talk About When We Talk
About Child Care ... 1

1. The Solidarity Case ... 15
2. The Community Case ... 30
3. The Family Values Case ... 45
4. The Patriotic Case ... 62
5. The Parenthood and Childhood Case ... 77
6. The Racial and Gender Equity Case ... 93
7. The Antipoverty Case ... 112
8. The Security Case ... 127
9. The Economic Case ... 141
10. The American Dream Case ... 158

Conclusion: The Child-Care System America Needs
and Parents Deserve ... 169

Acknowledgments ... 176
Endnotes ... 177
Index ... 198

Introduction

What We Talk About When We Talk About Child Care

The President of the United States was talking about child care. On a picturesque April day in the Rose Garden—one of those days that makes you forget Washington, DC was built on a literal swamp—he was surrounded by his Secretary of Labor, Secretary of Health and Human Services, members of Congress, business leaders, and the First Lady.

This was unusual: Generally, U.S. presidents paid little attention to child care. But William Jefferson Clinton was there, in 1998, to make the case that child care was an important part of the American economy.

"One of the reasons the business community is interested in this," Clinton asserted, "is that enlightened business leaders understand … if you permit people to do the right thing by their children, you wind up having a happier, more upbeat, more affirmative, more positive business environment, and ultimately the business enterprise will be more successful because the workers are also successful at home. That's what this whole business is about, taking care of their children and not asking their parents to choose between being good parents and good workers. It all comes down to that."[1]

Clinton's successors took up his rhetorical mantle. Barack Obama devoted significant time in his 2015 State of the Union address to the issue, declaiming that, "In today's economy, when having both parents in the workforce is an economic necessity for many families, we need affordable, high-quality childcare more than ever. It's not a nice-to-have—it's a must-have. So it's time we stop treating childcare as a side issue, or as a women's issue, and treat it like the national economic priority that it is for all of us."[2]

A few years later, even Donald Trump would concur. "With more women working today than ever before, we now have a historic opportunity to enact long-overdue reforms," President Trump declared in 2019, adding that, "In more than 60% of American homes, both parents work. Yet many struggle to afford child care, which often costs more than $10,000 per year. And it's devastating to families, frankly."[3]

Raising a Nation. Elliot Haspel, Oxford University Press. © Oxford University Press (2025).
DOI: 10.1093/oso/9780197799291.003.0001

Underneath all this speechifying was a challenge that Clinton laid out at the end of his Rose Garden remarks: "[W]e have a fundamental choice: Do you believe that the early years are as important as all the evidence says? Do you believe that we could hardly do anything better for America's families than to relieve them of the burden of being terribly worried about their children while they're at work? In other words, do you believe that this should be an urgent priority for America?"

The answer from government, and society more broadly, has been a resounding "no."

Although there have been modest increases in child-care funding, particularly at the state level, child care in America largely continues to be a hellscape more than a quarter-century after Clinton spoke. Parent fees are sky-high, supply is desperately low, child-care providers are paid a pittance, stay-at-home parents are ignored, and quality is questionable at best. Although the pandemic shone a bright light on how important child care is, it also took a sector that was barely treading water and dragged it into the deep.

The problem, I believe, is that we skipped a step, a step so fundamental that skipping it has torpedoed the chances of winning an effective child-care system despite decade after decade of pain that crosses geographic and ideological borders. We have never established that good child care belongs among the pantheon of American values. Because of what it means for the nation, that is exactly where child care belongs.

The economic argument for child care is valid—I have made it countless times myself—but far, far too narrow. It is a morally impoverished rationale that only gets the unconvinced to peek in the door. (It is also not new: scholarship on child care's economic return on investment goes back to at least the early 1970s.)[4] Far more compelling cases are needed in order to build the public opinion and political will to create a functional, sustainable, affordable, and high-quality system. Together, these cases can help create a societal mindset shift: taking child care from a private service useful only instrumentally to let parents work, to an essential support for strong children, strong families, strong communities, and a strong nation.

Indeed, given the amount of recurring public funding that needs to be unlocked to build a truly effective child-care system—experts calculate it will take at least $175 billion a year (in 2024 dollars), and I believe that's quite low—the economic argument does not offer a credible path to victory.[5] Yet major public funding is a prerequisite for a functional child-care system: As the journalist Annie Lowrey has written, when it comes to child care, "the math does not work. It will never work. No other country makes it work without a major investment from government."[6]

***

I argue in this book that there are (at least) ten distinct cases for why American society should invest in a strong child-care system, albeit tied together by common themes. The economic case is one of the cases, but only one of them.

I will note that you, the reader, are unlikely to find each of these cases equally compelling. That's fine. It's the same for me: I am not personally moved by the fact that child care has serious national security consequences. But there are those who are persuaded by such a case who are entirely unmoved by the cases that most move me. As the climate scientist Katharine Hayhoe has written, "on . . . issues with moral [or values] implications, we tend to believe that everyone should care for the same self-evident reasons we do. If they don't, we all too often assume they lack morals. But most people do have morals and are acting according to them; they're just different from ours. And if we are aware of these differences, we can speak to them."[7]

I also want to note that our values are significantly shaped by our life experiences and our identities. I am a white, middle-class male writing about child care, an issue that falls heavily on the shoulders of mothers and especially burdens mothers of color. Child care is also a sector whose workforce is almost entirely female and disproportionately made up of individuals who are lower-income, people of color, and/or immigrants. This does not mean I shouldn't comment on child care—in fact, I would submit we need a broad coalition of champions, very much including men—but it means my perspective around the ten cases is influenced by these factors. As for my personal child-care history, my two daughters have had a variety of child-care situations, including primary care provided by myself and my wife, a brief stint in a nanny share, years spent at a child-care center, and at ages seven and nine they now attend a mashup of after-school programs and summer camps. With that awareness in mind, I will try to bring in the voices of those with different experiences, different ideologies, and different identities.

Combined, these cases generate a framework for helping lawmakers and the public see that access to high-quality child care is not purely an individual family obligation but rather a societal imperative. That everyone—parents and nonparents alike—benefits mightily from a strong child-care system, and often in unexpected ways we too rarely consider. It may take a village to raise a child, but the raising of that child also benefits the village. We have forgotten the second clause.

Similarly, each case contains a rejoinder to the atomized stress-filled pressure cooker of modern life. By rebuilding bonds of solidarity, enhancing parents' sense of self-determination, and advancing a fairer and freer society, child care can be an entry point for restoring our weakened social fabric.

***

This book veers between the philosophical and the practical, and that is intentional. Unlike issues such as public education, environmentalism, or even warfare, child care has been subject to vanishingly little philosophical analysis. Although innovators like Maria Montessori certainly had something to say about child care—and arguments over the proper way to raise a child surely go back millennia—the work of such experts has been primarily concerned with early childhood pedagogy (*how* to teach), not whether and why a publicly funded child-care system should exist or what form such a system should take. The esteemed developmental psychologist Alison Gopnik has quipped that so little philosophical work has gone into caregiving generally that there cannot yet be conversations about "rethinking" care—we first need conversations about "thinking" care.[8]

Part of the reason, I surmise, is that modern child care—in the form of widespread, regular use of external non-kin caregivers—is a relatively new need. To be sure, there have been child-care providers of a sort for all human history, ranging from the communal "alloparents" of hunter-gatherer tribes to the multigenerational farms where most people lived until the Industrial Revolution. Similarly, mothers have worked in tandem with child-rearing duties since time immemorial, both on the aforementioned farms and, after urbanization, doing paid work at home such as making and mending garments. (Indeed, the single-earner "male-breadwinner" model was only a majority of marriages for a bare four decades, from the 1920s until the 1960s, and even then peaked in 1940 at only 57% of marriages.[9]) Some percentage of American mothers—particularly the poor, widowed, immigrants, and women of color—have always worked outside the home, to say nothing of the enslaved mothers forced to do so.[10]

It was not until the past fifty years, however, that America experienced a particular confluence of events: huge numbers of mothers—including middle-class and white mothers—entering the labor force as the economy, gender norms, and legal status of women were all reshaped and layered onto existing trends of mass urbanization and a precipitous decline in multigenerational households. The need for a true child-care system is thus a recent change, but also one that is almost surely permanent.

To put a fine point on it: In 1950, barely more than one in ten women with a child under the age of five worked outside the home (though again, plenty doubled up with child care and paid work done inside the home).[11] By 1975, the figure was well over a third, and grew steadily from there to its current level of more than two in three. In real terms, the changes over the past half-century represent upward of ten million more children needing care every year.

Given this history, child care is in (pardon the pun) its infancy. To continue the education analogy, versions of schools existed as far back as 2000–2500 BCE in ancient Mesopotamia and China. Figures such as Aristotle and Confucius contributed educational theories and frameworks. It's little wonder that child care is pigeonholed as a mere work support while K–12 education enjoys $800 billion a year in public funding and an entire layer of democratic governance in the form of school boards.

The framing we use around child care is far from an academic question. As sociologist Susan Prentice, who is also a Canadian child-care advocate, has written, "[frames] encompass not just what to think but how to think about something," and they can inspire entire social movements.[12]

Frames can be incredibly powerful, and they are frequently contested: Many experts credit framing changes as catalysts for major policy and public opinion shifts.[13] Examples range from the declining popularity of nuclear power as the focus veered from cheap energy to environmental and health risks, to how the marriage equality movement became far more successful when it changed course from legalistic arguments to the moral case that love is love.[14] Especially when an issue has more than one viable frame, which one becomes prominent in the public eye is highly consequential. For instance, schools, as we'll talk about more than once in this book, provide child care. Yet that is not how schools are primarily viewed.

Thus, there is a tremendous need to probe child care in order to develop the overarching frames and distinct cases that enable the necessary mindset shifts. These questions will echo throughout the book in such questions as: What is child care *for*? *Who* is child care for? What societal values does a nation's child-care system reflect?

***

Child care is a strange term because it encompasses so many different meanings. Writers' style guides can't even agree whether it deserves a space between the two words. At its core, child care is not a program or policy, but the human activity of caregiving for children. That activity has multiple components. When Dr. Benjamin Spock wrote his bestselling *Baby and Childcare*, he didn't mean, "Who's caring for the child?" He meant managing feeding, cleaning, sleeping practices, and other general care.

The problem is that alternative terms are inartful at best, and factually incorrect at worst. "Daycare" leaves out stay-at-home parents and family, friends, and neighbor caregivers, and ignores the fact that plenty of care happens at night (including overnight programs). "Early childhood education" conjures up narrow ideas of pre-Kindergarten and excludes school-aged children who need care before—and/or after—school and over summer break.

So, acknowledging its deficiencies, in this book I will use the term child care. By child care, I mean *the supportive care of children that occurs on a regular, recurring, and time-intensive basis*. Child care, in this formulation, can be delivered in any setting and by any caregiver. That means the term is inclusive of child-care centers, both secular and religious; family child-care homes; nannies and au pairs; family, friends and neighbor caregivers; and stay-at-home parents. It is also inclusive of what is called preschool or pre-K. Finally, this definition is agnostic on age: Care needs for children who are in elementary or middle school may be relatively less acute than in the early years, but settings that serve those kids are no less a form of child care.

Child care also inherently implies learning. Care and learning are inextricably linked, and not just in early childhood. As early childhood researcher and author Ellen Galinsky once told me in an interview, "All learning is relationship-based, all development is relationship-based. It's a fallacy that we can separate out our need to belong, to be respected, to be supported, to be challenged—all of those things that happen in an educational setting are relationship-based and come from care."[15] On a practical level, again, educational institutions like schools absolutely serve as child care. (If you don't believe me, ask any parent who had school-aged kids in 2020: My eldest daughter was part of the Dumpster fire known as Zoom Kindergarten.) So the idea that care and education are separate is simply wrong.

What "child care" is *not* referring to, in my usage, are specific child-rearing decisions a la Dr. Spock. Nor is it referring to mere "custodial" care, like hiring a babysitter; that is, very short-term, irregular care that is primarily devoted to simple supervision. Babysitters often play an important role in families' lives, but can reasonably be put outside the scope of this discussion.

So with those contours in mind, let's look at the current state of play in American child care.

A Child Care 101 Primer

If you're already well versed in child-care policy, feel free to skip the next two sections. If you're not, then these sections seek to answer two main questions: (1) What are the various types of child care? And (2) Why is child care so expensive, especially when child-care educators are paid so poorly?

Regular child care can be provided by any (or a combination) of the following. Importantly, high-quality care can be delivered in *any* of these settings*:

- *Child-care centers*: standalone multiclassroom facilities, or classrooms located within a bigger facility such as a school or house of worship. Centers can be secular or religious. With some exceptions for faith-based centers, centers must be licensed and regulated by their state. Center enrollments generally range from 20 to 200.
- *Family child-care homes*: programs operated out of the providers' home, where they care for a small number (usually between two and twelve) of children unrelated to the provider. Over a certain number of children—the threshold varies by state—family child-care programs must be licensed and regulated by their state.
- *Family, friends, and neighbor (FFN) caregivers*: as the name suggests, regular care provided by a trusted relative, friend, or a neighbor. These arrangements can be unpaid or paid. FFN caregivers may, in most states, optionally choose to register with their state and become

---

* A few nuances: "Pre-Kindergarten" (Pre-K) or "preschool" usually refers to child care geared toward four-year-olds, and sometimes three-year-olds. Forty-four states and Washington, DC offer some form of free public pre-K, although there is wide variation in eligibility criteria. Pre-K is most commonly provided via public schools, while many states allow private child-care centers to participate in their systems, and some allow participation from family child-care homes.

Head Start, and its companion program Early Head Start, are funded by the federal government. Head Start serves four- and three-year-olds with free child care and supportive services for the whole family, while Early Head Start serves children younger than three. Local entities, from school districts to nonprofit agencies, can apply to operate a Head Start program, and the services are again delivered mainly, though not exclusively, in school or center-based settings.

eligible to receive payments if the child they are caring for receives governmental child-care subsidies.
- *Nannies and au pairs:* domestic workers hired to provide child-care assistance among other services. Au pairs are foreign nationals approved by the U.S. government who live with the employing family, while nannies can be live-in or live-out.
- *Stay-at-home parents:* Parents who provide primary child care for their own child(ren).
- *After-school and summer programs/camps:* programs geared toward school-aged children outside of the normal school day/year. These programs are generally licensed and regulated by their state.

So where are America's children cared for? For the roughly 21 million children below the age of six, per 2019 data—the most recent year for which reliable numbers are available—about 40 percent receive primary care from a parent and have no regular nonparental care arrangement.[16] Among children who do receive care, around 65 percent attend a center-based program, around 20 percent attend a family child-care program, and 38 percent receive recurring care from a relative. Those numbers combined come to over 100 percent because many families utilize multiple care arrangements during any given week. (There are, as you might expect, important differences related to the age of the child: For infants younger than twelve months, for instance, center usage plummets while FFN usage spikes.)

School-aged children also have a variety of care settings. Approximately 10 million attend after-school programs, though surveys suggest at least 20 million more families would like to make use of these programs if slots were available and affordable.[17] Another 26 million children attend some form of summer camp.[18] A small percentage—4 percent of elementary schoolers and 18 percent of middle schoolers—take care of themselves, while the remaining families seem to cobble together a variety of FFN and parental care. Some family child-care providers also offer before- and after-school services in which school-aged children join the younger ones during those hours.

***

The financial equation for a given child-care provider naturally depends on the provider type. Child-care centers and family child-care homes, in particular, are marked by extremely high labor costs. That is the result of early child-care programs rightly requiring low (and legally mandated) adult-to-child ratios. While requirements vary by state, common ratios are

1:4 for infants, between 1:6 and 1:8 for toddlers, and between 1:10 to 1:12 for three- and four-year-olds.[19] This means child-care programs require *a lot* of staff. As a point of comparison, staff-to-user ratios are closer to 1:25 in an elementary school, 1:100 in a restaurant, and 1:1000+ in the case of airport gate agents to travelers. This is why there is no real way to innovate or otherwise overhaul the basic model of group child care: Because it requires a lot of grown humans to care for small humans, child care will always be—and should always be!—labor intensive.

To illustrate what this means in practice, consider a budget breakdown that a West Virginia center shared with American Public Media's *Marketplace*.[20] The program, A Place to Grow Children's Center, spends *78 percent* of its budget on payroll. The next highest expense is supplies, at 5 percent.

With labor costs so dominant, child-care programs respond by keeping wages low: As of this writing, child-care educators make a median salary of $14.60 an hour, or around $30,000 a year, on par with parking lot attendants and dog walkers.[21] A majority lack basic benefits such as employer-sponsored health insurance and retirement. Even still, many programs have trouble keeping the lights on. The problem is that despite charging parents $10,000 or more a year, programs are frequently *undercharging* parents compared to the true cost of running a sustainable program with well-compensated staff.

We understand this gap intuitively in other labor-intensive services and respond with public funding. Public school teachers and firefighters may be underpaid, but they make solid middle-class salaries with decent benefits; the median salary for an elementary school teacher is around $60,000, for firefighters around $52,000. There is no waiting list for your neighborhood public school and, in general, the fire department will show up to your house in short order if it's on fire. These realities are only possible because the United States spends, for instance, upward of $800 billion a year in public funding for K–12 schools. That's around $14,000 per student. By contrast, the United States spends less than $40 billion a year in public funding for child care, the majority of which is concentrated on four-year-olds. That translates to less than $1,000 per child below the age of three.[22] Imagine how things would go if we reduced the K–12 per-student expenditure to $1,000, and you'll start to understand the structural problem with our current child-care system.

It's worth noting that some of the economic strictures of child care in America and peer nations are the result of living in wealthy countries. Child care—like other human-intensive services such as elder care and K–12 education—is caught up in what is known as the "Baumol Effect."

Named after economist William Baumol, the concept means that increased productivity as a nation pushes up everyone's wages, but this also makes employees in sectors that are *not* getting more productive cost more. As economists Eric Helland and Alex Tabarrok wrote in a report on the Baumol Effect in health and education, "the higher prices of some goods are an inevitable consequence of economic growth."[23]

A simple way to think about the Baumol Effect is to compare a widget factory worker and a child-care educator. Thanks to advances in technology, the factory worker may be 100 times more productive at making widgets than they were a half-century ago. Because the widget factory is so much more productive and profitable, wages begin to rise, which in turn puts upward pressure on the cost of living. (One can argue whether they rise in fair proportion to workers' labor, especially compared to the salaries of the widget company executives, but that's a story for a different book.)

Our child-care educator, however, is not making widgets. There is no technological replacement for a human adult-to-human child relationship (sorry, Snoo bassinet!). Technology may be able to help on the margins, like making it faster to enroll a child, but generally one adult is caring for six or so toddlers now, then, and in the future. But the cost of living is still increasing for our educator, and the child-care program still needs to compete in a labor market where the widget factory is starting to offer considerably better compensation: Thus, the cost of child care rises.

The Baumol Effect explains why public investment in human services is so essential. K–12 education budgets have also been rising, but despite accusations from some quarters that this is due to administrative bloat or overregulation, Helland and Tabarrok—who are, it should be said, writing for the very libertarian Mercatus Center at George Mason University—conclude it is mainly about labor costs. The pair write that it is "fairly easy to explain why expenditures per elementary and secondary student increased by a factor of more than five between 1950 and 2013: the costs of instruction—most importantly higher teacher compensation, but also the cost of hiring more teachers—increased by a factor of more than five during this period."

Finally, the COVID-19 pandemic broke the child-care sector's fragile equilibrium. In the post-pandemic labor market, base compensation in other low-wage industries such as retail and fast food has risen significantly, in what is broadly a positive trend for American workers.[24] Regardless of whether the work of child care is more rewarding than packaging items in a warehouse, it is no wonder many child-care programs are struggling mightily to attract and retain staff.

Child care is an expensive service to provide. It will always be an expensive service to provide. That's OK. Although reasonable actions should be taken to limit costs, some services are by their nature not going to come cheap. Baumol himself points this out, writing that, "No matter how painful rising medical and educational bills may be, *society can afford them*, and there is no need to deny them to ourselves or to the less affluent members of our society, or indeed to the world"[25] (italics his). Instead of wishing it weren't so, what's required is figuring out how to unlock the necessary dollars to support our nation's children and families.

The Ten Cases, Briefly

The ten cases we will explore together are:

- The Solidarity Case—How child care can create bonds between parents that power broader positive societal changes.
- The Community Case—How child care impacts the vitality of communities, including public health and safety as well as the health of faith communities.
- The Family Values Case—How child care can be a support that leads to strong, healthy families able to pass on their values and traditions to the next generation.
- The Parenthood and Childhood Case—How child care not only supports healthy child development, but supports healthy parenting and optimal experiences in the early childhood years themselves.
- The Patriotic Case—How child care promotes democracy and a sense of patriotic unity, and how parents perform a public service.
- The Racial and Gender Equity Case—How child care is deeply intertwined with questions of gender and racial equity in ways that increase fairness for parents and nonparents alike.
- The Anti-Poverty Case—How child care is one of the most effective anti-poverty strategies available.
- The Security Case—How child care improves national and neighborhood security by helping the armed services have a robust recruitment pool, retain servicemembers, build America's global competitiveness, and maintain neighborhood cohesion.

- The Economic Case—How, now put in its proper context, child care is (despite my earlier barb) an essential piece of the infrastructure that keeps American businesses humming, and powers both innovation and entrepreneurship.
- The American Dream Case—How a strong child-care system moves the nation toward a place where all children and families can thrive with freedom and self-determination.

Together, these cases are like paints in a palette, illustrating the vibrancy of child care as a topic. In the modern era, child care and strong families—and, in turn, strong communities and a strong nation—are inextricably tied together.

Child care is, of course, not a panacea. To ensure widespread well-being and opportunity for families, America needs a holistic approach. As my colleague Joe Waters has written, "the United States has never had a comprehensive policy focused on ensuring the stability, flourishing, and health of American children and families."[26] Such policy includes child care and paid family leave and child tax credits, to be sure, and also requires affordable family housing and health care, as well as good jobs with predictable scheduling and family-sustaining wages.

Culture plays a crucial role as well. This can show up in the built environment of communities—for example, is there easy stroller access? Are there wide sidewalks, family-friendly restaurants, and ample parks and playgrounds? Do airports have a special lane for families with young children? And how are parents made to feel? Is the presence of children in public spaces like coffee shops and buses treated with disdainful glares, or is it embraced with smiles and offers of assistance?

But child care stands out as a unique doorway to larger social reform. The transition to parenthood is well-noted as a crucible that can spark personal and political transformation.[27] It is a period of exceptional vulnerability and need, of re-evaluating one's priorities and place in society. Next to pregnancy-related medical care, child care is the first major hinge point that most new parents face—and, as we will see, it quickly becomes a defining feature of life for years to come. If met with a policy and cultural response of welcoming abundance, we build toward an empowered society of collective care that is focused on human flourishing, with all its attendant benefits. If met with a policy and cultural response of do-it-yourself scarcity tied mainly to economic outcomes, we reinforce a low-trust society of winners and losers, with all its attendant ills.

On Flourishing

Before we begin, I want to spend a moment on the slippery-sounding metric of "flourishing." In recent years, Harvard University's Human Flourishing Project has been researching how to capture flourishing in a more definable sense. The Project, led by Tyler VanderWeele, posits five distinct domains of flourishing, along with one cross-cutting domain.[28] The domains are:

- Happiness and Life Satisfaction
- Mental and Physical Health
- Meaning and Purpose
- Character and Virtue
- Close Social Relationships

And the cross-cutting domain, as you might suspect from what is not on the list, is Financial and Material Stability, which the researchers consider not a dimension of flourishing in and of itself, but an enabling factor for sustaining flourishing in the other domains.

The words of another would-be president resonate here. In 1968, three months before his assassination, Robert F. Kennedy gave a speech at the University of Kansas. Kennedy offered:

> Too much and for too long, we seemed to have surrendered personal excellence and community values in the mere accumulation of material things… Yet the gross national product does not allow for the health of our children, the quality of their education or the joy of their play. It does not include the beauty of our poetry or the strength of our marriages, the intelligence of our public debate or the integrity of our public officials. It measures neither our wit nor our courage, neither our wisdom nor our learning, neither our compassion nor our devotion to our country, it measures everything in short, except that which makes life worthwhile. And it can tell us everything about America except why we are proud that we are Americans.[29]

The economy matters, and child care matters to the economy. No one can argue otherwise. But an effective child-care system fuels a broader sort of prosperity. If schools are primarily for conveying academic education and the electric grid primarily for generating power, then I submit child care is primarily for supporting the healthy development of children, families, and communities. It can move us toward a better America and, indeed, make us proud that we are Americans.

Let's see why.

Chapter 1
The Solidarity Case

Parents were in the streets demanding child care.

In New York City, in Philadelphia, in Cleveland, in Southern California, mothers and their toddlers—even a handful of men—marched. Their signs bore slogans like, "A Permanent Child Care Program Is the State's Responsibility!" and "Food Prices Rise—Mothers Must Work!"[1] Thousands of letters and phone calls poured into politicians' offices at the local, state, and federal level. The President of the United States got involved.

This wasn't the 2021 debate over President Biden's proposed Build Back Better Act. This was 1946. (It may fill one with rage to note that, as a benchmark of how little progress has been made over the past seventy-five years, one could colorize pictures from those protests, update the fashion, but need do little-to-no work on the slogans.)

For the briefest moment, America had a publicly funded child-care system of sorts. During World War II, as the men shipped out to the beaches of Normandy and Iwo Jima, women were needed in the factories. Tucked into an infrastructure bill known as the Lanham Act, the federal government (reluctantly) set up child-care centers accessible to all working mothers regardless of income. They were programs of remarkably high quality. At their height, around 3,000 of these Lanham Act centers served nearly 150,000 young children.[2]

Then the men came home.

A combination of traditionalist gender norms, concerns around government spending, and fear of returning men clashing with women over the same pot of jobs led to a prevailing sense among policymakers that mothers should, by and large, exit the labor force.[3] The overall feeling was summed up by Congressman Rolla McMillen, who stated bluntly in a 1945 committee hearing that women should be "discouraged [from working] and driven, if necessary, back to their homes, where they belong, to look after these children."[4] (Fritz Lanham, the committee chairman for whom the legislation was named, agreed "that is true as a general principle" and "of course, we all hope we can get rid of these projects as soon as possible and get back to a normal basis.")

Many mothers, however, were not ready to give up on the idea that they could contribute both inside *and* outside of the home; that, in fact, access to child care made them stronger mothers. This was not about the economy. This was about women seeking solidarity as they fought together for opportunities to continue engaging in both the domestic and public spheres—and for the idea that those spheres were not as separate as they might seem.

For instance, in a 1946 article for the magazine *The Child*, Glenna B. Johnson reported: "Through their wartime experience [mothers] now know there is something much better than the trial-and-error way of finding child care for their children . . . They know how much better children, mothers, and families thrive when they work out their child-care problems on a community basis."[5] Johnson goes on to talk about the fruitful partnerships between women and child development specialists at the Lanham centers, adding that mothers "learned that working out child care problems together produced results that working at them alone often failed to achieve."

Indeed, during this era many women pushed back hard against the idea that child care was a purely individual responsibility. No less an influencer than Eleanor Roosevelt wrote in one of her nationally syndicated *My Day* columns that "the closing of child-care centers throughout the country certainly is bringing to light the fact that these centers were a real need. Many thought they were purely a war emergency measure. A few of us had an inkling that perhaps they were a need which was constantly with us, but one that we had neglected to face in the past."[6]

Historian Natalie Fousekis records one mother's letter sent to California Governor Earl Warren that reads poignantly, "If there were fewer children affected by this action, I would not be writing to you. Because while this is a personal letter, it is *not* a personal program. There are so many of these children. Adequate care of children is the basis of things—the home, the government—even civilization itself. We cannot let the extended day care measure fall through. We must have your help."[7] Increasingly, these women began to talk about child care as a right akin to that of public education.

In the end, the pleas of working mothers fell mostly on deaf ears. With would-be allies like labor unions abandoning them in favor of male members, the Lanham Act funding was sliced and by the end of the decade guttered out entirely.

This type of parental solidarity has died in recent decades. There is no mass movement for publicly supported child care, paid family leave, or other family supports. Tens of thousands of parents are not crowding the streets of Washington, DC demanding change. Comedian Steven Haas has quipped, "If I had never heard of storming the Capitol, and you showed me that footage, I would have been like, 'Oh, this is about the daycare thing, right? These are the parents about the daycare thing.'"[8] But no.

This relative silence extends beyond child care. The expanded child tax credit that was part of the 2021 American Rescue Plan Act, which literally put money into the pockets of families every month, expired with more of a mewl than a cry. With a few notable exceptions like Moms Demand Action on Gun Violence and Moms for Liberty, organized parent voices tend to be small and politically weak. Polls show that parents themselves are highly unsure of their footing—Is it OK to expect government to step up, or is that stepping out of line?[9]

To be sure, there has always been a heavy strain of American thought that suggests the family should be sacrosanct and off-limits to the public sphere. Care work has long been devalued in comparison to manufacturing work, and each has been concurrently gendered as "women's work" or "men's work." However, the political isolation of households—the idea that government is toxic to the family, such that any attempt by government to aid families, or by families to seek government support, in fact weakens families—is a recent phenomenon that only came to full bloom in the 1970s. That loss of solidarity hurts the entire nation.

The Failure of 1971

You can't understand American child care without understanding what happened in 1971. President Richard Nixon had on his desk a bill known as the Comprehensive Child Development Act. The bipartisan legislation provided for a network of federally funded, locally run child care programs; in one version, the preamble declared such programs should be available "as a matter of right to all children regardless of economic, social, and family background."[10]

Pat Buchanan, arch-conservative advisor to the President, was having none of it. He went full Red Scare, pushing a line about how such a scheme would "Sovietize" American children by putting them under the thumb of the government. It didn't help that Nixon had recently announced he would be visiting China. Right-wing allies rallied to Buchanan's banner. Decades later, Buchanan bragged to journalist Brigid Schulte that "We wanted not only to kill the bill, we wanted to drive a stake right through its heart," adding, "that sucker was gone. Gone forever."[11]

Indeed, when Nixon vetoed the Act, he did so not on technical grounds or because of its cost, but with a philosophical missile strike: Child care was an individual family responsibility, not the government's business. "For the federal government to plunge headlong financially into supporting child development," the veto statement (written by Buchanan) read, "would commit the vast moral authority of the federal government to the side of communal approaches to child-rearing as against the family-centered approach."

The Nixon veto was one blow among many in a deliberate battle to throw child care—and child-rearing more broadly—into the form of a scarce market commodity as opposed to a social good. Doing so changed parents from people with common cause into competitors.

Market goods are, by their very nature, neutral and without moral valence. You are not entitled to any help in acquiring a car. You have no moral claim; terms and conditions of the social contract do not apply; the village is silent. You have no standing with which to go up to other people and say, "hey, let's work together on public policy that makes cars more affordable" (The Affordable Car Act?). In fact, in many cases that other person may be actively opposed to you because you're both reaching for the same limited resource, or maybe because they own stock in the car company.

The competitiveness required to secure child care in the United States is so extreme that news articles frequently refer to it as a "Hunger Games" situation.[12] Stories still pop up from time to time of parents literally camping overnight outside centers in hopes of being first in line, a scene more reminiscent of seeking out Black Friday deals than an essential element of family life.[13] In the post-pandemic era of child-care staffing shortages, sometimes even getting your child signed in for the day before their program hits its maximum adult-to-child ratio can cause a scramble. The *Anchorage Daily News* described one such situation in 2024:

> One of the worst things, [parent Tiffany] Hall said, was how it pitted parents against each other.
>
> "We used to hold doors open. Wait. Go slowly. Now people are speeding into parking lot, not holding doors," she said.

One morning there was a "little stampede" to get in the door. A mother was separated from her 4-year-old.[14]

And that's just on the buyer side of the equation. As sociologist Susan Prentice notes, "commodity exchange is inherently antagonistic. Buyers and sellers have opposing interests in market transactions, quite independent of their will or good character."[15]

When it comes to child care, the situation is even harsher than in a standard market transaction: Cultural shaming has been layered on. Have any discussion about child-care challenges, and inevitably someone in the room will bring up the point that couples should've thought about this before having a child. (The grossest version of this argument is fashioned with Socratic eloquence as "don't breed 'em if you can't feed 'em.")

It's as if you've been told that it is your responsibility to acquire a mode of transportation, and you are failing in your duties as a person if you struggle. Society does not judge families for needing access to schools or libraries or playgrounds, but not being able to figure out the child-care equation carries the scent of moral failing. "Don't bother asking for help" quickly becomes "how dare you ask for help?"[16] Or, in Prentice's formulation, "commodities are not the bearer of rights—certainly none transcendent."

The dominant economic case for child care reinforces this hyperindividualism by cementing child care as a mere work support—not so different from an employee's responsibility to figure out transportation to their job. It is vital to understand how ahistorical, modern, and dangerous this shift is. Families needing support is not new, and agitating for better policies is not breaking some unspoken rule. Even during earlier eras when cultural norms were deeply against working mothers and few middle-class mothers were in the labor force, parents often banded together to try and better the lot of mothers and children.

The Power of Women's Groups

Between the 1900s and 1920s, women's groups successfully rallied around a series of family policy changes (even if they weren't yet ready to push for major child-care reforms). Over the course of those decades, forty-four states passed laws enshrining protections for female workers, while "mother's pensions" were established to support widowed or destitute mothers.[17] In 1912, the groups lobbied the federal government to establish the Children's

Bureau, the first federal-level administration focused on kids and their families.

(Notably, these advances were primarily aimed at white mothers. Black mothers had long been expected to work outside the home with little social commentary. In fact, enslaved Black women were some of the nation's first child-care providers, forced to care for the children of their enslavers while their own children often went neglected. Mothers of color were deeply underrepresented as recipients of mother's pensions, with some Southern states excluding them entirely.)

The pièce de résistance of this era was the 1921 Sheppard-Towner Maternity and Infant Protection Act, often simply called Sheppard-Towner after its main legislative patrons. The legislation gave (in today's money) $66 million to be administered via the states to aid pregnant and new mothers—including with birthing support professionals such as midwives—that allowed their newly grown families to start life healthy and strong.

Passage of the Act was uncertain. But with women's suffrage in hand and a huge coalition of women's groups advocating for it, the Women's Joint Congressional Committee (WJCC) successfully made the case that maternal and infant health was a societal concern beyond the isolated family unit.[18] (Support was not across the board: A few women's groups and leaders disliked the legislation on grounds that it treated mothers as a distinct class, which they saw as opposed to social equality efforts.)

As one WJCC member, the social reformer Florence Kelley, testified pointedly before the U.S. House of Representatives: "The question that is arising amazingly in people's minds now is, 'Why does Congress wish to have mothers and babies die?'" The need to support families went far beyond welfare, advocates insisted. The Act's benefits were to be universally available, not income-tested; the Children's Bureau chief at the time declared that the intention was explicitly *not* to allow the services to "degenerate into poor relief."

The Sheppard-Towner Act passed overwhelmingly. Over the course of the next eight years, 3,000 infant and maternal health hubs were opened, and the infant mortality rate dropped by 20 percent. Although a later Congress failed to renew the law, much of the Sheppard-Towner framework would be incorporated into the Social Security Act.

Parents locking arms can be powerful, including in ways that go beyond matters of the family. Many mothers' groups were heavily involved, for example, in the fights against slavery and child labor.

Today, however, examples of organized parent advocacy—especially those including fathers—are few and far between. As author Dana Suskind has noted, parents may be the largest constituency without a major interest group: There is no AARP for parents.[19]

Toward the Free-Market Family

So what happened? Women were organized. More of them (including, importantly, middle-class mothers) were entering the workforce by the day, and ideas of publicly supported child care were fresh in the public mind thanks to the Lanham Act. Progress during the 1950s was halting at best, but by 1960, the U.S. Department of Labor concluded that a private child-care market "will never be able to meet the current national need."[20] President Lyndon Johnson provided new attention to the early years—and federal support of families in general—through the advent of Head Start as well as the Elementary and Secondary Education Act. In 1969, Richard Nixon was entering office talking about a guaranteed minimum income for families with children while signaling support for a greater federal role in funding child-care services. The path to a universal child-care system seemed almost inevitable.

Here's where things fall apart.

In the second half of the 1960s and throughout the 1970s, an alliance of religious conservatives and right-leaning economic libertarians—the latter often called "neoliberals," after the classical connotation of "liberal" meaning unbounded individualism, not the label sometimes used for Democratic political supporters—came together. They rapidly advanced a dual philosophy: Government needed to get out of the way of families, and the free market needed to get in.[21]

The early groundwork for the neoliberal philosophy had been laid way back in the 1930s by business leaders opposed to New Deal policies, and one can see seeds being planted in the intervening decades.[22] For example, an advertisement ran in the August 1958 edition of *McCall's* magazine, a popular women's publication, with the headline, "What Sort of World For Them?" showing a white boy hammering blocks while his sister plays with dolls.[23] It implored mothers to *"Be on the watch for ideas that could deprive them of their right to free and independent action,"* by which it meant government involvement in enterprise. In a sentence rich with irony given how many burdens neoliberalism has dumped on women's shoulders, the ad goes on to insist, "Use your 'woman-power' to refute this idea that 'government should run things.'" The ad was placed by, of all organizations, America's Independent Electric Light and Power Companies—an interest group of private power corporations that resisted government regulation.

Conditions finally ripened due to upheaval from the Vietnam War, anti-communist sentiment, the changing role and legal status of women, and economic pain from inflation. Anxiety about the decline of the country became wrapped up in anxiety about the decline of the family. In turn, mistrust of the government led to a receptiveness for drawing brighter lines around family units. The neoliberal–religious conservative alliance jumped through the open window head first.[24]

They were stunningly successful: With a combination of intellectual heft (seen in the rise of new economic schools of thought at places like the University of Chicago), populist tactics (such as Christian conservatives utilizing the new strategy of direct mail campaigning, as with Anita Bryant infamously fighting against gay rights), and corporate opportunism (more on that in a moment), these actors changed the entire American relationship with government and then convinced the country it had always been so.[25]

Consider that for the preceding forty years, the prevailing sense, first offered by Franklin Delano Roosevelt, was that America was "an interdependent country" where "primary responsibility for relief rests with localities now, as ever, yet the Federal Government has always had and still has a continuing responsibility for the broader public welfare."[26] Yet the famous University of Chicago economist Gary Becker asserted a different view: "The fact that fathers 'choose' to support wife and children and mothers 'choose' to perform most of the unpaid reproductive work of care, thus relieving the state of any such responsibilities, represents the equilibrium state of the family in a free-market order, a state of mutual dependence and self-sufficiency that . . . welfare reform must strive to restore."[27] Government, in this formulation, not only has no role to play in family life, it would actually be getting in the way by trying to advance the broader public welfare.

Sociologist Robert Bellah and his coauthors point out in their touchstone book, *Habits of the Heart: Individualism and Commitment in American Life*, that this new relationship was built on an insistence that social problems are solvable at the individual or neighborhood level, and that any broader breakdown is the fault of Big Government. After all, they write, "If we can take care of ourselves, perhaps with a little help from our friends and family, who needs the state? Indeed, the state is often viewed as an interfering father who won't recognize that his children have grown up and don't need him anymore. He can't help solve our problems because it is in large measure he who created them." Compared to the state, the authors note, the market in this formulation "seems benign."[28]

Similarly, for the religious conservatives, government made a convenient bogeyman as they fought back against the tectonic shifts that were threatening the "established order" of family structure. This is the era that witnessed the rise of James Dobson and Focus on the Family, Jerry Falwell Sr. and The Moral Majority, Pat Robertson and The 700 Club, and other famous preachers like Billy Graham using mass media to beam a reactionary, government-is-out-to-destroy-the-family message to millions.[29]

Child care was thus just one battlefield among many—but it was a big one. As Maxine Eichner writes in *The Free-Market Family*, in a matter of years "the widespread recognition at the beginning of the twentieth century that market pressures could be destructive to families, and that it was government's role to buffer families from these forces, was turned on its head. Government action was increasingly associated with damage to families. Meanwhile, government leaving families to fend for themselves against market forces was seen as healthy and normal."[30] And as we've seen, when we leave families to fend for themselves against a faceless market as opposed to a democratically elected government, they have little ability to band together and few means of influence.

The merging of conservative "family values" and free-market ideology found its knight, of course, in the person of Ronald Reagan. Although it would be many years before he declared as president that "government is not the solution to our problem, government is the problem," Reagan was in fact involved in the defeat of the Comprehensive Child Development Act.[31] While governor of California, he had a tape-recorded Oval Office meeting with Nixon lobbying for a veto:

> *Reagan:* Now, we started off again with the idea of childcare centers, so you can put a mother to work. But this isn't confined to welfare or anything else, this now has gone beyond. This is, my God; this is the state taking over the rearing of the child.
>
> *Nixon (conflicted, after a long pause):* I'm very aware of the bill. I understand that a childcare center has its purpose so that a mother can get

the hell out and work so they can grow up with something. When it goes beyond that, then you're going on a dangerous proposition. I think it's a dangerous proposition that the state takes the place of the family to raise the kids.

(Note that the bill did not require parents to do *anything* nor gave the state *any* new authority over families. It merely created an affordable system of federally funded, locally run centers parents could choose to use as they wished.)

Whipped up by Reagan, Buchanan, and others, the right-wing backlash against publicly funded child care verged on, in the words of historian Anna Danziger Halperin, "almost hysterical overreaction."[32] Opponent ads warned that "Big Brother wants your children," while one political cartoon showed toddlers behind bars in a U.S. government commune with the all-caps caption, "YOU DON'T HAVE TO GO TO RUSSIA TO SEE THE IRON CURTAIN." (Again: not what was in the bill!) Passionate opposition to public support of child care rapidly became an article of faith among social conservatives. When future iterations of the bill came up, Congresspeople's phone lines were flooded with calls of opposition over the perceived threat to the family.[33]

Despite what these conservatives wanted, however, mothers continued to flock into the workforce. They were driven both by preference and by need. During this period, manufacturing jobs and wages sharply declined, and the one-income household became increasingly hard to sustain. As one paper puts it, by the mid-1970s, "for many couples, two incomes were essential for economic survival."[34] Again: by 1975, nearly *half* of mothers of three-to-five-year-olds were working outside the home, along with a full third of mothers of infants and toddlers.[35] The middle-class working mothers had arrived—but instead of pushing the government to accept society's collective responsibility, they fell right into the waiting arms of the market.

Drive-In Daycare

There may be no better illustration of how quickly and successfully child care had been flipped into a private market good than a gloriously cringeworthy 1977 *New York Times* article titled "Drive-In Daycare."[36]

The piece was written by future *Times* Managing Editor and Pulitzer Prize winner Joseph Lelyveld. Here's the opening section:

ST. LOUIS—The shopping complex that's taking shape on McKelvey Road in suburban Maryland Heights, just off the Interstate, already has its McDonald's and its Baskin-Robbins. Its K-Mart is under construction across the road from its newly opened Kentucky Fried Chicken, which is roofed in red tiles that radiantly catch the midday sun, outgleaming all the other plastic landmarks in the vicinity except one: an equally radiant tower that appears to have been finished in the same red tiles. The first reaction is to wonder why the corporate keepers of Colonel Sanders allowed two of their outlets to be established so close together. Then you draw near enough to read the logo. It's not Kentucky Fried Chicken. It's Kinder Care—a chain of day-care centers that's relentlessly replicating itself near the Interstates and Beltways that funnel suburban American to work.

Its promoters confidently promise that Kinder Care will be to the preschool child what McDonald's was to fast food and Holiday Inn to the salesman's one-night stand.

This direct linking of child care to fast food is as remarkable as it is skeevy. This is not a country panicking about the state takeover of the family or reluctantly offering welfare help, this is *capitalism, baby!* (or, capitalism about babies? For what it's worth, those promoters turned out to be right: KinderCare is now the largest private provider of child care in the United States, serving around 200,000 children in over 1,500 centers, a larger capacity than many states).

Lelyveld goes on to note that one reason KinderCare's model works is because it pays its staff poorly. "Does it sound a little mercenary?" he muses, "I suppose it does, but the idea that parents and children are consumers is also a little refreshing. It implies they are entitled to choices and their money's worth." This, again, is how you talk about buying a car, not how you talk about a human service that cultivates young children's brains and carries wide societal implications. Lelyveld then explicitly ties the rise of such individual consumerism with the demise of public solutions, writing that "when you opt for competition in this country, that's what you get. Now, in the absence of comprehensive day care, commercial operations like Kinder-Care may be more than an alternative. They may be the future."

Sadly, articles like these did not cause the revulsion you might expect. Overwhelmed by the opposition and riven by internal conflict, child-care advocates gave in. No longer were they arguing that child care was a collective responsibility, that it should be a right and entitlement for all Americans. Instead, as Halperin writes, "following this narrowing of political possibilities and shift of the policy landscape to the right, by the 1980s advocates ... began to adapt, and no longer pressured policymakers for universal approaches. Instead they focused on more limited provisions, like tax incentives for employers to provide child care." The entire child-care debate had shifted away from one around universal policies to one around, at best, reluctant welfare for the poor.[37]

Child care was now fully individualized, and parents were out on a ledge. The risk and responsibility for their work-care situations fell entirely on the shoulders of each household, and in truth on each mother. Parents were set against one another in a competition for slots and a competition to justify the pain they were absorbing to make life work.

But here's the thing about competition: When you take sides, you often start disliking the other side.

Rise of the "Mommy Wars"

The so-called "Mommy Wars" arose in the 1980s. Cultural conflict around motherhood and work had certainly existed earlier, but the first recorded instance of the term is a 1989 *Texas Monthly* article wherein Jan Jarboe, a senior editor at the paper, wrote about the conflict between working mothers and stay-at-home mothers: "So much for sister-hood. So much for tolerating another woman's choice of lifestyle. She was an angry stay-at-home mom. I was a guilty working mom. We were natural enemies."[38] Within a few years, this formulation had engulfed the highest levels of popular culture and politics in the form of a lightning rod known as Hillary Clinton.

A group of researchers led by Melissa Milkie tracked how the Mommy Wars played out in the media over the course of the 1990s and 2000s. They note that among the many problematic aspects of the Mommy Wars—very much including its name, which infantilizes women—was how much of the debate rested on questions of choice. Choice rhetoric was variously used as a way to support stay-at-home mothers (it's their choice) or to support working mothers (it's *their* choice), as a way to cast doubt about the legitimacy of options (is it a real choice or a forced choice?), and as a way to call for peace (let's all respect every mother's choice).

Yet the researchers argue such choice rhetoric is actually insidious. "Such an emphasis on choice deemphasizes the *social* aspect of the problem," they write (italics theirs), "instead individuating the problem and its solution to mothers themselves, thus leaving the weighty burden of responsibility for mothers to bear alone—and a symbolic wedge between them and other mothers."[39] Indeed, the entire construct lets both fathers and government off the hook!

Choice is incredibly important, of course, but choice can exist *within* a universal system (you can choose to homeschool your child or exercise your legal right to send them to the free local public school) as opposed to being the entire system. Halperin told me in an interview that the prevailing philosophy quickly became, "if you want to go to work, it's your choice, but you're responsible for figuring it out through the private market. If you're relying on the government, there's something wrong with you." Indeed, a 1986 *Cosmopolitan* magazine article about an "urgent crisis" in child care explained that "every working woman perceives the day-care dilemma as her own problem, because she's been made to feel that if she 'chooses' to work, it's her responsibility to make arrangements for her children. (The truth is that no one's doing us a favor by allowing us to work. Without female labor and female paychecks, this country would grind to a halt.)"[40]

The difference between an individuated challenge and a collective challenge is often the difference between inaction and action. The sociologist Sandra Levitsky has noted that "the conceptual shift away from thinking about one's situation as an individual problem or as a problem caused by fate or nature, to thinking about it as a social or public problem, is widely understood to be a necessary, if insufficient, condition for political action."[41]

So the individualized, market-based turn had, and continues to have, a devious built-in power source. The worse child care got, the more parents would blame one another, the harder it became to unite and fight for structural change. As Milkie and her coauthors conclude, "The 'real' war against mothers is a cultural one that pushes them apart and polarizes the community of mothers."

Reclaiming Parental Solidarity

If there's one thing the pandemic proved, it was how cross-cutting child-care needs are, and how much parents are struggling without a real system of support. If we can reclaim a sense of collective social responsibility around child care, we may yet be able to reclaim the immense power of parental solidarity. Angela Garbes writes in *Essential Labor: Mothering as Social Change* that "Raising children is not a private hobby, not an individual duty. It is a social responsibility, one that requires robust community support. The pandemic revealed that mothering is some of the only truly essential work humans do. Without people to care for our children, we are lost."[42] (Garbes uses "mothering" in a nongendered sense—that is, she means the act of caring, delivered by a parent of any gender.)

I would go so far as to suggest care writ large offers one of the few universal human bonds and therefore one of the best opportunities to heal our fragmented nation and world. As scholars at the Salzburg Global Seminar have asserted, "Every individual will need care at some point in their lives; every individual will give care at some point in their lives. Care for self and others is fundamental to building and maintaining social relations and its value to individuals, families and societies is truly incalculable."[43] The importance of those bonds is difficult to overstate. As my colleagues at the think tank Capita, Joe Waters and Ian Marcus Corbin, have written:

> Progress toward solving society's greatest challenges is possible . . . [but] there is no getting around our need for spiritual renaissance. A culture of daring, future-facing innovation is best fostered by dedicated groups that willingly pool risk and reward, but this kind of pooling—also known as solidarity—generally springs up where there is a deep, shared vision of what is good and beautiful and worth pursuing.[44]

Make no mistake, it will not be easy: It is difficult to overstate how hard it is to build a mass movement for government action when the people most impacted have been made to feel it is transgressive to push for government action. As the eminent child development expert Edward Zigler reflected in a 2009 book, *The Tragedy of Child Care in America*, "it is no surprise that [many] parents claim full responsibility for child care, since admitting anything less in a system where 'government steps in by necessity when families have failed'"—a line pushed by Jimmy Carter, of all people—"would be tantamount to conceding an inability to care for one's own children."[45]

Moreover, there are still foes out there spouting the same pablum that has poisoned the well since the 1970s. In January 2022, amid a tough re-election race in a major swing state, Wisconsin GOP Senator Ron Johnson had this to say about child care: "People decide to have families and become parents. That's something they need to consider when they make that choice. I've never really felt it was society's responsibility to take care of other people's children."[46] Johnson's sentiment was echoed in December 2023 by South Dakota Governor Kristi Noem, who stated that "The one thing I'm not willing to do is directly subsidize child care for families. I just don't think it's the government's job to pay or to raise people's children for them."[47]

It will likely require an active campaign to build a renewed path—one whose messages do not rely on economic value. The eminent sociologist Theda Skocpol, to whom we will return in a later chapter, made a call in 1997 for the creation of a "Parents First" movement. "You may think that talking about parents as people who serve their nation by doing their job well is rather trivial," Skocpol offered, "But I think this formulation has a real cutting edge. Although Americans today engage in a lot of rhetoric about families and children, our economic and political arrangements are making it harder and harder for parents to do their jobs effectively." She added that "a citizens' movement—of, as well as for, parents—is the best route toward effective advocacy for children in the United States today."[48]

Skocpol's suggestion was never taken up, but it is as needed now as it was a quarter-century ago. Until we solve child care, America will continue to suffer as atomized families are subject to the raw, amoral churn of the market. Not only does that leave a potential force for good untapped, it does direct damage to entire communities—the second case to which we now turn—making them less safe, less healthy, and less vibrant.

Examples of "Solidarity Case" Messages:
- "Having access to affordable child care means parents don't have to compete for scarce slots and can focus on working together to better their communities."
- "America is strong when we are united. Our inadequate child-care system drives families apart. It didn't always used to be this way: We should get back to an era when Americans understood parents need support for the nation to thrive."
- "Parents know what their families and communities need. The way America tells families it's their fault if they struggle with child care creates unnecessary polarization, silences parents, and hurts everyone."

In a sentence: A dysfunctional child-care system forces parents to be competitors in a soulless market instead of making common cause, depriving America of a powerful force for positive change.

Chapter 2
The Community Case

I can still remember looking around my one-bedroom San Francisco apartment and thinking, "well, so much for living here." That was still the favorite dwelling of my life: sun-filled with bay windows, situated near the bustling Haight-Ashbury neighborhood but far enough away from the chaos, within walking distance of Golden Gate Park and a million cafes, right next to several public transportation lines. My daughter, however, was starting to crawl, and the lack of space was becoming an insurmountable problem. My wife and I ran the numbers: We could scrape together enough for a two-bedroom place, but rent plus child-care costs were a dealbreaker. A few months later, we bid adieu to The City.

The presence or lack of affordable child care has enormous consequences for communities—consequences that have nothing to do with the employer–employee relationship—because child care helps drive both population dynamics and the well-being of families. Healthy communities need healthy families with children. The reasons, which we'll get into throughout this chapter, are as practical as they are varied: For example, those parents are doctors and firefighters and ambulance drivers; under-enrolled schools are huge headaches at best and civic rifts at worst; aging faith communities wither and die without young blood.

The impacts on communities also extend into less measurable domains. Place matters, and rootedness matters. Edmund Burke, the conservative thinker, famously wrote of associative life that "to be attached to the subdivision, to love the little platoon we belong to in society, is the first principle (the germ as it were) of public affections."[1] In our increasingly atomized society, being able to set down roots is particularly important. My wife and I had begun to enmesh ourselves deeply into the beating heart of San Francisco. We were engaged in political activity, volunteering on a campaign to tax sugary beverages in order to pay for pre-K services, as well as tutoring at a local school and participating in leadership roles with our local church. When we left, we lost our community and I dare say the community lost out, too.

It's one thing if individuals or couples have long planned on returning to their hometown upon having a child. It's quite another if they are forced out because of a lack of child care. Take Qweyonoh Parker, a public school teacher and mother of three in the Minneapolis region. Parker wrote in a 2024 letter to the *Minneapolis Star Tribune* that "I can either sideline my career to care for my three children or go into debt to pay for child care ... I am seriously considering moving to Illinois, where I have family, not because I want to, but because I cannot see a path that allows me to work and raise my children in Minnesota."[2]

Parker is not alone. A recent study found that among parents who do not use formal child care, one in five had moved closer to family primarily so they could get child care help.[3] That's a lot of involuntary unmooring, unmooring that can be dangerous to individual and communal well-being. Photojournalist Chris Arnade, author of the book *Dignity*, writes that "there is value in home, but isn't just the value of the house or the yard. It is the connections, networks, friendly, family, congregation, the Little League team, the usuals at the hairdresser, regulars at the bar, the union hall, the crew at the vape store, the regulars at the half-price movie night, the guys for Tuesday night basketball."[4]

Of course, one does not need to physically leave a community to be unable to engage with the little platoon. We will talk about this in more detail in the next chapter, but unaffordable and unreliable child-care offerings can be enormous financial and psychological stressors on parents. Inadequate child care can also force parents into undesirable care situations, such as working multiple jobs or parents working back-to-back "laddered" shifts so that one is always available to provide care. Exhaustion, anxiety, depression, and a plain lack of time are all correlated with reduced civic engagement.[5]

That's a problem, because concentrations of children and their civically active parents indelibly influence a community's built and social environments.[6] Families are the most compelling reason—and most compelling advocates—for parks and playgrounds and well-maintained sidewalks; slow streets around schools and child-care programs; festivals and children's museums; and splash pads and parades. Nearly all of these carry what civil rights advocate Angela Glover Blackwell calls a "curb-cut effect": actions taken to aid a specific population that end up benefiting the general public.[7] (Blackwell recounts how in the 1960s some early curb cuts were unsanctioned cement ramps poured in the literal dead of night by disability advocates in Berkeley, California, yet now they are used every day by millions of all ability types.)

Making communities places where families with young children can remain rooted helps those with older children and those who do not have children at all. Toddlers are not the only ones who benefit from wide sidewalks, vibrant colorful streets, ample shade, and verdant parks. All residents' ears can be filled by either the roaring of endless streams of cars or by trilling birdsong, their lungs by exhaust and pollution or by crisp clean air. More ineffably, as children's play advocate Tim Gill has said, children can be an antidote to stale and isolated communities; they bring a welcome jolt of creative chaos and "exemplify a degree of tolerance and conviviality, the idea that life is about more than work and money and restless grown-up intensity."[8]

Without adequate child care, though, communities bleed families—and everyone loses.

When Families Leave

Child care is a rare need that unites rural and urban communities. Although the phenomenon of urban dwellers fleeing for the suburbs upon having kids is well-known to the point of cliche, child-care options in rural regions tend to be even scarcer. As one report put it, rural areas are "far more underserved than urban areas, making it even harder for rural parents to access child care within an already fragile system."[9]

Because rural towns are so small, any depopulation poses an existential threat. Some out-migration may be due to unavoidable circumstances, but when child care is the forcing function, population movement is a policy choice. In Woodstock, Vermont (population: 3,005), a picturesque and literal no-stoplight town nestled by the Green Mountains, the local economic development commission in 2022 "discovered that 27 families in Woodstock that have a child under 3-years-old don't have care and that six of those families were moving away because of the issue."[10] Six family trees uprooted by the lack of care.

Similarly, a 2021 survey of rural Kansas residents between the ages of twenty-one and thirty-nine found that "the lack of quality child care is keeping young people in rural Kansas from taking jobs or even having kids—and may be pushing them away from rural Kansas."[11] The threat is so significant that rural, conservative towns from Nebraska to Minnesota have begun taking it upon themselves to create child-care options through taxpayer-funded initiatives.[12] Although these towns do not have the tax base to build a sustainable solution, the desperation and willingness to set aside antigovernment attitudes is telling. It is hardly an exaggeration to say that without child care, much of small-town rural America has no future.

Within cities, while part of the story is certainly about housing, child care remains an unpulled lever for retaining families like Qweyonoh Parker's. Brent Toderian is a leading urbanist and was the chief planner of Vancouver (British Columbia) from 2006 to 2012. Vancouver has defied trends by keeping a large number of families with children in the city core. In a 2018 interview with *Vox*, Toderian explained that:

> Even if you have [enough family-sized] homes, you need the services and amenities that support family living. Those start with daycare and schools. We put a lot of attention into schools, but you can't underestimate the importance of daycare . . . we have pretty good daycare service by comparison to other cities, although we are constantly struggling to keep up with demand.[13]

(Notably, since Toderian's interview, Canada has been implementing a massive new investment in child care, pumping in what would be, adjusted for the U.S. population, the equivalent of $250 billion over five years to create a national "$10 a Day" system. British Columbia has already seen an increase of more than 30,000 child care slots.)[14]

Cities that have shrugged off the need for child care—relying on the idea, as one writer puts it, that "childless singles and couples pay their taxes without demanding much in the way of services, at least in terms of schools and playgrounds"—are finding out the hard way how unsustainable that monoculture can be.[15] As the rise of remote work brought by the COVID-19 pandemic continues to wreak havoc on office building-driven downtowns, many cities have no bedrock of families with children on which to fall back.

Combined with lower birth rates, family migration has another knock-on effect: There aren't enough children to fill local public schools. Because public schools are mainly funded on a per-pupil basis, and because under-enrolled schools still have costs for such things as the building upkeep and utilities, under-enrollment can quickly push school districts into crisis. For instance, as of 2023, Minneapolis Public Schools is on the brink of fiscal insolvency, Chicago Public Schools is over $1 billion in debt, and it took a voter referendum to prevent a rural Kansas district from being dissolved. School closure debates are emotional, painful, and can create serious civic discord. When the San Antonio school board voted to close fifteen schools, one news article reported:

> After the vote, dozens of parents stormed out of the board room, some thanking trustees who voted against the closures and vowing to remember the decision in upcoming school board races.
>
> Responding to shouts from the audience before the vote, board President Christina Martinez urged the crowd to model good behavior, but it wasn't until district Police Chief Johnny Reyes called for quiet that civility was restored.[16]

An effective child-care system will not solve these types of multifaceted problems in their entirety, but such a system is a deeply underappreciated influence. From every angle, building a community without child care is building a community on sand.

And at some point, when a lack of child care makes a community unpalatable enough to families, it starts becoming unsafe.

Child Care's Impact on Community Health and Safety

Montrose is a small city of 20,000 in western Colorado. Situated on a valley floor surrounded by a stunning amount of natural beauty, including the Black Canyon of the Gunnison National Park, the city is a gateway hub for commerce and tourism in the region. It is deeply Republican; 67 percent of residents voted for Donald Trump in 2020, and the city was until recently represented by the controversial firebrand Representative Lauren Boebert. It is also a town gripped by a child-care crisis.

The lack of child care in Montrose is so bad, it is having consequences for public safety. On a video produced as part of a community process for identifying possible actions, Blaine Hall, Chief of the Montrose Police Department, states plainly: "Police officers have come to us and said they are looking for affordable and accessible child care and are not able to find it in this community, and so they moved on."[17] Hall adds later, "I will have a deficit in the number of police officers serving directly in the city of Montrose, and that affects our crime rate, our response times to calls."

It's clear that those dealing with the daily reverberations of inadequate child care realize that this is more than an individual problem and more than an economic problem. Hall's deputy said in the same video, regarding officers who have to stay home with their children due to child-care breakdowns, "The person who calls for our help may not have children, and may not think of it that way, but they would get better public service [if there was effective child care]."

In fact, police departments across the country are struggling so badly with child care's impacts on recruitment and retention that some have begun starting their own child-care centers. San Diego became the first department to open a program in January 2024, with St. Louis County (Missouri) close behind. The *St. Louis Post-Dispatch* reported that "the project was launched about a year ago when officers were asked to identify the major challenges that come with the job. Many cops pointed to child care, especially after the department moved to 12-hour shifts last year."[18]

It is not just police officers. Nearly 40 percent of registered nurses in the United States are between the ages of twenty and forty-four, and close to 90 percent are female. Nursing job openings are projected to grow throughout the 2020s at one of the greatest rates of any occupation; the federal government expects nearly 200,000 new registered nurses will be needed nationwide by 2032.[19] That translates to a huge swath of a critical profession deeply affected by child care. Unsurprisingly, research suggests that the lack of child care leads to issues around nurse recruitment and retention. As one nurse, Sherrie Page Guyer, wrote in a 2022 *Newsweek* op-ed:

> When I became a mother, I didn't want to pause my career as a psychiatric nurse. My work with homeless veterans made a difference; I helped connect them to health care and housing. But when the birth of my second child coincided with a move to a different state, I suddenly found myself without a trusted provider for my toddler and newborn. This, combined with now double child care fees, made taking an eight-year hiatus from the job I loved seem like the only option.[20]

Guyer goes on to cite a colleague in Boston, who "reports that a common reason nurses decline to interview for jobs where she works is the high cost of daycare in Massachusetts." A 2023 survey of nearly 600 parents who are medical professionals in the United Kingdom found that 93 percent have experienced child-care challenges, and it was impacting the pipeline of doctors and nurses.[21] One in-training practitioner recorded that "the whole thing is a total nightmare. I am seriously considering resigning based on the stress and cost of [child care] alone."

By contrast, hospitals that take steps to address child care, such as by having an on-site child-care center or partnering with community child-care programs, show significantly increased recruitment and retention. A *Stat News* article that references Wellstar Health in Marietta, Georgia, notes:

> Staff members who used the child-care center at Wellstar Health had the lowest turnover rate—only 1.5 percent—among staff, according to an internal study which analyzed turnover and benefits.
>
> "Basically no one leaves that utilizes the child care center," said Penny Ferrell, the executive director for employee wellness and services at Wellstar.[22]

(We will talk about on-site child-care centers in a future chapter, but for now know that a tiny percentage of U.S. workers have access to them, and they face serious challenges around fairness and scalability. They can, however, be wrapped into a comprehensive, publicly funded child-care system.)

Child care thus exacerbates or helps relieve nursing shortages. The effects of nursing shortages are about what one would expect them to be. One research paper concludes that "nursing shortages lead to errors, higher morbidity, and mortality rates. In hospitals with high patient-to-nurse ratios, nurses experience burnout, dissatisfaction, and the patients experienced higher mortality and failure-to-rescue rates than facilities with lower patient-to-nurse ratios . . . when staffing is short, ratios go up to meet the need."[23]

A similar, if not identical, story can be written for other key public health and safety professions: firefighters, emergency medical technicians, ambulance drivers, and so on. Public school teachers and child-care educators themselves are caught in the whorl. In an era where two-thirds of young children have all available parents in the workforce, a substantial percentage of those parents will work jobs that undergird strong communities. The idea that child care is an individualized responsibility whose impact is circumscribed by the moat of the household is as inaccurate as it is foolhardy. So is the idea that child care is needed purely to support the abstract Economy. No, child care is woven into the daily fabric of small towns, sprawling suburbs, and big cities—we've just failed to notice.

That has to change, because there is almost no aspect of American life untouched by child care. Consider that beyond health and safety, child care also implicates another crucial community contributor: faith communities.

Staunching the Great Dechurching of America

America is experiencing what authors Jim Davis, Michael Graham, and Ryan P. Burge have termed a "Great Dechurching."[24] They write that "About 40 million adults in America today used to go to church but no longer do . . . For the first time in the eight decades since Gallup has tracked American religious membership, more adults in the United States do not attend church than attend church. This is not a gradual shift; it is a jolting one." Although most pronounced among Christians, declines in religious membership are occurring across nearly all major U.S. faith groups; instead, there has been a pronounced rise in the "nones," those with no faith affiliation whatsoever. By one estimate, over 100,000 houses of worship will close between 2020 and 2030.[25]

That is a challenge because, beliefs aside, attachment to faith communities has a host of positive benefits for individuals, and strong faith communities have a host of positive benefits for the broader community. One review notes that the presence of faith communities is correlated with "providing help to poor and vulnerable individuals in the community, improving marriage relationships, decreasing violence among women, increasing moral community obligations, and promoting charitable contributions and volunteering."[26] Moreover, as the *Chronicle of Philanthropy* reports, a quarter of the charitable organizations in the United States are directly operated by a faith community.[27] The *Chronicle* goes on to note that:

> Researchers also talk of the "invisible safety net" in congregations—informal support among members when someone meets adversity like losing a job or falling behind on rent. Counseling by clergy also can help stop problems—a rocky marriage, substance abuse, depression—from becoming crises.
>
> "I don't think anyone understands how big the invisible social safety net is," says [Ryan] Burge, the Baptist pastor and political scientist. "And they don't understand what it's going to mean in 20 or 30 years when it's gone." Nonprofits that serve the vulnerable can expect their workload will only

grow. "The people who will fall through the cracks will be those we should be looking out for the most—the lonely, the addicted, the depressed, the poor, the marginalized, the sick. Those are the people who are going to be hurt the worst when religion goes away."

Faith communities can also be deeply influential in striving for beneficial policies and laws. The most famous example of this advocacy came during the civil rights movement, but efforts continue today as networks of faith communities push for everything from clean air to reduced gun violence to affordable housing.

What dying congregations need more than anything is to attract and retain families with young children. This is feasible: Families with children are one of the groups most likely to attend church. Moreover, the transition to parenthood is a crucible that opens the door for potential religious attendance by those previously unattached. In a 2009 paper, *The Challenge of Faith: Bringing Spiritual Sustenance to Busy Lives*, scholars Kimberly Morgan and Sally Steenland explained that,

> Young people often reconnect with or participate for the first time in organized religion when they get married and have children. Starting a family seems to trigger the desire to belong to a faith community, as new parents seek help giving their children a moral and spiritual foundation for growing up. New parents also look for others like themselves to find support and community.[28]

That support is particularly crucial in the early years of parenthood: another facet of the invisible safety net. Jessica Calarco, a sociologist we will hear more from in a moment, told me that the mothers she has interviewed who feel most surrounded by a village of support upon having a baby—whatever the other tradeoffs—are conservative Christian women.

As one might by now expect, child care influences faith communities in several ways. First, of course, are impacts on macro-level trends in family mobility and birth rates, both of which shrink the potential universe of congregants. Then there are the consequences of sacrifices parents make to deal with child care. Morgan and Steenland cite research that "for both men and women, long hours spent at work is related to lower levels of church attendance, less involvement in other congregational ministries and a reduced sense of the importance of religion . . . these problems [may be] particularly acute for workers in lower-paying service and blue-collar jobs, who may not have resources to pay for services that help them cope with the time squeeze." Those services very much include child care.

Acknowledging these realities, many faith communities have stepped up to provide child care directly, including some denominations that railed against it in the 1970s. Morgan and Steenland report that:

> Between 1992 and 2008, there was a 76.4% increase in child care provided in Protestant institutions, a 52.6% increase offered by Catholic institutions, and a 47.7% increase by Jewish institutions. Today [in 2009], one-quarter of children under the age of 5 who are in center-based child care are in programs located in churches, synagogues, and other places of worship. This figure may even underestimate the proportion of children in religiously affiliated child care because many children are in "faith-affiliated" and "faith-infused programs" that are located outside places of worship.
> *[Note: Not all child-care programs located in a house of worship are sectarian in nature; at times, secular programs merely lease the space]*

Since Morgan and Steenland wrote their paper, however, faith-based child care has gotten caught up in the same broken system and lack of public funding as secular programs. Although faith-based programs may have lower facility costs, recall that child-care program budgets are dominated by personnel, befitting the need for many adult humans to care for small humans; staffing frequently makes up 70 percent or more of a program's expenses.[29] Faith-based child-care programs, then, are generally not able to offer better compensation than other programs, and they are competing for the same scarce and beleaguered child-care workforce.

So, even though faith-based programs are generally eligible for federal and state child-care funds, the paucity of money in the system has begun to take its toll. A 2021 report from the Bipartisan Policy Center found that, "Like many child care programs across the country, the faith-based organizations we spoke with faced challenges in keeping their child care programs financially solvent . . . interviewees dispelled a commonly held and incorrect belief that faith communities are able to provide child care services without external financial support."[30]

In practice, that looks like the abrupt closure in 2022 of Leland Christian Academy preschool in North Carolina, located within the First Baptist Church of Leland, because "unfortunately, like others, we have been impacted by staffing shortages."[31] It looks like Good Shepherd Lutheran Church in Sioux Falls, South Dakota, shuttering its daycare in 2023 because "it was no longer financially feasible to continue operating a child care center."[32] It looks like Jewish child-care providers coming together to urgently seek philanthropic funding so they can offer staff wage supplements and avoid the same fate.[33]

That faith communities continue to try and find a way forward for child care speaks to how important it is to them, and how much more vibrant America's congregations could be if there was a universal child-care system in place. In 2023, the Christian magazine *Sojourners* ran an article titled, "The Solution to Unused Church Space Might be Toddlers."[34] It expounds on a nascent effort by the Texas Conference of the United Methodist Church to help churches start and financially sustain child-care centers. The article explains that:

> The main benefit to churches, [Rev. Jill Daniel, the initiative's leader] said, is rejuvenation, bringing life back into long-shuttered corridors. The churches have learned that just because the halls are full during the week doesn't mean the pews will be full on Sunday, but it has encouraged them to engage the young families, let them know about other services the church can provide, and in a few cases, she said, families have found a church home through enrolling their kids in the school.

In essence, child care helps faith communities stay healthy as well as fully imbue their role as community hubs—a role child-care providers themselves can play if society supports them.

Child-Care Programs as Community Assets

At their best, child-care providers create a linkage point between often-isolated new parents and other parents, and between those parents and the broader community. Child-care programs should be seen as, in the words of one scholar, "an adjunct to parental primacy and family stability, not their antithesis."[35] That role comes into sharp relief during disasters. A report from the U.S. Early Years Climate Action Task Force (an effort I helped coordinate), recounts the story of one such provider:

> Susan Gilmore runs North Bay Children's Center, a California child care network with 13 locations. Her network contended with wildfires and their

effects. She and her staff tracked children and families: who was evacuated, who lost their homes, and who needed resources. They set up a command center and created a spreadsheet to track every family—a difficult feat since many of the families they serve don't own their home, or had evacuated, or were staying with relatives. Many families lacked power and food. Staff linked them to food banks and, when it was safe, brought resources to them.[36]

That's not the output of a service that exists just to help parents work and keep the national GDP rising; that's the output of essential societal infrastructure.

Providers are also key sources of parenting advice and can help identify potential challenges in young children that require additional intervention. Next to family members and pediatricians, child-care providers are frequently cited by parents as one of the most trusted sources of guidance.[37]

These providers can also be enormously important in offering support and a safe, stable, nurturing relationship for children whose families are facing challenges. In the documentary *Make a Circle*, preschool educator Dan recalls how important his child-care providers were as he grew up with a single mother and struggled with learning disabilities. "My mom was both my parents, and my other parent was my preschool teachers," Dan says, voice thick with emotion. "They helped my mom when she needed assistance. They helped me. They helped my family. They, in essence, I feel, saved my life."[38]

One way to see the vital role of child-care programs is to consider what happens when they close. In 2023, Chabeli Carrazana of *The 19th* reported about the ripple effects of a twenty-six-year-old center shutting down in the small town of Lancaster, Wisconsin (population: ~4,000).[39] The center, Giggles & Wiggles, could no longer maintain reasonable staffing levels as it fell victim to the harsh economics of child care and the expiration of pandemic-era government funds. As Carrazana wrote:

> When a child care center closes, especially in a small town, it frays the ties that keep a community together. Children become scattered, separated from the only caregivers most had ever known. Families are left scrambling to find alternate care in a system known for years-long waiting lists. And working parents are stymied, making impossible decisions around leaving their jobs or cutting back hours.

The consequences included parents "putting their kids on waiting lists for care in neighboring cities," reducing work hours, or trying to juggle caring for their child while working from home. One mother "told [Giggles & Wiggles owner Kristin] Holman-Steffel she was putting her plans for another child on hold. She had expected Giggles & Wiggles could care for them." The closure—which likely could have been avoided had there been adequate public funding available—was devastating for center leadership, too:

> Giggles & Wiggles hasn't just been a job . . . [i]t's been a community. It's been about the back-to-school potlucks for all the parents and the Halloween open house, the library art show. It was about when a storm knocked down a tree and a dad offered to saw off the broken limb. Or the time parents chipped in to rent out an ice cream truck to deliver cones for all the kids.
>
> "When you care for their children for 10 hours a day, you really get to be part of that family's life," Holman-Steffels said. Now that the center is closing, "you just feel like you're letting everybody down."

This community feel can be especially true of family child-care providers: those who offer care in their home for a small number of unrelated children. Family child care is especially preferred among rural and immigrant populations, and they are often the only providers in an area who offer care during nontraditional hours—that is, nights and weekends. In addition to young children, many serve school-aged kids before and after school. Because of the small size and long hours and years of engagement, these providers commonly become, in more ways than one, part of the family. That familial connection is an asset that can be long-lasting and life changing. I have a former colleague who credits his family child-care provider with altering his life trajectory. When he was having a difficult time as a child, she got him involved with the football program at a local church, and it ended up becoming a critical source of support.

That's why it is so worrisome that America's family child-care providers are disappearing. Between 2005 and 2017, the last year for which full data is available, the country lost more than half its small family child-care programs, a plunge of 90,000 distinct providers.[40] Given trendlines and the impact of the COVID-19 pandemic, it is almost certain the decline has continued if not accelerated. In many cases, family child-care providers are hanging up their hats because it is an enormous amount of work for insultingly little pay or because they are reaching retirement age. Not surprisingly, there is no queue of young providers lining up to replace them.

Conclusion

It's worth coming back to that most irritating of arguments—why should society pay to help people raise kids they chose to have? It's cathartic to give a snarky answer, like the British writer Rhiannon Lucy Cosslett, who offered this rejoinder: "Why should any of us pay for anything? Why don't we just, I don't know, roll around in our own excrement? Because what is society? What is humanity? Let's just all be chimps, picking fleas off each other. Which is actually quite a nice communal childcare model, come to think of it. At least when compared with what is available."[41]

But the real answer is that nearly every facet of healthy communities is caught up in questions of child care. One danger of the economic case's dominance is that it further blinds us to the way child care pulses like an artery within communities and the body politic, helping carry the nutrients needed for health and vitality. The more advocates, elected officials, and the public can start loudly observing all the ways in which child care supports everyday community life, the less frequently we may hear what in Cosslett's world might be called daft whinging.

Still, the wording of Richard Nixon's 1971 veto statement continues to hang over the debate: "For the federal government to plunge headlong financially into supporting child development would commit the vast moral authority of the federal government to the side of communal approaches to child-rearing as against the family-centered approach." I would hope that it is clear by now that this is an irreparably false dichotomy. But to put a final nail in the coffin of Nixon's syllogism, let's look at all the ways a publicly funded child-care system actually helps parents be the parents they want to be.

Examples of "Community Case" Messages:
- "Child care is essential to letting families stay rooted in and contribute to the communities they love. If we want rural America to remain vibrant, or the great American cities to prosper, we need a strong child-care system."
- "Child care undergirds public health and safety. Without adequate child care, our police departments and fire departments and hospitals cannot remain adequately staffed. You might not be thinking about child care when the police are slow to show up at your house or your

Continued

Continued

> loved one gets an infection in a short-staffed hospital, but child care is part of the story."
> - "Faith communities are so important to healthy towns and cities, but one reason so many are aging and dying is because they can't attract young families with children. America's neglected child-care system is driving families away, forcing parents to work multiple jobs so they don't have time to attend a house of worship, and closing faith-based child-care programs left and right."

In a sentence: Child care is a foundational element of strong and vibrant communities, influencing everything from public health and safety to faith communities to whether or not parents can remain rooted.

Chapter 3
The Family Values Case

Any parent can tell you that a family does better when its members have regular quality time with one another. Chronic stress and a lack of being in the same place are thus squarely opposed to family flourishing. More tragically, so is being unable to choose to have the type of family you want.

Inadequate child care fuels the dynamo of all these challenges. In fact, a strong and inclusive child-care system is a prerequisite for strong families—and, as we have been seeing already, strong families are a prerequisite for a strong nation.

It may be an obvious point, but families, whatever their shape, are the core unit of social reproduction. When parents spend time with their children, they pass on values, stories, traditions, and beliefs. Family life inherently teaches lessons of communication, compromise, and selflessness, and teaches the tension of individuals and a group together seeking the higher good for all. A maximalist argument for the importance of healthy families was laid out in 1976 by the philosopher and author Michael Novak, who expounded in *Harper's Magazine* that the family is,

> the most potent moral, intellectual, and political cell in the body politic ... the family is the seedbed of economic skills, money habits, attitudes toward work, and the arts of financial independence. The family is a stronger agency of educational success than the school. The family is a stronger teacher of the religious imagination than the church. Political and social planning in a wise social order ought to begin with the axiom *What strengthens the family strengthens society* ... one unforgettable law has been learned painfully through all the oppressions, disasters, and injustices of the last thousand years: *if things go well with the family, life is worth living; when the family falters, life falls apart.*[1] (emphases his)

And contrary to those who argue that a robust child-care system hurts the family, it turns out the family has a frightening future without one.

Child Care and Stress

Stressed-out, exhausted parents don't tend to parent at their best. I understand this all too well, as I expect you do; one doesn't need research studies to prove that when you're at the end of your rope, you're more likely to be snappish and less likely to be present or want to play pretend. (There are reams of such studies, though![2])

As things stand, trying to find and afford child care causes parents an enormous amount of stress. We'll return to the financial burden, which frequently rivals that of rent or mortgage payments. But even finding a program at which to become financially burdened can be hellish. America's ongoing refusal to publicly fund child care and instead let it operate as what former U.S. Treasury Secretary Janet Yellen has called a "textbook example of a broken market" creates a badly supply-constrained system.[3] Parents in many communities face epic waitlists, lists that are only growing longer. An analysis commissioned by the news site *The 19th* found that between February 2020 and February 2023, the average waitlist length at the analyzed child-care centers rose 28 percent to a whopping 236 children.[4]

This lack of options takes a toll on parents already contending with the daily stresses of raising young children. Molly Dickens is a stress physiologist and founder of the Maternal Stress Project. Along with a reproductive psychiatrist, Lucy Hutner, Dickens penned a *New York Times* op-ed in early 2024 titled, "The Stress of Finding Child Care Is Hurting Parents' Health."[5] The pair begin:

> On a Saturday morning last May, Julia Sachdev, a mother of a 2-year-old and 4-year-old, woke up to an email from her children's preschool. The school—which her children adored and had been in operation for over 50 years—announced that it would be closing in a month.
>
> In the following days, she and her husband scrambled to find an alternative that was a reasonable driving distance from their home. Most of the places they reached out to had long waiting lists. Some said their waiting lists were full. Some never even called them back.
>
> "It was so stressful," reflected Ms. Sachdev. "There was this suffocating anxiety that ruled my day. I couldn't concentrate on other things. It kept me up at night."

Even absent a crisis brought by child-care program closures, the process of trying to find a reasonable child-care situation is fraught in such a supply-constrained market. This is yet another consequence of miscasting child care as a market to begin with. Dickens and Hutner note that "the task of finding care can also increase parents' mental labor load, which can erode psychological health, particularly for mothers." In one 2024 survey, fully 70 percent of mothers agreed that managing child-care decisions such as securing care was "overwhelming."[6]

Unsurprisingly, the counterfactual holds true as well. As one Australian study concluded, "an increase in the availability of center-based childcare is associated with a decrease in perceived difficulty in finding 'good quality' childcare, as well as an increase in mothers' satisfaction with the amount of free time available."[7]

Yet even when families are lucky enough to secure a spot, the stress doesn't end there. Because there is so little child-care supply in America, parents can't be choosy: In many cases, the first option is the only option. But this is not like settling for a burger at Wendy's because other restaurants are full or closed (no offense to Wendy's), this is handing one's child—in many cases, one's preverbal child who cannot accurately report what's going on—to a near-stranger.

Parents' feelings of satisfaction and security with their child-care arrangement are paramount, otherwise it can naturally lead to them spending their days anxious and unhappy. (This is one reason why family child-care providers, family, friends, and neighbor caregivers, and stay-at-home parents are such an important part of a comprehensive system—some parents will never feel comfortable if their child is not with a known and long-trusted caregiver.) Indeed, research studies have found that parental stress spikes when parents are dissatisfied with their child care.[8] Moreover, as the Sachdevs found out the hard way, in the weak American child-care system finding a slot doesn't mean keeping one. "Unpredictability itself is a source of stress," Dickens and Hutner note. "Even when parents manage to secure care for their children, it can be unreliable, and they never know when it might go away."

In this sense, America's consistent neglect of child care has created a vicious cycle: underfunded programs with high staff turnover have questionable quality and sustainability, which leads parents and policymakers to be wary of child care, which generates less political will for putting in the funding that would lead to higher quality. It's true that modern parents may not face the Satanic and sexual abuse panic of the mid-1980s. (Although this turned out to be a fiction, the damage was done: Media outlets lapped up the narrative, as with NBC running a *Nightly News* segment titled, "Daycare

Nightmare."[9]) Still, child-care programs are not always held in particularly high regard—and the policy choices behind their struggles frequently go unremarked—which gets in the way of both building a movement for universal child care and the well-being of families.

To see how this plays out in the real world, consider how Dickens and Hutner conclude the story of the Sachdev family:

> In the end, they found another preschool for their children, but it didn't have the same learning environment as their previous school, and they didn't know the community there. Without the luxury of being able to carefully consider which school would be the best fit, they made their choice, at least in part, out of necessity.
>
> "We just went with a place that had an available spot," explained Ms. Sachdev. "And then we had more anxiety for months over whether it was the best place for our kid."

But say a family has managed to find a spot in a child-care program they are thrilled with. Now it's time to talk about how they pay for it.

Child Care is Expensive: How Expensive Is It?

It's well-known that child care in America is expensive, but it's worth emphasizing just how unsustainably expensive it has become. In 2022, the U.S. Department of Labor (DoL) published the first-ever "National Database of Childcare Prices."[10] The DoL data found wide variation in cost across U.S. counties, although nowhere was particularly affordable. Consider toddler care in center-based programs. Looking at programs in "large" but not "very large" counties—defined as those with populations between 500,000 and 1 million, so leaving out the most expensive locales such as New York City and Los Angeles—a slot ran on average nearly $12,500 per year.

Family child-care homes cost less but prices are still painful; the DoL data show that care for the same toddler at a family child-care home in a medium-sized county (population 100,000 to 500,000) costs over $8,100 a year. Those types of numbers are torpedo blasts into the side of family budgets when you consider that nearly 40 percent of households with children make less than $75,000 a year, plus the rising cost of housing, food, and other goods. And woe to families with two or more children below school-age! (Not that after-school and summer child care is a picnic once kids reach the pearly gates of Kindergarten, with parents paying an average of $400 a month for after-school care and often thousands for summer camps.)

Worse yet, the DoL numbers are already outdated: Throughout 2022 and 2023, child-care prices rose at twice the overall rate of inflation as programs tried to keep up with a changed post-pandemic labor market and rising costs of supplies such as diapers. Then, in September 2023, $24 billion in pandemic-era stabilization grants that went directly to child-care programs expired. Particularly in states that did not use state money to extend the stabilization grants, parents are facing huge fee increases, often $200 a month or more. In the two months following the funding expiration, nearly one-third of parents reported seeing fee increases.[11] This isn't greed; the alternative for these programs is closing up shop.

The situation isn't much better for the small number of lower-income families able to get government aid to defray child-care costs. (Due to inadequate funding and bureaucratic hurdles, only one in nine eligible families receive these subsidies.)[12] As journalist Stephanie H. Murray explained, citing the work sociologist Amanda Freeman (from whom we will hear more in the Anti-Poverty Case) has done interviewing low-income mothers:

> [Many] of the women Freeman interviewed depended on various forms of means-tested social assistance that are issued for brief and varied intervals and subject to stringent income limits and work requirements. Hanging on to them requires, among other things, regularly reporting detailed information about their earnings or work-related activities, creating an additional axis of work-family conflict. This triple load of work, parenting, and navigating public benefits is a direct by-product of America's view of public support for parents as something you are not supposed to need, Freeman told me. It's not something that happens when programs are universal.[13]

It should be noted, again, that the migraine-inducing expense and stress of child care is a policy choice and not a given (perhaps most obviously contrasted by the seven hours a day, 180 days a year worth of free care in public schools that all Americans are provided as a matter of state constitutional right). A few years ago I attended a wedding in Seattle where I struck up a conversation with a guest in from Berlin. He and his partner had an eighteen-month-old, and he got an almost rueful smile when I asked him about how child care was going. He said that when talking with his friends at the reception who also had young children, he was having to try hard to stop gloating. He explained that he had access to a German *kita*, or child-care center, seven hours a day while he worked full-time, and his spouse worked part-time. It was an excellent, updated facility with a loving staff. For this privilege, he paid 50 Euros a month (about 55 dollars), which he described as the "top end" of the fee scale.

He also looked more relaxed than any of the other parents there. There is a reason why a different German couple mused on the popular child-care podcast *No One is Coming to Save Us* how, in their much family-friendlier nation, "we can focus on being good parents, not on how to afford being good parents."[14]

But here in America, when the child-care slot won't come open or the family budget won't balance, something's gotta give. Too often, it's marriage and parent-child relationships.

Sacrificing at the Altar of Child Care

Emily Guendelsberger is a journalist who spent several years working at places like McDonalds and Amazon and wrote about her experiences in her book, *On The Clock: What Low-Wage Work Did to Me and How It Drives America Insane*. When it comes to parents, she writes that child-care pressures make already tough circumstances nearly untenable:

> So, so many working parents I met in the course of writing this book sacrificed their relationships with each other for the sake of their kids. Like Hailey [and her husband], working opposite shifts so one can always be home. 'We have Sunday if I'm not working mandatory overtime, and occasionally we have Monday morning—if I don't have to work Monday morning—to see each other, and that's pretty much it.' Could you maintain a marriage living like that? A sex life? Could you be a good and loving partner if both of you were constantly stressed and irritable?[15]

Could you, I would add, be the type of parent you want to be?

These types of sacrifices are all too frequent. Tens of millions of Americans work low-wage shift jobs in industries such as retail and fast food, and one-third of them are parents; in fact, research from Harvard's Shift Project reveals that "one in ten American children has a parent working in the retail or food service sectors."[16]

A 2023 article from Seattle's NPR affiliate explained one family's laddered-schedule plight by saying, "Lara Allen and Rob Butler couldn't afford the high cost of child care for their three kids, so they pay with other resources—sleep and time."[17] Later, the article quotes a Washington State child-care leader: "It just puts a real strain, because essentially what ends up happening is despite there being two adults in the home, you end up with the children in a way that feels very single parent. You don't get the support of two adults in the home being with the children, but rather you're tag teaming it and creating this handoff system."

This, again, is true of families across America. Sociologist Jessica Calarco recounts the story of a married couple she interviewed called Erin and Mark (not their real names), who moved to Mark's rural hometown and took low-wage jobs.[18] When Erin got pregnant, child-care options were scarce, and Mark's parents still worked full-time to pay their bills. They decided to ladder their schedules. As Calarco summarized, "That split-shift arrangement took a toll on Erin and Mark's relationship and left Erin constantly exhausted. 'It was terrible,' Erin recalled. 'It was really hard. I was ALWAYS tired.' Eventually, Erin quit her job and the family scraped by with help from public assistance programs."

There are certainly other aspects of the modern U.S. economy that do badly by families, such as persistently low wages, "just-in-time" scheduling that reduces scheduling predictability, and the lack of robust paid leave policies. We will return to these in more detail in the Economic Case chapter. But because of its outsize role and expense, stress from trying to find and afford a quality child-care situation puts enormous pressure on family dynamics.

All that stress and lack of time together—exacerbated by self-reinforcing cycles of poor sleep—is terrible for "the most potent moral, intellectual, and political cell in the body politic." America's neglected child-care system is turning a fair number of two-parent families into essentially a pair of single-parent families who happen to share the same home. Having two parents is important: As economist Melissa Kearney wrote in *The Two-Parent Privilege*, "A strong, stable family life is the foundation upon which children find their footing in this difficult world . . . the two-parent family structure is, in general, advantageous for children."[19] (Kearney notes, of course, that these are averages and there are plenty of times, such as in the case of an abusive parent, when children are better off in one-parent households).

Moreover, chronic stress is linked to depression and anxiety, particularly among mothers.[20] In turn, this has negative impacts on marriages and parenting relationships, leading to higher relational conflict and more childhood behavioral problems. Tying into other cases for child care, this is also not the profile of individuals apt to be deeply engaged in community or civic life. Eventually, the swirl of stressors starts substantially spiking the risk of parents—whether married, cohabitating, or otherwise—splitting up.[21] One North Carolina mother, Lindsay K. Saunders, shared in an op-ed that the stress of trying to afford child care, alongside a lack of paid leave, was a major factor in her and her husband separating. "I wondered," Saunders wrote, "If only we'd had more support, would we have made it?"[22]

Although child care is not the only culprit, it is worth noting that we live in an era of declining parental mental health. One study found that between 2016 and 2020, parental mental health in the United States was on a steep fall, and this conclusion was drawn prior to the full force of the pandemic. The percentage who reported that their mental health was "excellent/very good" dropped nearly 5 percent over this period, while the percentage saying they were coping "very well" with parenting demands went from 67 percent to 60 percent.[23]

Single parents—of whom there are over 13 million—face additional challenges, given that they are one of the groups most likely to experience loneliness and social disconnection.[24] Indeed, by nearly any measure, single parents struggle more with child care. (I do not believe anyone's reason for being a single parent should be judged, and it is worth remembering how many become single due to leaving abusive or otherwise unhealthy relationships, due to a partner's death, and so on.) They are simultaneously a population with an acute need for care and one that commonly has limited economic resources. The Federal Reserve Bank of St. Louis has noted that "many single mothers have very low levels of financial reserves. For example, about a third would not have been able to handle a $400 emergency expense in 2019."[25]

Notably, this is a gendered story. The Federal Reserve went on to look at wealth—not just money in the bank, but assets minus debts—and concluded, "The motherhood wealth penalty is clear: Single women without children had over nine times more median wealth than single mothers, while the median wealth of single childless men and single fathers of minor children did not significantly differ, indicating there wasn't a commensurate wealth penalty for fatherhood."

Yet the story goes beyond finances. As journalist and former public radio host Tanzina Vega wrote in an op-ed:

Here's the thing: Single parents don't just need to work, many of them, including me, want to work. But we can't do that effectively if child-care costs represent half or more of our take-home pay or if we have jobs that don't allow us the flexibility we need to care for our children. Work is not just a necessary break from parenting but something that allows us to contribute to society in a meaningful way beyond being a parent. We need cost effective child care to be able to be our full selves for the benefit of our own personal development and that of our children.[26]

Sometimes, the lack of child care impacts not only parents' mental health, but their physical health. A 2017 survey by Kaiser Health Systems of more than 2,700 women found that "14% of women missed or delayed their own healthcare because of lack of childcare."[27] This can have devastating consequences, as in the case of Alexandrea Ruiz. The *Fort Worth Star-Telegram* reported in 2022 that:

When Ruiz was diagnosed with an advanced stage of cervical cancer last year, she missed multiple early appointments, delaying the start of her treatment. The single mom knows only a few people in Dallas, and said she had no one she could ask to safely watch her daughters while she got care day after day, sometimes for hours on end. She couldn't afford traditional day care or a babysitter.[28]

All of this suggests America should be doing everything it can on the grounds of family health and stability to reduce the child-care burden, even if there were no economic impact at all. In fact, a strong child-care system can be a *protective* factor for families; one study concluded that "mothers' perceptions of having good choices for care were associated with a reduced likelihood of clinical depressive symptoms, even after controlling for prior depressive symptoms and concurrent parenting stress."[29]

But what about families where child care is handled in-house?

Valuing Stay-at-Home Parents

Stay-at-home parents are too often left out of child-care conversations, despite the fact that nearly one-third of families with young children have one. As Ivana Greco, a colleague and stay-at-home parent herself, as well as an advocate for inclusion of stay-at-home parents in public policy, has noted:

> During the 1960s and 1970s, when American women left the home in large numbers to pursue paid work and greater educational opportunities, [many] politicians rightly applauded the tearing down of legal and cultural barriers that had kept women on an unequal footing with men. But at the time, and ever since, few policymakers appreciated the key role played by homemakers in America's social, economic, and political fabric. Homemakers raise children, care for the sick and elderly, and steward family economic and physical health. They also knit neighborhoods and communities together through volunteering, social events, and religious activities.[30]

On the merits—and frankly on the politics, since they are often used as a tripwire in child-care debates—it's important that stay-at-home parents are supported to flourish. And here's a secret: Stay-at-home parents need child care, too. In a 2024 survey commissioned by Capita, the think tank I work for, nearly 40 percent of stay-at-home parents reported needing child care at least a few times a week, with another 22 percent needing it a few times a month.[31] Yet despite this, only a quarter of respondents said they had access to the child care they needed all the time, with 40 percent saying they "rarely" or "almost never" had the care they need.

Parents require breaks for their mental and physical well-being, as well as practical needs like going to doctor's appointments. Child care—even part-time, and whether delivered by a grandparent or a center—provides those breaks. One research paper found that reducing parenting hours by nine to thirteen hours per week through offering high-quality child care had a substantial benefit for child outcomes. The benefits were primarily achieved, the authors conclude, by increases in parenting quality. As they put it, "allowing parents to parent less may allow them to parent better."[32]

Those breaks are also essential for marriages, self-care, and having a social life. In 2023, the organization Mother Untitled commissioned a study that included a survey of 1,200 college-educated stay-at-home mothers.[33] Although most of the mothers surveyed were glad they had the chance to be home with their children, half said leaving the workforce shrunk the size of their mom friend circle, with a similar number reporting it is hard to make friends as a stay-at-home parent.

Relatedly, and concordant with the Capita results, the Mother Untitled survey also found that few stay-at-home parents were regularly using child care. In fact, nearly one-third *never* use child care, not even asking for help from relatives. The reasons are a combination of concern about cost and concern about social stigma. One mother offered that "There is some judgment of why you would need childcare if you aren't going to work. I think there is also the judgment that you chose to have children and stay at home so why do you need a break if this is what you wanted."

If that's the case for parents who elected to become stay-at-home parents, those forced into it by the lack of open or affordable child-care slots face an even harder road. Jessica Calarco records that Erin, the rural mother, struggled with the monotony of stay-at-home motherhood. Erin told Calarco, "you don't necessarily notice it right away. It kinda builds up slowly over time. And then you get to the point where, like, two weeks have gone by, and you haven't really talked to another adult, and you're emotional and you feel kinda crazy. And it's like, I gotta get out! I need a break!"[34]

It does not have to be this way. It is useful here to once again contrast the public school system. Although schools inarguably serve a child-care function, they do not exist only for the benefit of "working families," and therefore stay-at-home parents have equal ability to send their children to school without fear of social reproach. (Although, to be fair, schools do not provide one-off breaks.) In countries like Finland and Norway, stay-at-home parents are incorporated into the child-care system as a matter of policy. That includes giving stay-at-home parents access to cash stipends; operating municipal "open centers," which are staffed drop-in child-care programs; and promoting "family cafes," low-cost offerings where parents of young children can go to socialize while volunteers help care for the children.

Yet when economic logic dominates, it makes little sense to incorporate stay-at-home parents. After all, their contributions have been deliberately excluded from economic indicators. As Greco writes:

> In 1934, Simon Kuznets presented Congress with the research that would become today's GDP calculation. However, he cautioned that it omitted the "services of housewives and other members of the family." This omission had significant and lasting impacts on how American policymakers view homemaking. There is an aphorism in business that "what gets measured gets managed," with the corollary that "what gets measured, matters." The value of homemaking was not measured in the GDP, and so—in the eyes of many economists and politicians—it did not matter.

(Later research proved that unpaid domestic labor in the United States is worth upwards of a trillion dollars per year.[35])

A similar if not identical point can be made around family, friends, and neighbor (FFN) caregivers. I would argue that in most cases—to use an example first posited by advocate Katie Albitz—it would be better for all involved if a seventy-year-old grandmother is caring regularly for their grandchild rather than serving as a Walmart greeter (assuming that is their preference). Although FFNs may be eligible for limited government aid depending on the income level of the children they are caring for, these programs generally involve onerous hoops for miserly pay: as little as $15 a day. It is fair to say there is no widespread public support available to help FFN caregivers, given that less than two in ten receive any above-the-table pay at all.[36]

At times, these policy directions can lead to truly bizarre outcomes that sharply demonstrate the inadequacy of our current approach. Consider neighbors who are stay-at-home parents, both with toddlers. If they decided to swap children during the day, they could each hypothetically register as a family child-care program and, if low-income, qualify for state reimbursement—while remaining ineligible for any support for taking care of their own child.

Such underlying assumptions and delineations have even made their way into left-leaning child-care proposals: The most prominent Democratic bill, with over forty Democratic Senate co-sponsors, is notably titled the Child Care for Working Families Act. The legislation is entirely silent on stay-at-home parents. When one steps back from the free-market child-care system—and the ways it has piled titanic responsibility and stress on the shoulders of mothers and then cleaved homemakers from those working outside the home—it becomes clear that a different foundation is needed to support healthy families across the board. America's failure to do so has now begun taking away a most elemental part of families: the presence of children.

Children as a Luxury Good

There are few freedoms more fundamental than choosing to grow your family on your terms. Such an intimate decision calls for the whispered conversations that sidle up to the idea, so it doesn't startle and flee, those sidelong glances and growing smiles that finally lead one partner to bravely manifest the concept long before conception: "Do you think we're ready?"

Yet for far too many American couples, "ready" is not driven by desire. It is not even driven by the ability to conceive. Readiness, instead, takes on a new meaning in 2020s America: Are families ready to navigate the isolation, expense, and child-care stress that enters the world attached like downy hair to a squalling baby?

Consider Brittany Kjenaas, a married mother who lives in northern Minnesota. She is a healthcare supply manager and her husband is a miner; they are, in other words, a fairly typical middle-class American family. Yet Kjenaas told *Vox*'s Rachel Cohen, "We waited until we were in our 30s to start a family and . . . it's not an exaggeration to say that the decision was based on the cost of child care. She is our only child, and unless something changes in the cost of child care, she will remain our only child."[37]

To see how this plays out on a national scale, consider that having the number of children you want is increasingly a choice only afforded the rich. Children are becoming, in short, a luxury good.

Conventional wisdom—which, for many decades, was correct—is that those at the lower- and moderate-income levels are most likely to live that minivan life, while the wealthy set are content with one or two scions. Nowadays, however, the affluent are the group with the highest relative share of families with three or more children. A group of researchers reported that "the relationship between income and fertility has flattened between 1980 and 2010 in the U.S., a time of increasing inequality, as high income families increased their fertility," a fertility trend that has only continued since.[38] ("Fertility" is used here as an admittedly awkward academic term for how many children a woman has, on average, by the end of her childbearing years.)

Although fertility involves a complicated web of influences, one major change in those decades was families' ability to put the child-rearing—and, specifically, child-care—puzzle together. The phenomenon is not subtle: As one rich Manhattan father told *The New York Times* in 2014, "At some level, the third child is a proxy for having enough wealth to have a very comfortable life."[39]

Indeed, the underlying reasons for this shift aren't shocking. As Michael Bar, one of the economists looking at the income-fertility link, put it: "Richer families can now afford home-care services—like prepared meals, babysitters and day care—because of the continued rise in income inequality."[40]

Similarly, there is strong evidence that women with graduate degrees (a proxy for high earning potential) are utilizing high levels of paid care. Their robust income, a different report notes, has "weakened the trade-off between career and family life and enabled highly educated women to pursue demanding careers without giving up on their desired family size."[41]

We can also see the counterfactual at play. In a 2018 survey commissioned by *The New York Times*, among couples who said they had fewer children than they wanted, the number-one reason was that "child care is too expensive."[42] The rest of the top-five reasons were littered with concerns about finances. A few years later, Pew polled childless adults and found that, among those who desired children, financial reasons trailed only medical reasons in why they didn't have kids.[43] As one mother told the *Times* in 2022 of her child-care challenges, "Realizing how expensive everything is, and then the instability of it, the cost, material and psychological? It really makes you question whether expanding your family is the right thing to do."[44]

This is not a small problem. A 2021 survey from the right-leaning think tank American Compass found that "nearly half of parenting-age Americans say they would ideally have more children than they do."[45] Among married respondents, the overwhelming reason given by all but upper-class parents wasn't about lifestyle or career but that "I don't think I could afford to have more children." According to demographer Lyman Stone, the average American woman's desired fertility has not met her actual completed fertility since, at best, 1982. As Stone says, "unobtained childbearing is a large-scale social problem to be considered alongside of unwanted childbearing."[46]

At times, the two collide. One of the most visceral ways this shows up is with regard to abortion. Although there is plenty of evidence that financial concerns drive abortion decisions around unplanned pregnancies, it is less commonly understood that women not-infrequently terminate *wanted* pregnancies because of child-care costs.

In 2022, a U.K. advocacy group named Pregnant Then Screwed surveyed over 1,600 women who already had at least one child and who had an abortion over the past five years.[47] Some 60 percent said that child-care costs influenced their decision, with nearly one-in-five reporting that the costs were the "main reason" they chose to have an abortion. (While this data comes from across the pond, there is absolutely no reason to think it doesn't apply to the United States; the American child-care system is by any measure equal to or worse than the United Kingdom's.)

One woman shared this wrenching story:

> I have found it heartbreaking that I have had to have an abortion primarily because we could not afford the cost of childcare. If I had continued my pregnancy of a much wanted child, I would have had to quit my job to care for them, this would have meant we had to sell our home as one salary would not cover the bills. This would have been detrimental to my 1 child. The system is a shambles and it is so upsetting. It is horrendous that myself and my husband are both professionals yet we cannot afford a second child due to the first years of their life requiring child care.

That how many kids one can have is connected to whether one completed a postgraduate degree or have a six-figure salary is anathema to modern values. By now, it should be clear the idea that removing the family from the public sphere somehow strengthens the family is simply a falsehood. Instead, the results are harming individuals, households, and the whole of society.

Declining birth rates, particularly coupled with a rapidly growing and longer-lived senior population, have tremendous society-wide implications. Whether one leans conservative or progressive, almost every priority is under threat by demographic change because there is almost no postindustrial social or economic system that isn't predicated on continued population growth or at least stability. As demographer Phillip Longman wrote back in 2004, "population growth underlies our modern concept of freedom."[48] (It should be said that immigration can be a short-term salve to low birth rates, but with rates falling globally and the majority of the world living in depopulating countries, it is not a sustainable answer.)

Although it is beyond the scope of this book to get into all the reasons low birth rates are dangerous—and not withstanding that some of the reasons behind the declines, such as increased education and agency for women, are unalloyed positives!—several consequences of population decline are direct threats to family life.

As mentioned in the previous chapter, depopulating communities with underenrolled schools are not usually thriving places in which to live and raise children. And when population pyramids become top-heavy with the elderly far outnumbering the young, social spending—which tends to shrink in aggregate as nations age and economies slow down—shifts away from families with children and toward elder care. Consider U.S. Census Bureau projections that while 15 percent of the U.S. population was over age sixty-five in 2016, that figure will rise to nearly one-quarter by 2050.[49] The number of people over age eighty-five will more than double. Such a "gerontocracy" also dilutes the voting power of parents and makes it harder for them to force politicians to pass laws that benefit families.

Moreover, when would-be parents are artificially deprived of the opportunity, they lose out on a unique human experience. While I have not one iota of judgment toward those who choose not to raise children (and ample judgment for those who cast aspersions, as if we don't also need a cadre of loving aunts and uncles), philosopher Anastasia Berg and writer Rachel Weisman aptly point out that parenting can yield a deep perspective shift. They write in their book, *What Are Children For?: On Ambivalence and Choice*, that while parents may gain individual fulfillment from parenting, "to have children is to allow yourself to stand in a relationship whose essence is not determined by the benefits it confers or the prices it exacts. That's what it means for it to be not just another good among others. People say that having a child is a gift, but if that's true, it's not because it's like getting a gift. If having a child is a gift, it's because it's like giving one."[50]

It is important to note that an effective child-care system isn't a birth rate panacea. Even nations with the best child-care systems in the world have seen birth rate declines. But good child care has been shown to help mitigate and slow the *rate* of decline.[51] One 2024 paper found that even modest reductions in child-care costs can have significant impacts on reducing the gap between desired and realized family size, boosting fertility rates by around 13 percent.[52] That matters; when it comes to birth rates, small changes have cascading impacts. As the writer and researcher Paul Constance has explained:

> At a fertility rate of 1.85, the [depopulation] process is so gradual that it can take more than two centuries for the number of newborns to shrink by half. But at lower fertility rates, depopulation accelerates because of reverse momentum. At a fertility rate of 1.6, it takes around 90 years for the number of newborns to drop by half. At 1.3, it takes some 50 years. And at a fertility rate of one child per woman—a level already common in many parts of Asia—it can take less than 30 years: Each generation has half as many children as the previous one.[53]

(Note: As of this writing, the U.S. fertility rate is slightly below 1.7.)

Imagine how many couples could meet their desired family size if child care was free.

Conclusion

One cannot square the importance of families with America's ongoing neglect of such a core family issue as child care. If, as Michael Novak opined, what strengthens the family strengthens society, then public support of child care is not to be provided reluctantly but should be proffered proudly. In fact, as we will see in the next chapter, because healthy child-rearing provides a service to the nation, child care is downright patriotic.

Examples of "Family Values Case" Messages:

- "Families are the cornerstone of society. But the lack of child care makes families sick. It forces parents to spend less time together and with their children, and it adds so much stress into families. We need a strong child care system for strong families."
- "Parents deserve support to be the parents they want to be, whether it's a family with two earners or a stay-at-home parent. Public funding of child care helps parents pass on their values and traditions."
- "Families are losing the chance to choose how many children they want to have not due to desire or ability to get pregnant, but just due to child-care access and affordability. That's wrong and un-American."

In a sentence: The availability of good child care strengthens family life, family stability, and even family formation; the artificial lack of child care hurts the American family.

Chapter 4
The Patriotic Case

What do you call someone who voluntarily chooses to serve their nation by courageously putting their bodies on the line, sacrificing ease and comfort for the harder path, and in doing so helps ensure the country is strong, safe, and prosperous?

You call such a person a patriot.

You can also call them a parent.

My tongue is, of course, in my cheek, and there are blindingly obvious differences between parenthood and soldiery. But the fact is for much of American history, child-rearing was considered a service to the nation in addition to a private choice and responsibility. In fact, the above analogy is not mine; it was laid out in 1908 by none other than President Theodore Roosevelt. Speaking to a conference organized by the National Congress of Mothers, Roosevelt inveighed:

> There is no other society which I am quite as glad to receive as this. This is the one body that I put even ahead of the veterans of the Civil War; because when all is said and done it is the mother, and the mother only, who is a better citizen even than the soldier who fights for his country.[1]

Roosevelt was in some ways echoing the great labor activist and social reformer Florence Kelley. Writing in 1905, Kelley asserted that the American Republic "must perish if it should ever cease to be replenished by generations of patriots," who can only be raised through a "long-cherished, carefully nurtured childhood for all the future citizens." This, of course, requires the service of parents. Kelley concluded that "the care and nurture of childhood is thus a vital concern of the nation."[2]

If parenthood is patriotic, then a service such as child care that supports parents in doing their important work is also patriotic. The idea that child care can help create a stronger nation has long been present in both American thought and action, even when cast in contradictions. Moreover, we'll see in this chapter that child care has direct and meaningful impacts on the very exercise of American democracy.

The framework for understanding the patriotic case comes from sociologist Theda Skocpol, whom we met back in Chapter 1. In 1992, Skocpol wrote an award-winning book called *Protecting Soldiers and Mothers: The Political Origins of Social Policy in the United States*.[3] Skocpol shows that in the early twentieth century, a sense of parenthood's vital role in society, combined with intentional movement-building by women's groups, led to a series of astonishing political victories. Harkening back to the Solidarity Case, it is notable that this movement largely crossed class and ideological lines (although not always racial lines—white-led women's groups frequently discriminated against women of color).

Those victories were all the more impressive because they happened in a period when the national mood was opposed to large-scale government programs—and by the fact most of them occurred before women had the right to vote! These wins included securing labor protections for women workers, "mother's pensions," the federal Children's Bureau, and (post-suffrage) passage of the Sheppard-Towner Act aimed at preventing maternal and infant mortality.

To illustrate her point, Skocpol includes as one of the book's first epigraphs a quote from G. Harris Robertson, President of the Tennessee Congress of Mothers, who stated in 1911 that:

> We cannot afford to let a mother, one who has divided her body by creating other lives for the good of the state, one who has contributed to citizenship, be classed as a pauper, a dependent. She must be given value received by her nation, and stand as one honored . . . If our public mind is maternal, loving and generous, wanting to save and develop all, our Government will express this sentiment.

Today, we can update the language to be more inclusive of different family types. It is also rightly offensive to many modern ears (mine included) to see women's value tied so tightly to their reproductive abilities, as if those who cannot or choose not to bear children are undeserving of respect. Asserting any public interest in women's bodies is also fraught territory. There is a reason, as Skocpol writes, that modern feminists have tended to reject this framing: deployed badly, it can veer between insulting and destructive. Yet the underlying sentiment remains powerful.

It is worth emphasizing how pervasive the sense of child-rearing-as-national-service became. Skocpol notes that in the first decade of the twentieth century, progressive reformers ran into judicial roadblock after judicial roadblock trying to defend laws intended to better the lot of the working class. For instance, in 1905's *Lochner v. New York*, the U.S. Supreme Court struck down a law that would have capped working hours for bakers at sixty hours a week, or ten hours a day.

Yet three years later, in *Muller v. Oregon*, the Court issued a very different opinion, upholding a law that established a cap of ten hours a day—for working *women* only. Justice David Brewer wrote in the (rather patronizing) opinion that "[a]s healthy mothers are essential to vigorous offspring, the physical well-being of woman becomes an object of public interest and care" in order to ensure the strength of subsequent generations.

If you are a parent, you may protest here that your motivation to have children had little to do with the good of the state—I would say that thought never entered my or my wife's mind—but in a sense this does not matter. I expect that many of those who have contributed to American greatness, whether scientists like George Washington Carver or authors like Louisa May Alcott, did not do so with the explicit goal of bettering the nation.

Interestingly, civically minded language around family formation has begun to make a resurgence around the world. In 2024, while allowing that "we must not make those who don't want children feel guilty," French president Emmanuel Macron announced a package of policies intended to increase births, including improved parental leave. In doing so, Macron declared, "France will only be stronger if it revives the birth rate."[4]

As we have begun to explore, all countries, very much including America, require strong and healthy children. Nearly every social and economic system that allows the nation we hold dear to prosper relies on children consistently entering the scene. Although the next chapter is dedicated to taking childhood on its own terms, children are undeniably tomorrow's workers and drive an enormous amount of consumption today (toys alone are more than a $100 billion industry in the United States, to say nothing of how children increase consumption needs around basics such as food and clothes). Children are the ones who will pay into social insurance systems such as Social Security and Medicare. They are tomorrow's innovators. They are tomorrow's soldiers. They are tomorrow's voters. Those who raise them deserve our thanks.

The Contributions of Parenthood

Parents serve the nation by more than just producing the next generation of citizens: They also sacrifice their time and treasure. The money parents spend on children's clothing and toys and extracurricular activities, the unpaid time they spend shuttling kids to said activities and participating in school bake sales and talent shows, all contributes to the growth of those strong and healthy children. There is also an opportunity cost: That money and time could be used elsewhere. As a group of researchers put it in a 2023 paper:

> The relative invisibility of parental transfers is what allows welfare states to implicitly freeride on the cost of producing their own future taxbase. To the degree that current policies and accounting procedures do not fully take into account how the next generation of taxpayers was produced in the first place, they adhere to an erroneous "stork theory" of child-rearing.[5]

Put another way, when a child grows up to get a stable job and pays taxes that benefit everyone via filling Social Security coffers and highway trust funds, we don't tend to see all the uncompensated inputs that went into shaping that child's future. The researchers note that in the past, it was more difficult to isolate the contribution of parents because there were so many contributors to child-rearing: grandparents, neighbors, community members, and so on. The village, in essence. Today, with the nuclear family still exceedingly dominant (although there has been a recent uptick in multigenerational households), nearly all the costs are borne by parents.

Although Western nations offer parents varying levels of benefits to defray the cost of child-rearing—from child tax credits to public subsidy of schooling (or, yes, child care)—these generally amount to less than half of the total costs of raising a child. Taking into account all the invisible parental expenditures, the researchers calculate that even in Europe, where nations offer more generous family benefits, parents contribute on average 2.6 times as much to national economies as nonparents. That is not a dig at nonparents, but a lens highlighting that parents are doing more for their country than we commonly acknowledge.

U.S. economists such as Nancy Folbre have confirmed that this holds true in America as well: Folbre has suggested that "as children become increasingly public goods, parenting becomes an increasingly public service."[6] If one replaced all the unpaid hours of parental care with hours from paid child-care educators, Folbre calculates, one would need over *30 million* child-care educators—or five times the total number of existing child-care *and* K-12 educators combined![7] She also cites a study that found when children's future tax revenues are taken into account, the average U.S. parent "contributes about [$300,000 in 2024 dollars] more than the average nonparent in net taxes." Such a lens can help us understand that public spending on child care is not some sort of handout, but rather at long last making things square.

I would nuance the parenting-as-service concept in one important way. Soldiers' pensions and the GI Bill—as well as elder care provisions such as Medicare—are ways of honoring service *after* the service is complete. It is the promise (one that is questionably fulfilled, to be sure) that for the labor you voluntarily give now, you will be compensated later.

Providing affordable, high-quality child care is more like ensuring soldiers have the supplies they need in terms of uniforms, food, and tools of the trade. (And, as we will see in a future chapter, child care is quite literally one of those basic military needs.) Because parents are serving the country, it is incumbent on the country to ensure they have what they need to maximize their chances of success.

I hope it is becoming clear this is actually a very American concept.

Supporting Early Child Care Is Deeply American

Despite the national mythos around hyperindividualistic self-sufficiency, there is more of a history of American support of families with children than commonly realized. (This is true beyond child care: The author Alissa Quart notes that "pulling yourself up by your bootstraps" started as an absurdist and mocking phrase, because boots in the era when the phrase originated required human or mechanical assistance to get on.[8])

Would it surprise you to learn there was a movement to provide care and education for children between eighteen months and four years of age in the late 1820s? As in, during the presidency of Andrew Jackson? When the must-have toy for children was a wooden cup-and-ball known as a *bilboquet*?

Termed the "infant school" movement, this was an import from Great Britain, and it took hold most firmly in Massachusetts.[9] The Boston Infant

School Society promised these programs—operating from 6 AM to 7 PM in the summer and 8 AM to 5 PM in the winter—would provide "eminent service, both to parents and to children." How? "By relieving [working-class] mothers of a pan of their domestic cares, it would enable them to seek employment," while helping children of working-class families "be removed from the unhappy association of want and vice, and be placed under better influences." (It was the 1820s.) Bronson Alcott—yes, Louisa May's father—was a well-known infant school teacher.

Nor were infant schools only for lower-income families. Historian Emily Cahan has written that a good number of affluent families sent their young children to infant schools.[10] She cites an 1829 article in *Ladies Magazine* in which the author mused (presaging much later arguments in favor of early childhood education):

> And why should a plan which promises so many advantages, independent of merely relieving the mother from her charge, be confined to the children of the indigent? It is nearly if not quite impossible, to teach such little ones at home with the facility they are taught in an infant school. And if a convenient room is prepared, and faithful and discreet agents employed, parents may feel secure that their darlings are not only safe, but improving.

Although infant schools varied widely in their quality, target ages, and class clientele, they were a decidedly communal approach. Infant schools were an affordable early care and education option from very early in America's history, free for the poor and within easy reach for the working and middle classes. One such school, which was opening in Jacksonville, Illinois, advertised its quarterly fees as $2—all of $70 in today's money.

In the end, the infant school movement failed more for politics than mores. Although some religious fundamentalists did object, the bigger issue was that nascent public school districts weren't keen on sharing government grants with the infant schools. When a well-known child psychologist declared that too much "mental excitement" was harmful for young children (it was, by then, the 1830s), interest and funding dried up; the country moved on.

Still, the idea of the public assuming some measure of responsibility for early child care lingered until a stricter school enrollment age was put into place. As infant schools faded, public schools picked up many of their students. Although detailed records from the era are scarce, one researcher has calculated that in the 1839–1840 school year, fully 40 percent of three-year-olds in Massachusetts were enrolled in public schools.[11] (For context, less than a quarter of Massachusetts three-year-olds are currently enrolled in public pre-K programs.[12])

Traditionalist resistance to external child care has also long melted away when inconvenient, most notably during wartime. The first federally funded child-care program in America was established in Philadelphia in 1863, long before the World War II Lanham Act centers or the Depression-era Works Progress Administration emergency nursery schools that preceded them. The Philadelphia site was opened in order to serve the children of women working in clothing factories and hospitals during the Civil War.[13] Even after the Civil War, the government continued to support the program for children of working war widows.

The Curious Case of Pre-K

In the modern era, American society is actually fine with the idea of paying quite a lot of money for the care and education of young children—it just depends on how the question is phrased. The first universal public pre-K systems were established in the mid-1990s in surprising states: Georgia and Oklahoma. In Oklahoma, for instance, pre-K is funded as part of the state's public education system; the service is available to every resident for free, and it is delivered through a variety of public school classrooms, child-care centers, and other community-based programs. Currently, around 70 percent of Oklahoma's four-year-olds attend. Nearly every state now has a version of public pre-K.

Pre-K for four-year-olds has been able to escape the culture wars around the role of the state versus the mother by attaching like a barnacle to another great American institution: public education. The patriotic understanding that strong public education is essential for a strong nation goes back to the literal founding of America, as thinkers from Thomas Jefferson on have forcefully made the case that the nation has no future absent a system of schooling. (How that system should look and what it should teach, of course, have been and remain the subject of intense debate.)

As previously noted, public education receives around $800 billion a year in public money. Despite all the flaws and inequities, education is the first- or second-largest line item in every state budget, and every state constitution contains a right to free schooling for its residents. The inclusion of such a right was seen as so important to the American social fabric that Congress made it a de facto requirement for Confederate states' re-entry into the union.[14]

Sociologist Sandra Levitsky, who has studied how pre-K came to be accepted, notes that advocates built from the Georgia and Oklahoma precedents with an intentional campaign to place child care inside the education circle. Levitsky writes that "this education narrative was a powerful reframing of the necessity of state intervention in the lives of families with small children."[15]

Yet glomming onto the education frame came with a cost. Unlike the women's movement in the early twentieth century, these investments were purely about the child. Parents, and the family more broadly, were somewhere between ancillary and absent. Levitsky writes that "early childhood programs can achieve their goals in ways that do not necessarily support ... the needs of working families." For instance, many pre-K programs run on a school-year, school-day schedule, which is misaligned with work schedules. Levitsky goes on to argue that, in a deeper sense,

> [W]hile considerable public discourse has focused on the educational development of three- and four-year-olds, the needs of working parents with babies are rarely mentioned at all. Perhaps more insidiously, the logic of "social investment," which drove the political shift from childcare to early childhood education, generally construes children as a "good investment" in ways that implicitly suggest that women are *not*. (emphasis hers)

What Levitsky is getting at is the legacy—and fallacy—of treating child care and education as separate ideas, something I touched on in the Introduction. Historian Barbara Beatty calls that schism "the big divide, the flood when early education and child care got separated and put on different arks."[16] An in-depth study of that particular history is beyond the scope of this book. Suffice it to say that the tension remains unresolved and has made it more difficult to secure a functional child-care system that is inclusive and goes across both the early years and elementary school years.

The challenge and opportunity, then, is to knit these two ideas together: parenthood-as-service, and young-children-as-within-bounds. Combined, they form a solid bedrock for building out a real child-care system. It would form the philosophical basis for seeing all investments in the early years being as equally patriotic as investments in preK–12 public education, and do the same for school-aged child care like after-school and summer needs.

Given that American society and voters are already on board with public support of child care in some forms and for some settings, there is immense potential in breaking down the artificial walls.

Accomplishing that task will be much easier with a strong democracy in place that fully includes parents.

Vote, Mama

In a very real sense, the lack of child care hurts American democracy by narrowing the pool of people who can reasonably serve in elected office.

Whereas women are already underrepresented in elected offices—in state legislatures, women make up roughly 30 percent of the seats despite being half the population—mothers of minor children are stunningly absent. Reports from the nonprofit VoteMama Foundation found that in the early 2020s, less than 7 percent of Congress and a hair more than 5 percent of state legislators were mothers with children under the age of 18.[17] (Full disclosure: I served on the VoteMama Board from 2021 to 2022.) Whereas upwards of four million American women give birth each year, in 2021 a grand total of twelve(!) state legislators did. The first U.S. Senator to give birth in office was Illinois' Tammy Duckworth, who did so in 2018.

Child care is a huge barrier to having these vital voices shaping policy decisions. Until the past few years, campaign funds could not be legally spent on child care—though they could be spent on transportation and coffee. Even once legislators and other officials are elected, child-care pressures don't abate. The VoteMama report notes that Georgia State Representative Rebecca Mitchell spends 237 percent of her state legislative income on child care. And, of course, innumerable would-be candidates don't run because of child-care challenges or because they move away from districts in which they have roots in search of affordable care.

Child care may be a consideration for fathers who want to run for office, but this dimension clearly impacts mothers more acutely. As Becca Balint, now a U.S. Representative from Vermont, said to VoteMama, "Government at any level was not designed for women, let alone mothers. When I ran for Congress, I was constantly questioned on the campaign trail. 'Who will take care of the kids?' 'Have you thought about how this will impact your family?' I don't think men running for office get asked these questions."

Although the mere presence of mothers with young children is not a slam dunk for family-friendly policies like child care—and again, fathers have a huge role to play—history shows they can be vital champions. As Balint told journalist Rebecca Gale, when Balint first became a state legislator back in 2015, most of her colleagues were men over the age of sixty. "They hadn't been thinking about the issue of having two [parents] in the workforce . . . they would tell me [child care] was strictly a personal issue, and say 'someone should just be home with the kids.'"[18] Partisan ideology remains a strong brew, but there is some evidence that having more mothers in office can help advance viable solutions. Kelly Dittmar, director of research at the Center for American Women and Politics, told Gale in the same article that "Even more traditionally conservative women might be more amenable to thinking about solutions [to different public policy problems] because they understand the challenges."

Perhaps unsurprisingly, then, Quebec's efforts in the late 1990s to make child care deeply affordable (less than $10 a day for most families) was led by Education Minister Pauline Marois, who later became the province's first female premier. Similarly, German Chancellor Angela Merkel oversaw tremendous child-care reforms, including a 2013 law that guaranteed child-care slots for all German families. These effects are measurable: One study found that U.S. Congresswomen with minor children introduced more legislation "specific to the needs of parents and children" than their counterparts.[19]

The availability of child care can also, as we have seen, take the boot at least partially off the neck of exhausted, stressed-out parents and caregivers. Doing so can add capacity, enabling them to participate civically by engaging with community groups, going to rallies, attending school board or legislative committee meetings, and so on. This can start a virtuous cycle. In 2023, *The New Republic* reported on a New Mexico grandmother, Patricia Bustillos, whose grandchildren had benefited from the state (temporarily) making child care free for families making up to around $110,000 a year. The article states that:

> The stability has helped to open further doors for Bustillos. Having both grandchildren in childcare means she's been called on less to care for the girls herself, freeing her up to work more. She's putting more hours in at a nonprofit that offers parenting skills, working both morning and afternoons, while she spends the rest of her time cleaning offices. "Eso para mi es un ingreso extra," she said: For me that's extra income.
>
> She's also able to participate more in nonfinancial activities. She's a member of OLÉ, a grassroots nonprofit that has advocated for more

investment in childcare and early childhood education, and she traveled to the state Capitol to lobby for investment without worrying about having to care for her grandchildren. She also participated in a training with the nonprofit National Women's Law Center to do public speaking about social justice and equal pay for women, especially Latinas like her. The NWLC has taught her "como cuidar a yo" and "como relajarme": how to take care of herself and relax.[20]

Indeed, child care matters not just for candidates and elected officials, but for those doing the voting. One recent study found that mothers with infants are 3.5 percent less likely to vote, and fathers with infants 2.2 percent less likely, than their peers without children.[21] Other research suggests the impact is most concentrated among lower-income families.[22] The story appears to be about child-care availability more than the exhaustion of early parenthood: Universal vote-by-mail systems cancel out the negative effects. Although these percentages are not earth-shattering, the impact can be significant, especially given that parents of young children are already outnumbered by those who are not.

What's more, insofar as child care reduces poverty (the subject of its own upcoming chapter), child care enhances voting rates. It is a well-established finding that voting propensity correlates strongly with income. For instance, in 2020, around 65 percent of those making under $40,000 voted, versus 88 percent of those making more than $75,000.[23]

This has something to do with practical barriers, such as getting time off a shift job to go vote or having the mental bandwidth to fit that in when juggling more first-order needs such as paying bills, but it is also strongly a matter of how lower-income and working-class Americans perceive themselves in relation to the government. Here again, we see influences starting in childhood. The eminent political scientist Robert Putnam has noted that "high-quality national surveys of high school seniors confirm that kids from less educated homes are less knowledgeable about and interested in politics, less likely to trust the government, less likely to vote, and much less likely to be civically engaged in local affairs than their counterparts from college-educated homes."[24]

From both the candidate and voter angle, a vibrant democracy requires vibrant child care. That's true from another angle: the generation that can't even vote yet.

Civic Readiness

A great deal of the U.S. focus on child care revolves around the idea of "school readiness," which we will delve into during the next chapter. Yet these settings—especially more formal child-care programs such as centers—are also key sources of what might be considered "civic readiness": preparing children to engage in American democracy and learn to appreciate the country in which they live.

Child psychologists Jennifer Astuto and Martin D. Ruck have written that "Early childhood settings . . . are the first representation of greater society for young children. Not only does this context function to introduce young children to democratic processes and values, but it also may be the most fundamental context in developing the necessary competencies and skills for future civic engagement in the polity."[25]

For better or worse, these early experiences form the foundation for a child's understanding of society. Do they live in a society where their voice is valued or where they are subject to authoritarian whims (other than the whims of Nap Time, of course)? What is to happen when there is a disagreement over how to allocate scarce resources (say, wooden blocks)? These are not minor questions: As we will see in a later chapter, they are also questions frequently coded along lines of class and race. Obviously, toddlers are not engaging in intellectual debates—nor, thankfully, sniping at each other on social media—but they are gaining knowledge and skills through everyday play. As Astuto and Ruck write:

> [I]f play provides opportunities for young children to function in democratic ways, solve problems, communicate effectively, and express opinions, then a quality play context also provides a unique template for engagement in society. It is here where children learn to become an active member of a group, follow rules, and contribute to the development of ideas. These foreshadow the skills (and behaviors) of a civically engaged adolescent.

Perhaps even more importantly, child care helps children develop critical executive functioning skills. Brain architecture, it can hardly be repeated enough times, develops like building a house: cumulatively, and from the foundation up. Executive functions such as self-control, working memory, and shifting perspectives depending on the situation (developmentally speaking, "cognitive flexibility") are all linked to prosocial behaviors. Such skills and behaviors are particularly crucial in our age of anxiety and rancor. The old Robert Fulghum book, *All I Really Need to Know I Learned in Kindergarten*, turns out to have picked a too-late starting point.

Moreover, the early years are where national pride and traditions begin to be passed down. Especially as children pass out of infancy, a high-quality child-care program or unstressed parent is likely to be able to read books and teach age-appropriate lessons around America's founding and values, to visit museums and parades, to begin to help kids understand what that big, oddly shaped map on the wall represents. This is doubly true for school-aged child-care programs. These implicit and explicit lessons go beyond an anodyne sense of Americanness anchored on construction paper turkeys: As the Albert Shanker Institute's Rachel Wessler, a former early childhood educator, has written, "These early experiences help young children grow an awareness of their civic agency and a caring for communities. Developing these democratic dispositions at an early age can support students' ability to solve problems of injustice throughout their lives—forging a path toward a more equitable and just future for all."[26]

A more ineffable democratic value also would be conveyed by creating a universal child-care system. Universal, free-at-the-point-of-service institutions are a vital part of the national fabric, a form of connective tissue. If you look through the early arguments for "common schools," including from luminaries such as Thomas Jefferson and Horace Mann, an overriding theme is the need for mass education in furtherance of democracy, that all Americans would have the knowledge and skills needed to be an informed and active citizen.

What's more, such institutions themselves serve as hubs for social connection, what sociologist Eric Klinenberg, from whom we will hear more around the Security Case, calls "social infrastructure."[27] There is a reason why we use public monies to fund not only schools, but libraries and parks, and make them free to all regardless of one's ability to pay. Bill Gates or Warren Buffett can check a book out at their local library for free, picnic in their local park for free, send their children to their local public school for free; we ask them to pay more in taxes (hypothetically), but we do not begrudge their use of these public commons. Child care belongs among this pantheon of universal services.

Any way you cut it, patriotism starts early.

Conclusion

America needs patriots. According to Gallup polls, as of 2023, just 39 percent of adults said they were "extremely proud" to be American (with another 28 percent saying they were "very proud"). That extremely proud number was down from 57 percent ten years earlier.[28] Less than one in five eighteen-to-thirty-four-year-olds reported being extremely proud. Trust in institutions, from government to public schools, is at or near all-time lows. A 2023 Pew survey found that Americans on average feel far less close to other people in the country, or in their local communities, than residents of peer nations.[29] There are complex factors behind these numbers, but surely one of them is that the social contract has frayed: Too many Americans, including parents, no longer believe—sadly, with good reason—that the country has their backs, or perhaps worse that the country has any interest in having their backs.

That is a dangerous brew. As the German-American political philosopher Hannah Arendt detailed back in 1951 in her book, *The Origins of Totalitarianism*, when individuals—whether their beliefs lean conservative or progressive—feel abandoned by their society and government, they are susceptible to the sway of antidemocratic, authoritarian movements. As one scholar of Arendt's work explained, "When a person feels isolated, a political movement offers them a sense of belonging, purpose and meaning... when there is no longer basic kindness, trust and human decency, and people feel thrown into the world to make it on their own, [they] will go looking for a movement to belong to."[30]

Yet patriotism can be a powerful antidote. The economist and writer Noah Smith has asserted, after reviewing relevant research, "People want to like their country. They can be disappointed in it or mad at it or frustrated with it, but ultimately they want to think that they're part of something good. And that desire can be used to great effect if a political movement manages to capture it, uphold it, and validate it."[31]

Although the history of American support of families is checkered, we would do well to recapture the idea that parenthood provides a crucial service to society. This can open the door to powerful arguments: Instead of begging for scraps, parents are positioned to demand that government make good on their obligations. Child-care funding is not something to be reluctantly handed out by legislators busy with other priorities; it is *owed* to parents who are, every day, thickening the threads on the skein of American society.

Moreover, as we've seen throughout the book already, child care is deeply tied up in questions of freedom and self-determination. Belief in individual freedom remains perhaps the most American of values: One 2021 survey found that 95 percent of Americans think believing in individual freedoms is important to "being truly American."[32] When our failure to invest in a functional child-care system detracts from those freedoms, it injures the national character.

Child care therefore belongs in the constellation of great American institutions and social services. As we've seen, if you squint or tilt your head a certain way, it already is: We just need to refocus our eyes and realize government support of child care is not some alien intrusion but the natural extension of our country's history and values. Doing so will not only strengthen American families, but American democracy—both now and for the future. To be a child-care champion is to be a patriot. In doing so, as we will now see, these patriots improve the very experience of being a parent and being a child.

Examples of Patriotic Case Messages:
- "Having and raising children is a service to the nation. America owes it to parents to provide them with the support they need to thrive."
- "Public support of child care is an American idea. We've been offering help in various forms since the 1820s. It's long past time to make good on that promise and make America a place parents are proud to raise kids."
- "The country is only as strong as its democracy. The lack of child care makes it hard for mothers with children to run for office, and makes it hard for parents to vote. A good child-care system is good for American democracy."

In a sentence: Parents provide a public service by raising children, and for much of America's history we honored parents for that service with public support; for the sake of our democracy, we need to recapture that sense of parenthood-as-patriotic by creating a real child-care system.

Chapter 5
The Parenthood and Childhood Case

Childhood as we know it is a modern invention. As historian Steven Mintz explained in *Huck's Raft: A History of American Childhood*:

> During the nineteenth century, only a small minority of children experienced the middle-class ideal of maturation taking place gradually, in carefully calibrated steps, within institutions segregated from adult society. The vast majority of families ... continued to rely heavily on children's labor and earnings. On farms, children as young as five or six pulled weeds and chased birds and cattle away from crops. By the time they reached eight, many tended livestock, milked cows, churned butter, fed chickens, collected eggs, hauled water, scrubbed laundry, and harvested crops. In urban areas, working-class children ran errands, scavenged, participated in street trades, or took part in outwork, namely, forms of manufacturing that took place in the home.[1]

The question of child care was, therefore, in large part nonsensical: Most of the country lived in multigenerational homes tending the family farm or working the family business. Care of those too young to contribute was juggled between mothers, grandmothers, and older siblings. (At least for those who were free: In the antebellum South, enslaved women and girls were commonly forced into service as caregivers for the children of their enslavers, and enslaved children writ large forced to work from extremely young ages.[2])

Thankfully, the status of children changed dramatically over the twentieth century. A confluence of social, economic, and scientific factors led to children's role in society being repositioned. Children transformed, in the formulation of sociologist Viviana Zelizer, from being "economically useful" but not sources of deep sentiment to "economically useless but emotionally priceless."[3] (There are, of course, exceptions in both directions: One should not think our ancestors heartless nor our era a paragon of child welfare.) For the first time, childhood could be taken on its own terms. And—not for the first time, but certainly with unprecedented acuteness—parents became extremely concerned with how their parenting was affecting their children's well-being and future prospects.

A strong child-care system—which, again, means a system covering support of stay-at-home parents alongside child-care centers and everything in between—bolsters the lot of both children and parents. It allows us to take childhood as a valuable period in itself, instead of only "investing" in children for their future returns. It is also part of an antidote to America's dangerous dominant philosophy of "intensive parenting," the idea that parents need to curate children's experiences and maximize their chances of success given the uncertainty and chaos of the age. In the simplest sense, it helps everyone take a deep breath.

If we want healthy, happy children having healthy, happy childhoods alongside their healthy, happy parents, America needs child care.

What Children Need

It is worth reiterating the science of early childhood development. Whereas for much of human history children were generally considered small adults at best or inferior impulse-driven creatures at worst, we have for several decades known better.[4] The now-classic metaphor remains accurate if crude: Human brains and bodies develop like building a house, and the early years are the foundation.

In recent years, aided by cutting-edge technological tools such as functional MRI machines, researchers have uncovered even more detailed blueprints for human development. We now understand there are prenatal and even preconception influences; that the presence or absence of safe, stable, and nurturing relationships are key mediators of stress; and that the developing body and brain are deeply impacted, in intertwining ways, by their physical environment.[5]

These advances make our era an exciting one for early childhood. Yet in many ways we have swung the pendulum too far. Instead of treating young children like tiny adults, too often we now approach the early years—and our ability to intervene in them—only for their usefulness in shaping children's later lives. Here, again, the shadow side of the Economic Case becomes visible. For instance, in 2017, the U.S. Chamber of Commerce Foundation released a report called *Workforce of Today, Workforce of Tomorrow: The*

Business Case for High-Quality Childcare. Although the report has useful elements, it states the underlying assumption on page one: "A broad set of socially and economically valuable skills start developing in children's very first months, build over time, and are critical determinants of academic and economic success."[6]

Sociologist Susan Prentice calls this concept that of "the investible child."[7] Children's value is wrapped up in what they can produce in a future state, not unlike an investment vehicle such as a stock or bond. This frame can be helpful in attracting the attention of previously indifferent, yet powerful actors—such as, say, the U.S. Chamber of Commerce—but in many ways it is wedging a door open by breaking the wood: There is a cost, and the resulting opening is narrow. "Economic reframing displaces the justice-based rationale for childcare," Prentice writes, adding that "The business case for child care builds an ideological/conceptual bridge to contemporary wealth production, not to social transformation." (Indeed, the U.S. Chamber of Commerce would later put up a six-figure ad buy as part of a lobbying blitz opposing the 2021 Build Back Better Act, which contained in part $400 billion in child-care funding.[8])

Few people these days question the logic of the investible child—the economic rationale for childcare is exceptionally dominant and deployed by leaders of both political parties as well as even very progressive advocates. This is a sign that the status of children has again changed. Researchers Nina Bandelj and Michelle Spiegel note that Zelizer was writing about the priceless child in the early 1980s. Since then, animated by ideas like economist Gary Becker's human capital theory, children have again become economically useful: It's just that their usefulness is cast into the future.[9] If the name Gary Becker sounds familiar, it's because he was one of the core intellectuals behind neoliberalism, and his ideas deeply influenced America's slide into a market-based child-care system and the "free-market family" more broadly.

The Problem with "School Readiness"

A similar philosophy animates the common refrain that child care is needed to ensure "school readiness." While I, of course, concur that early childhood experiences provide the foundation for academics, it is worth considering to what school readiness refers. Today, the common understanding is that school readiness means early child care should prepare children for school so they walk into Kindergarten on day one with a baseline of academic (and, secondarily, social) skills. Hence, alarming headlines like "New report: Majority of kids in Illinois not ready for kindergarten,"[10] and, from Florida, "Is your child kindergarten ready? 43% of students are not, according to state data" appear regularly.[11]

But dig a bit deeper. Inherently, the concept of school readiness is tied up with the concept of the investible child: It asserts that the value of the early years is only in relation to later educational attainment. Indeed, the modern concept came out of panic about the nation's educational performance, and in turn global competitiveness, following the 1983 *A Nation At Risk* report. A few years later, the National Education Goals Panel stated that the country's first goal should be, "All children in America will start school ready to learn."[12]

What's more, tethering child care's value to children's future production begins at the earliest of ages, thereby enforcing norms of winners and losers. Even though any expert—and any parent with more than one kid!—can explain that child development is wildly variable, there are lines of demarcation when viewed backwards through the lens of "academic and economic success." This group of children are on track, those children are a problem.

Such a view of childhood can carry nasty implications. For instance, while the Head Start program has done an immense amount of good, it began not as a way to ensure a positive childhood but as a kind of inoculation against the pathology of (Black) poverty. In announcing the program, President Lyndon Johnson was not subtle, invoking a sort of proto-investible-child frame in declaring that "Five- and six-year-old children are inheritors of poverty's curse and not its creators. Unless we act these children will pass it on to the next generation, like a family birthmark." (We will have more to say in the next chapter about the consequences of a racialized system aiming at school readiness.)

When we see childhood as instrumental rather than inherently valuable, it can also lead to damaging policy decisions. Consider a 2022 study of Tennessee's public pre-K program. Contradicting many other pre-K studies, this one found modestly *negative* effects on students' academic and behavioral outcomes by the time the cohort reached sixth grade. Although there were many possible explanations—including the idea that too much emphasis was being put on one year of pre-K versus the rest of the elementary school years—the lead researcher offered that one challenge was an inappropriate focus on academics.

Jackie Mader of *The Hechinger Report*, a nonprofit news site that focuses on early childhood and K–12 education, reported that, "Across the Tennessee pre-K classrooms that were observed, teachers spent too much time on transitions and whole group instruction. When content was taught, it was almost entirely focused on literacy."[13] (Tennessee state officials say that, since the study period, they have made adjustments to ensure program curricula are developmentally appropriate.)

Findings like those out of Tennessee also reveal a real political danger in resting the case for child care only on future academic and economic impacts. What happens if the "return on investment" stops looking so robust? Indeed, opponents of public child care funding gleefully jumped on the Tennessee report. Barbs came in from sources such as the *Wall Street Journal* editorial board, who used the results to cast doubt on the entire pre-K enterprise.[14] The more research that comes out which fails to replicate the same outstanding ROI of earlier, smaller studies—and in nearly every social science field scaling tends to reduce effect sizes, which is why one set of researchers calls it "naïve" to think those earlier results will generalize—the easier it becomes to hand-wave away the need for major public money.[15]

Finally, all of this takes families and communities out of the equation, instead zeroing in on children as the unit of change. There was actually a moment when the train could have been rerouted. In the early 2000s, a group of seventeen states and several philanthropic foundations came together around what was known as the National School Readiness Indicators Initiative.[16] The Initiative posited a "ready child equation": ready families + ready communities + ready services + ready schools = children ready for school. The effect on children here is the *output*, not the *input*. Children were not asked to bear the burden of readiness. Sadly, the work of the Initiative was largely swamped by the rising focus on the investible child and the No Child Left Behind "accountability era" of education reform.

Making the childhood case for child care can help put early childhood back in its proper place, push back on opponents, and win more widespread support from those who look at the over-academized and over-economized system and find themselves wanting nothing to do with it. Otherwise, we will continue to fall prey to a dangerous temptation: When we are so focused on what children might become, we forget who they are and what they need.

Childhood for Childhood's Sake

The alternative to economic and school readiness frames is to honor the early years in their own right and on their own terms. To declare that there is an elemental beauty and goodness to giving children the ability to play, roam, delight, wonder, laugh, and be joyful. Supporting young children and their families—not just rhetorically, but with society's cultural attention and taxpayer dollars—is an inherently proper and right goal.

This view resonates with a Catholic social teaching (one that itself has echoes in many faith traditions) known as "integral human development."[17] Pope John Paul VI first detailed the concept in 1967, writing in an encyclical that "[Human] development cannot be limited to mere economic growth. In order to be authentic, it must be complete: integral, that is, it has to promote the good of every person and of the whole person." Integral human development rests on the irreducible dignity of every human being—child and adult—and demands consideration of all dimensions of well-being: not just financial but social, spiritual, creative, and so on. Many of these elements show up in measures developed by Harvard professor Tyler VanderWeele as part of the Human Flourishing Project he leads.[18]

Interestingly, we grasp the negative formulation of childhood-on-its-own-terms. Several bestselling books in recent years, such as Bessel van der Kolk's *The Body Keeps the Score* and Bruce Perry's *What Happened to You?*, have reinvigorated conversations about how deep-seated and long-lasting traumas can be, even if some of those traumas occurred before our long-term memory came online. Yet instead of coming from the angle of post-hoc response or even prevention (which, while surely important, still feels more like steering away from a boulder as opposed to never getting in the rapids in the first place), what if we flipped the script and began from an ethic of maximizing contented childhoods?

Approached this way, the fact that helping children have good childhoods causes positive impacts down the road in the form of better academic performance and better lifetime earnings is nice, but hardly the point. If I may be permitted a pointed analogy, that is like suggesting the purpose of striving for a good marriage is regular sex. The latter may be welcome and naturally come with the territory, but it is not the organizing principle. Instead, as writer Rob K. Henderson puts it in his memoir, *Troubled*, about a childhood in which he was neglected and abused:

Unstable environments and unreliable caregivers aren't bad for children because they reduce their future odds of getting into college or making a living; they are bad because the children enduring them experience pain—pain that etches itself into their brains and bodies and propels them to do things in the pursuit of relief that often inflict even more harm. Credentials and money are not antidotes to the lingering effects of childhood maltreatment.[19]

When you take childhood on its own terms, the goal shifts to being what child psychologist Alison Gopnik calls "a gardener." Speaking specifically of parents, but applicable to caregivers and child-care policy more generally, Gopnik writes in *The Gardener and The Carpenter* that:

> When we garden ... we create a protected and nurturing space for plants to flourish. It takes hard labor and the sweat of our brows, with a lot of exhausted digging and wallowing in manure. And as any gardener knows, our specific plans are always thwarted ... The good gardener works to create fertile soil that can sustain a whole ecosystem of different plants with different strengths and beauties—and with different weaknesses and difficulties, too ... our job is to provide a protected space of love, safety, and stability in which children of many unpredictable kinds can flourish. Our job is not to shape our children's minds; it's to let those minds explore all the possibilities that the world allows. Our job is not to tell children how to play; it's to give them the toys and pick the toys up again after the kids are done. We can't make children learn, but we can let them learn.[20]

A comprehensive, affordable, high-quality child-care system is a key nutrient in that garden soil—like nitrogen or phosphorus—and it is difficult to imagine a healthy garden without it. Moreover, a garden desperately needs a healthy gardener. If a gardener is sick or so stressed that they cannot do the work of cultivation, or if gardeners keep changing and needing to re-learn the specifics of a particular plot of land, the plants are likely to suffer. This is one reason why the exceptionally high turnover among low-paid child-care educators, and the exceptionally high stress experienced by many parents, is so destructive: It disrupts children's stability and metaphorical soil. Hence, garden and gardener both need child care.

Stress + Scarcity = Intensive Parenting

Over the last half-century, so-called "intensive parenting" has become the dominant parenting philosophy in the United States. As I explained in an article for *The Atlantic*:

> Often used interchangeably with more derisive terms such as helicopter parenting, bulldozer parenting, and snowplow parenting, intensive parenting has its appeal. Scholars suggest that it first arose among middle-class families in the mid-to-late 20th century, amid shrinking manufacturing jobs, globalization, growing wealth inequality, a sense that children were both "vulnerable and moldable," and a general feeling that American triumphalism was perhaps not a guarantee. In response to this anxiety, parents started pushing harder to ensure their kids' future stability. Throughout the 2010s, as precarity continued to increase, the intensive-parenting ideology stretched its tendrils across class lines.
>
> Rafts of research prove that intensive parenting mainly serves to burn out parents while harming children's competence and mental health. But the facts are losing. In a 2018 survey, 75 percent of respondents rated various intensive-parenting scenarios as "very good" or "excellent," and less than 40 percent said the same about scenarios showing a non-intensive approach. (An example that respondents grappled with: When a child says they're bored, should a parent find an activity to sign them up for or suggest they go outside and play?)[21]

In Gopnik's metaphor, intensive parents are carpenters. Rather than create the conditions for healthy yet unpredictable growth, they are driven to build to specifications, one hammer-stroke at a time: "essentially your job is to shape [your] material into a final product that will fit the scheme you had in mind to begin with. And you can assess how good a job you've done by looking at the finished product... Messiness and variability are a carpenter's enemies; precision and control are her allies. Measure twice, cut once."

The instinct to grasp for control amid stressful, scarcity-driven circumstances like modern parenthood is understandable. I have certainly experienced it myself. That control-seeking can at times be adaptive. If you are in a war zone, you likely do not want to let your children roam freely. There is a reason why your body quite literally clenches up when you are walking a tightrope or about to be struck. Scarcity shows up through both physical and psychological means.[22] On top of everything else, stress and scarcity often lead to poor sleep—already an infamous hallmark of parenthood—and we are rarely at our parenting best when chronically exhausted.

The challenge for contemporary American parents is that this chronic scarcity and stress is largely artificial. We do not live in a war zone: We live in the wealthiest country the world has ever known; it just happens to be one that throws its parents to the wolves.

As Fabrizio Zilibotti and Matthias Doepke explored in their book, *Love, Money & Parenting: How Economics Explains the Way We Raise Our Kids*: "Differences in child-rearing practices are rooted in the socioeconomic environment in which parents themselves grew up, in which they interact with their children, and in which they expect their children to live as adults." The pair add that, "in countries with high inequality and a high return to education, parents are both more authoritarian and more prone to instill in their children a drive to achieve ambitious goals." It is not surprising, then, that American intensive parenting rose alongside American inequality.

Now put all of this in the context of child care. Acquiring child care is couples' introduction to the way society treats parents and children, and to the institutional support available. When parents are plunged into the cold, deep waters of America's child-care system (or lack thereof), they are being given the implicit and explicit messages that they have entered the Hunger Games arena and better buckle up.

I have been told more than once by new parents a variation of, "I knew finding child care was going to be hard, I had no idea it was going to be *this* hard." The challenge can be one of supply, as we have seen, as well as one of finding a provider with whom parents feel comfortable handing over their child. These foundational experiences can set the stage for approaching parenthood in a defensive crouch rather than with open-armed abundance, always wondering what limited resources will have to be fought over next. In this way, intensive parenting makes it much harder to take childhood on its own terms: It is difficult to breathe in and look around when you're constantly running for cover and preparing for the next crisis.

Welcome to the Summer Hunger Games

Unfortunately, scarcity does not much improve when the children reach Kindergarten. Trying to find and afford summer care in America falls somewhere between maddening and madness. Summer care programs—as well as before- and after-school programs—are subject to many of the same pressures as early child-care programs, albeit with looser child-to-adult ratios.[23] They also have unique considerations that are squeezing them, such as fewer teens interested in working summers, higher minimum wages, and aging facilities. This aspect of child care is also a failed market, as sky-high demand has not resulted in widespread supply.

Increasingly, summer camp registrations open in the dead of winter, and frequently all slots are gone within minutes. Even nonspecialty day camps, like those offered by the YMCA, can run well over $1,200 a month for one child. There can be excellent low-cost municipal options, but these are limited and not always able to cover the needed hours. Moreover, many parents have internalized that summer is a place to lean into intensive parenting curation, focusing on finding the most "enriching" options or those that will look best on a college application. The combined result is parents commonly spending hours creating elaborate spreadsheets and then sitting around frantically hitting refresh like they are trying to score prime concert tickets.

Sadly, that description actually represents something of a best-case scenario. Summer camps are disproportionately utilized by middle- and high-income families and those with high levels of educational attainment. One study found that in the summer after their Kindergarten year, close to half of the children of parents with a bachelor's degree or above attended a day camp, versus merely 6 percent of those whose parents had a high school diploma or less.[24]

For families on the lower end of the income spectrum, these camps are largely out of reach, so they substitute other sacrifices for the time and money their counterparts spend on the camp scramble. Sociologist Jessica Calarco told writer Anne Helen Petersen that several of the women Calarco interviewed recounted, "how they made their own career decisions around the fact that their kids would be home in the summers and after school."[25] Those decisions ranged from turning down better-paying jobs to only taking part-time roles, frequently not out of preference but for lack of a better option. Parents who have children with special needs face their own hellish path.[26]

(This discussion leaves out families with a stay-at-home parent, which we will get to shortly.)

At nearly every income level, summer care and after-school care are tremendous pain points that only stoke the intensive parenting fire with more logs of stress and scarcity. Contrast this, again, with the line from the German couple: "We can focus on being good parents, not on how to afford being good parents." I found that in Germany, many cities and towns "organize comprehensive holiday programming, often in partnership with local schools."[27]

Funding a functional child-care system, then, can be a significant step toward cooling the intensive parenting inferno.

Toward "Good Enough" Parenting

I argued in my *Atlantic* article on intensive parenting that the goal should be calibrating parenting practices toward a concept known as "good enough parenting":

> The phrase was coined in 1953 by the British pediatrician and psychologist Donald Winnicott, and we can now update his work. Winnicott pushed back strongly against the idea that children require perfection from their parents, or that children should be perfectible. "There is room for all kinds of [parents] in the world," Winnicott wrote. "And some will be good at one thing, and some good at another. Or shall I say, some will be bad at one thing, and some bad at another." He added another idea, too: That no one-size-fits-all parenting model exists. "You are specialists in this particular matter of the care of your own children. I want to encourage you to keep and defend this specialist knowledge. It cannot be taught."
>
> "Good enough" does not mean mediocre or apathetic (the *not*-good-enough parent is real), but requires acknowledging the point beyond which attempts at further optimization cause more harm than good. Given reasonable conditions and plenty of love, there are many ways in which kids can have happy childhoods and emerge as healthy, conscientious, successful adults.[28]

This recalibration—setting down our collective hammers and picking up our gardening trowels—will be made far more possible if America adopts a real child-care system, ideally alongside robust paid family leave and a suite of family-friendly community offerings. Doing so would wrap parents in abundance and let them know it is OK to stand down and just enjoy life with one's progeny.

I don't want to overstate the case. Intensive parenting has other fuel, perhaps most notably America's competitive college admissions process that has many parents feeling like they need to run what economists Garey and Valerie Ramey have termed "the rug rat race."[29] While overall income inequality has narrowed modestly in recent years, many parents still feel paths to success in the modern economy are narrow and few. Broader shifts in economic and social policy will be required to fully put out intensive parenting. But focusing on child care is certainly a good first step toward, as well as a prerequisite for, containment.

A robust societal approach to child care can also aid parenting practices by providing access to other parents as well as early childhood professionals. Despite being inarguably one of the most difficult periods of parenthood (I'll say "one of" as I have not yet had the pleasure of parenting teenagers), parents have little experience to fall back on. Whereas we all remember the pleasures and difficulties of the school years and can refer to them as a sort of lodestone, the early years are opaque. The great child psychoanalyst Selma Fraiberg put it like this back in 1959: "The first period of childhood, roughly the first five years of life, is submerged like a buried city, and when we come back to these times with our children we are strangers and we cannot easily find our way."[30]

Having guides who have gone before can help. In 2018, the nonprofit group Zero to Three surveyed 1,000 parents of young children about where and why they get information and resources around parenting.[31] Child-care providers were one of the most trusted sources of advice, with 85 percent of parents reporting they trust these providers "some" or "a lot," coming in only behind immediate family and healthcare providers. This echoes part of the Community Case: The less isolated parents are, the more likely they can be the parents they want to be.

This is also a place where the need to support stay-at-home parents looms large. Likely reflecting the isolation we discussed in the Family Values Case, a 2012 Gallup survey found that stay-at-home mothers were substantially more likely to report worry, sadness, and depression compared to employed mothers.[32] Research shows that they can experience significantly hampered physical and mental health relative to their counterparts; echoing the Gallup finds, one study concludes that in addition to a tighter family budget, "Women who stay at home may face reduced social networks, financial dependence, and greater social isolation, all of which may place a strain on health."[33]

To be clear, these results do not suggest there is a problem with parents staying home with their children. It suggests they need more support—both for their own sake and that of their kids. To play off the gardening metaphor, one cannot starve a plant (in this case, the parent) of water and then blame the plant for struggling. As we have touched on, strained health, stress, and depression are all correlated with suboptimal parenting practices.[34] And recall the research finding that "allowing parents to parent less may allow them to parent better."[35]

A comprehensive child-care system, then—one which is inclusive of all caregiving setups—stands to improve parenting across the board. Calmer parenting, in turn, stands to improve the experience of childhood for millions. Which brings us to a final way in which child care impacts childhood and parenthood: It can stand as a shield against the changing climate.

Childhood Warming

In 2022 and 2023, I helped to coordinate an effort known as the U.S. Early Years Climate Action Task Force. The Task Force was made up of experts in child care, climate action, and pediatrics, as well as business leaders, philanthropists, and parents. The Task Force heard months of testimony from researchers, practitioners, and families about ways in which our disrupted climate systems were impacting young children, parents, and the systems that serve them. In October 2023, the Task Force released an Action Plan, the first paragraph of which reads:

> In the earliest stages of life—from before birth through age 8—children develop rapidly and have a distinct biology that makes them uniquely sensitive to their environments and exposures. As the effects of climate change intensify, so do the risks to children. It is hard to overestimate the potential impacts on children's health, well-being, and opportunities. In turn, it is hard to overestimate the potential impacts on the trajectories of their families and the nation.[36]

Climate chaos—what climate expert Katharine Hayhoe calls "global weirding"—can impact childhood in several ways: Young children are particularly vulnerable, even more so than older youth, to hazards like air pollution and heat waves. For instance, they can dehydrate substantially faster because, as one expert group writes, "their smaller bodies heat up more quickly, and they have less capacity to release heat via sweating. The biological systems that regulate body temperature in infants and young children are less developed and, therefore, less efficient. Infants and young children also can't seek out cooler environments or get water to drink without relying on adults."[37] In a different vein, the U.S. Environmental Protection Agency has noted that alterations in temperature and precipitation patterns are changing the habitat and range of disease-carrying creatures such as ticks: Pediatric Lyme disease cases are projected to rise in the eastern half of the country by 31 percent to 272 percent, depending on the extent of global temperature change, compared to a nonwarming world.[38]

A more pervasive impact is that climate change simply makes it harder for children in many parts of the country to go outside and play as much as they used to.[39] Longer and more intense heat waves (even famously hot places like Arizona are becoming dangerously hot), raging wildfires, and widespread flooding reduce this most quintessential of childhood activities. As the United States found out dramatically in the summer of 2023, as smoke from Canadian wildfires blanketed the Midwest, Northeast, and mid-Atlantic, one does not need to live in a particular environment to be affected by climate-change-enhanced events.

Child-care programs can provide a layer of resilience against such hazards—if they have the resources to do so. These are settings where millions of young children are spending time every day. We have already seen how they can be vital community assets during climate-enhanced disasters. Disaster response aside, however, when child-care programs have good cooling systems, air filtration, stormwater infrastructure, and shady outdoor areas, they provide a safe and healthy environment for children to grow and play.

Child-care providers can also leverage their relationship with parents to provide guidance, helping families understand climate risks and think about ways to adapt. Providers and parents can work together (solidarity!) to reduce risks, for instance by lobbying local governments to follow the lead of cities like Paris and London and establish "low-emissions zones" that restrict car idling—and, in some cases, cars altogether—around child cares, schools, and other places where children congregate.[40] And yes, all of this both improves the broader community (clean air and shade have a big curb cut effect) and sets us up to have generations of healthy children with the capacity to tackle the climate challenges that lie ahead.

Our national neglect of child care restricts programs' ability to serve in these roles. When programs are forced to exert every ounce of their energy on keeping the lights on, they are not able to think about questions like climate preparedness, nor act even if they do. Instead, climate hazards frequently strain or disrupt our fragile child-care programs, causing them to temporarily or permanently close and depriving parents and children of a critical resource. As disruptions continue, we can no longer talk about child care without talking about climate change, nor talk about climate change without talking about child care.

Conclusion

Robust public funding of child care gives providers the capacity they need, and gives parents the support they deserve, to maximize the chances children have an overall positive childhood. A good experience of childhood—and a good experience of parenthood—does not need to have a future return on investment to be a worthwhile and virtuous goal. We have an opportunity to enhance the day-to-day, the small interactions, the moods and moments.

Properly understood, an effective child-care system focuses as a first principle not on the investible child, nor the child-as-tiny-adult, nor the sacralized child; rather, it focuses on the child as an individual who deserves to be surrounding by the conditions to grow and flourish within their personality. Centering the garden of childhood, and placing child care as a greenhouse of sorts, calms the need for a wild-eyed focus on school readiness and intensive parenting. It allows us to stretch child care to its appropriate range, broadening it on one axis to include stay-at-home parents and on the other to include school-aged care. It offers, in short, better years ahead.

There is, however, an important question looming over this discussion: If that's the Edenic vision of a childhood garden, who gets through the gates?

Examples of "Parenthood & Childhood Case" Messages:
- "A strong child-care system helps children have a happy, healthy childhood. The benefits for later school and work are nice, but shouldn't we want all children to experience joy and wonder as they explore their world? Good, stable child-care providers help make that happen."
- "Parenting these days is needlessly stressful. Having a good child-care system reduces the strain and scarcity parents experience and gives them a resource to lean on, helping them parent the way they want. That system must include helping stay-at-home parents and parents with kids in school who have to scramble for after-school and summer care."

Continued

Continued

- "Climate disruptions like extreme heat waves, wildfires, and flooding are making it harder for today's children to play outside and opening them up to environmental threats. Funding a good child-care system not only gives kids access to safe and healthy environments, it also lets parents work together with child-care providers to navigate this predictably unpredictable era."

In a sentence: If we want children to have the best childhood possible and parents to be able to parent the way they want, we need child care as an enabling condition, like soil in a garden.

Chapter 6
The Racial and Gender Equity Case

Enslaved Black girls and women were among the first non-kin child-care providers in American history.[1] Conditions were brutal. Frederick Douglass recounts this appalling story:

> The wife of [slave owner] Mr. Giles Hicks, living but a short distance from where I used to live, murdered my wife's cousin, a young girl between fifteen and sixteen years of age, mangling her person in the most horrible manner, breaking her nose and breastbone with a stick, so that the poor girl expired in a few hours afterward. She was immediately buried, but had not been in her untimely grave but a few hours before she was taken up and examined by the coroner, who decided that she had come to her death by severe beating. The offence for which this girl was thus murdered was this:—She had been set that night to mind Mrs. Hicks' baby and during the night she fell asleep, and the baby cried. She, having lost her rest for several nights previous, did not hear the crying. They were both in the room with Mrs. Hicks. Mrs. Hicks, finding the girl slow to move, jumped from her bed, seized an oak stick of wood by the fireplace, and with it broke the girl's nose and breastbone, and thus ended her life.[2]

Distressing as it is to read, this episode illustrates why we cannot wrestle with child care's place in American society without reckoning with race and gender. These two topics could certainly be separated and each made into its own chapter, but they intersect so intensely that I will address them together. Issues of poverty and class also constantly dialogue with those of race and gender. With that linkage in mind, in this chapter I will foreground race and gender, and in the next chapter poverty and class. I want to acknowledge again that I am writing about this topic as a white man, so I will seek to lean on voices other than my own whenever possible.

In this chapter, we will look briefly at the racialized past and present of child care, and explore why building an effective child-care system would be a strike for both racial and gender equity. Those positive impacts surround not only children and parents, but the 97 percent female child-care workforce—over a million strong just in formal licensed programs—which is disproportionately made up of people of color. Similarly, even white women suffer from a "motherhood penalty," while the United States is an outlier in lacking any national paid family leave policy. Our collective march toward a more just society must have child care as one of its pillars.

Child Care's Racialized History

The outsized role enslaved girls and women played in keeping the South's economy humming shaped views that still haunt us today. Fatima Gross Graves, president of the National Women's Law Center, explained why in a 2021 op-ed:

> The invisibility of child-care workers today can be connected directly to the invisibility of Black women who provided care both as coerced labor and underpaid workers before and after the Civil War in conditions that made it difficult to also care for their own children. While white womanhood in the Antebellum South was depicted as embodying grace and leisure, the labor of Black women they relied upon, from domestic chores to feeding white infants at their own breast, was rarely noted nor mentioned. Even contemporary depictions of slavery—including Oscar winners "Django Unchained" and "12 Years A Slave"—continue this trend, rarely focusing on the role of enslaved people in raising and caring for white children to the benefit of white families.
>
> After the Civil War, many white families still relied upon the unpaid or underpaid service of Black domestic servants for their most valued treasures, a status quo many white families worked to further invisibilize through the proliferation of the "mammy" stereotype. Usually portrayed as a rotund and joyful Black woman, the "mammy" existed to frame the fair compensation for the labor of Black women as in tension with the close personal bond white families were depicted as having with their servants. Child care wasn't business, the mammy suggested, just personal.
>
> So devoted to the "mammy" mythology, the Daughters of the Confederacy successfully lobbied the U.S. Senate to authorize a (never built) statue on the National Mall "in memory of the faithful slave mammies of the South," whitewashing the exploitation at the heart of much domestic labor.[3]

Indeed, this racialized approach opened up two tracks in the American mind: While it was frowned upon for white women to work outside the domestic sphere, there was no such compunction about Black women. Enslaved women were frequently pressed into service either in the fields or, like Frederick Douglass' relative, forced to care for the children of their enslavers. (It is worth reiterating that most working- and middle-class white women in this time period contributed enormously to their "corporate family" through helping to run the family farm or business.)

Who was left to care for the children of the enslaved? Historian Steven Mintz records that at times, one or two enslaved adults were left to care for forty to seventy young children. Worse yet, sometimes the young children themselves were pressed into service: "children as young as two or three rocked babies and made sure they didn't crawl too near the fireplace."[4]

As Gross Graves notes, the post-Civil War period was hardly a renaissance for Black women and their children. Even as America began to have charity-funded "day nurseries" for the children of poor or widowed mothers—miserable as conditions in those nurseries could be—Black families were often excluded. The sociologist Casey Stockstill, from whom we will hear more shortly, has written that, "Having been enslaved mothers and then working mothers for decades, Black mothers were defined by white day nursery reformers of the Progressive Era as workers who could support white middle-class mothers, rather than as mothers in their own right."[5]

Immigrant mothers were, to be sure, another group that society had no problem seeing working outside the home. The 146 women who perished in New York City's 1911 Triangle Shirtwaist Factory fire were almost all Italian or Jewish immigrants. Their number included Providenza Panno, mother of six. Discrimination against these groups, however, looked different than the rank segregation experienced by Black families.

In response, Black women's clubs began to form at the end of the nineteenth century; the first national organization was called the National Association of Club Women (NACW). The Center for the Study of Child Care Employment notes that "Black club women's commitment to early care and education in the form of kindergartens and day nurseries was a key component of the NACW's overall strategy that encompassed a range of broader activities, including anti-lynching, temperance, adult education, and women's business exchange efforts."[6]

This history is notably different than that of "nursery schools." Where day nurseries existed as a sort of custodial holding pen for large groups of children "unfortunate" enough to have mothers who needed to work, nursery schools were established with ostensibly loftier goals. They were, as historian Emily Cahan writes, designed not only to give children needed skills, but to "provide children with an opportunity to develop socially through association with peers under the expert supervision of a trained teacher."[7] Many started as lab schools attached to universities. It should come as no surprise that these nursery schools were forerunners to today's pre-Kindergarten programs.

Nursery school advocates took pains to distinguish their offerings from child-care programs, leading to child care being treated, says another historian, Sonya Michel, as a "poor cousin."[8] As a result, Cahan adds, "Nursery schools catered almost exclusively to children of the middle and upper classes. In short, the nursery school persisted as a track for affluent parents and their children." Again, many nursery schools were segregated either by policy or in practice. As with day nurseries, Black groups did try to create their own offerings—a lab nursery school was opened at Spelman College in 1930, for instance—but most Black families were boxed out.

Many Black leaders clearly understood the connection between child care and prosperity. Prominent members of the civil rights movement were involved in crafting and pushing what would become the 1971 Comprehensive Child Development Act. As the scholar William Roth has written, if welfare reformers were one parent of the legislation, "the other parent was civil rights."[9] Ultimately, as we have talked about in previous chapters, these efforts fell short when Nixon vetoed the bill.

We are still living today with the two-tiered legacy around child care. The artificial distinction between "child care" and "preschool" has been damaging enough—we know by now that preschool is merely one form of child care, akin to how all squares are rectangles, but not all rectangles are squares. But pretending pre-K is distinct has led to a devaluation of care and made the path toward a comprehensive child-care system that much steeper. That damage is exacerbated further when we consider how the lack of good child care leads to immense segregation during early childhood.

Segregation Starts Early

In 2019, researchers Erica Greenberg and Tomas Monarrez of the Urban Institute conducted one of the first comprehensive analyses of segregation in child-care settings. Their conclusions were startling:

Nationwide, early childhood education is more segregated than kindergarten and first grade, even while enrolling a similar number of students. Early childhood programs are twice as likely to be nearly 100 percent black or Hispanic, and they are less likely to be somewhat integrated (with a 10 to 20 percent black or Hispanic enrollment share).[10]

(As a note, the pair use "early childhood education" to refer to any home-, center-, or school-based program for children not yet in Kindergarten.)

Unsurprisingly, research has also shown that children of color attend, on average, early childhood programs that are more poorly resourced.[11] Even systems intended to level the playing field, such as child-care subsidy programs, inherently reinforce disparities. In the vast majority of states, the per-child funding attached to subsidy vouchers—the child-care equivalent of a Medicare or Medicaid reimbursement—is far below the true cost of providing high-quality care.[12] Considered alongside segregation, which concentrates not only children of the same race but of the same socioeconomic status, it is easy to see why these programs may struggle to provide the care and learning they want and that the children deserve.

To be fair, some of this segregation is the result of preferential choices made by parents. It is not necessarily problematic if a family child-care program led by a Spanish-speaking educator and located in a heavily Spanish-speaking Latino community enrolls mostly Latino children. And, indeed, Greenberg and Monarrez found segregation was significantly greater in family child-care programs versus center-based programs. Much of this segregation, however, is the result of policy choices rather than preference and could be reduced if there was a universal (and ideally free) child-care system in place.

Consider Head Start. While laudable in its attempt to bring quality child care to lower-income children—and, indeed, the positive impacts on children and families can be seen as a strike toward equity—the program has never had its eyes on integration. In her book *False Starts: The Segregated Lives of Preschoolers*, Casey Stockstill details how the origins of Head Start were explicitly and unapologetically grounded in a pathologized view of poor families—and especially poor Black families—as deficient.[13] Given Head Start's poverty means-test and the racial makeup of poverty in America (another set of policy choices), how could it be integration focused? As of 2022, the bulk of Head Start enrollment was made up of 37 percent Latino, 28 percent Black, and 23 percent white children.[14]

To understand how this segregation plays out on the ground, Stockstill embedded herself at two preschools in Madison, Wisconsin: a Head Start program almost entirely populated by children of color, and an affluent private center that was predominantly white. She found explicit and implicit differences in the day-to-day experiences for children, families, and educators. Stockstill writes that:

> When we center segregation as an operating force in preschool children's experiences, it becomes clear how family circumstances crystallize in different, unequal ways within a classroom. This affects the feeling of classrooms: from how teachers and children spend their time to scripts for pretend play to access to toys to conversations between parents and teachers.

There are practical problems with this segregation, as well as moral ones. Concentrating poor children in one classroom tends to concentrate the likelihood of behavioral problems (not because there is something inherently wrong with these children, but because of the correlations of poverty and chronic stress on parental well-being and on child development). This makes it more difficult for educators to get through lessons or projects, despite the best intentions. Stockstill records that frequently, by midmorning, the class in the affluent center had read four books while the Head Start classroom had not read any. On average, the Head Start classroom read one book and spent "about five minutes on reading" versus six books and thirty minutes at the affluent center.

When policy reinforces segregation, Stockstill goes on, it builds on the racist and classist history of America's early childhood system. For poor children of color, preschool is seen as compensatory, making up for shortfalls in their families and communities. For wealthy children, especially wealthy white children, preschool is seen as supplemental. Yet, she writes, "affluent children, too, are harmed by segregation—they can develop an outsized sense of entitlement to adult attention, become unprepared for changing classroom conditions, and learn about economic need as an abstract problem rather than an embedded aspect of daily life."

Indeed, decades of research in K–12 education confirms myriad benefits from integration for all involved.[15] These range from better academic outcomes to improved creativity to bolstered self-confidence to reductions in anxiety and, yes, racial bias. Would universal child care instantly break down the barriers of segregation? Of course not. Our universal, free public schools remain persistently segregated, and patterns of residential segregation fueled by racist policies such as redlining are a large factor.[16] Such a system would, however, massively increase the options available to families of color, and in doing so increase opportunities for both children and parents—especially mothers.

Child Care Improves Opportunity for Mothers

It's now time to bring gender into the bias-laden mix. Here, we turn our attention to mothers of all races, keeping in mind that just about every factor that impacts white mothers has an even greater impact on mothers of color. It will likely come as no surprise that child-care access is deeply correlated with maternal employment. This is sometimes known as the "motherhood penalty." (This section focuses on women who work outside the home, but rest assured we will return to stay-at-home parents shortly.)

Although the concept is not without controversy—as with the gender wage gap, some argue that the penalty is reflective of different choices and preferences as opposed to structural discrimination—research suggests women take an earnings hit of 4 percent each time they have a child (while men actually *gain* earnings).[17] The theory behind the penalty involves a combination of women experiencing more career interruptions and employers perceiving mothers of young children as less committed to the workplace, whereas fatherhood conveys a sense of responsibility and maturity. Layered onto gender norms, such treatment can lead to wild outcomes: For instance, in a study Jessica Calarco fielded during the first year of the COVID-19 pandemic, "84% of moms in mom-dad families said they would be the ones primarily responsible for caring for a child who got sick or had to quarantine."[18] Perhaps more eye-popping, *even when the woman was the primary breadwinner in a couple*, this remained the case for 77 percent of mothers.

These differential earnings can have lifelong effects. Research from The Century Foundation found that "While 47% of fathers and 52% of nonparents say they have saved enough for retirement, a mere 33% of mothers feel that they have saved enough."[19] What's more, individual financial security is strongly linked with women's ability to extricate themselves from abusive or otherwise unhealthy relationships.[20]

Good child care can help mitigate the motherhood penalty. It can open the door to paid work generally, and also to entrepreneurship. The latter is particularly important both for economic dynamism and because mothers who start their own business are naturally protected from employer discrimination. Yet a survey of working mothers who are interested in starting their own business and have children younger than age six found a whopping 61 percent said access to affordable child care was a barrier.[21]

Interestingly, there is wide variation among U.S. states in how child care intersects maternal employment, and the answers may surprise you. Sociologist Leah Ruppanner conducted a deep analysis for her book *Motherlands: How States Push Mothers Out of Employment*. Broadly speaking, Ruppanner summarizes, "A large body of literature documents that mothers who remain in the labor market experience inter-role strain in balancing work and family demands ... as a consequence of the incompatibility of work and family demands, mothers are particularly vulnerable to labor market exits when young children are present in the home ... a lack of high-quality, reliable, and affordable child care is a key reason mothers 'opt out' of employment at higher rates than men."[22]

Among married mothers, the states with the highest maternal employment rates are actually those in the "heartland," including a bevy of strongly Republican-leaning states. This group includes the Dakotas, Iowa, Nebraska, Kansas, Oklahoma, Mississippi, and South Carolina. The lowest maternal employment rates are found in West Coast and some Northeast states. The reason, Ruppanner's analysis suggests, is a collision of factors including the cost of child care (which is substantially higher in wealthier coastal states) and the length of the school day (which is modestly shorter in those states). Lower median incomes and higher poverty rates in the heartland states may also induce mothers to work as a matter of economic necessity. Although Democratic-leaning states such as California may offer more generous family policies than their counterparts, it has not been enough—at least as of Ruppanner's analysis, which used averaged data from 2011 to 2015—to offset these other influences.

The school day length factor points again to the importance of including school-aged child care in the conversation. As Ruppanner writes, "simply getting children into public school is not an effective child care solution for mothers in states with short instructional days and difficult-to-access after-school care, which illustrates the importance of conceptualizing child care resources in terms of holistic regimes that continue to support parents as their children grow older."

Maternal employment—again, when chosen, not coerced—has positive effects that go beyond the individual woman and her family. Paid work can be conducive to growing political awareness and coalitions. Although this can certainly happen outside the workplace (plenty of early American feminists led from the home), access to work outside the home is a major catalyst. The sociologist Alice Evans, who studies gender and society worldwide, has observed that, "through paid work in the public sphere, women gain esteem, build diverse friendships, discover more egalitarian alternatives, collectively criticize patriarchal privileges, and become emboldened to resist unfairness."[23]

A comprehensive child-care system, then, is essential for gender equality and true freedom of choice for all women. That includes those doing the caring.

Raising the Workforce

We have been talking in this chapter about the impact of child care on mothers and people of color. It's time to circle back to who is providing the care: women, and disproportionately women of color. Based on the most recent data available, the child-care workforce in licensed programs is nearly 97 percent female, 58 percent white, 17 percent Black, and 16 percent Latino, with other demographic groups making up smaller percentages.[24] Nearly one in five identify as immigrants. These numbers do not account for the huge numbers of diverse family, friends, and neighbor (FFN) caregivers, nor stay-at-home parents. (Among stay-at-home parents, defying stereotypes, half are non-white, a third are immigrants, and a third live below the poverty line.[25])

This workforce is, as we have discussed, deeply, badly, absurdly, insultingly underpaid: Child-care compensation ranks in the lowest 5 percent of all occupations.[26] The impact of this underpayment is difficult to overstate; it sets the contours for the entire field and shapes the life experience, health, and well-being of educators. One ongoing survey of child-care providers found that as of summer 2023, half the providers surveyed were experiencing at least moderate symptoms of anxiety and depression.[27] In a 2024 op-ed, family child-care provider Tonia McMillian wrote about those in her subsector:

> I retired from the practice of family child care last December after 29 years. That same month, I attended a funeral for Deanna Robles, an amazing

family child care provider and early care and education advocate who was 53 years old.

In January, I attended another funeral for another family child care provider in her mid-60s. Renaldo Sanders was not only a professional who had done this critical work for over 25 years, but also a dear friend. Both died from "natural causes," but there is nothing natural about working 60, 70, or 80 hours a week for 20 or 30 years.

These were women who worked in a field with little, no, or all-too expensive health care, who struggled to provide for themselves and their families on wages far below the minimum. These were women who couldn't get a good night's rest trying to figure out how to take pennies and create a million-dollar early learning environment within the walls of their homes. These were women who sacrificed and gave their lives to children and early learning.[28]

This brew of low pay, slim benefits, and poor working conditions didn't happen by accident; it bubbled up from a legacy of sexism and racism. A functional child-care system that compensates its educators with reasonable, family-sustaining compensation would thus do enormous good toward gender and racial equality. In a single stroke, we could raise more than two million women toward the middle class. We could also make it blindingly clear that child care is important and skilled work to be valued and respected. (As an added benefit, this would massively reduce caregiver turnover and improve the quality of child care across the board.)

There is, however, no way to elevate the child-care profession without immense amounts of public money flowing in every year. As detailed in the Introduction, the economic strictures around child care are such that the market will simply never be able to get compensation to a decent level. We do know, however, that public funding can.

In 2022, Washington, DC launched a permanent Pay Equity Fund intended to move its early educators toward an equivalent salary level as elementary school educators.[29] The Fund is fueled by a tax on very high earning households. In the first phase, DC sent $14,000 checks to full-time child-care educators and $10,000 to assistant educators. As of 2024, the money is flowing to child-care programs themselves in exchange for adopting robust salary scales. DC is also offering child-care educators low- to zero-cost health insurance via a special program run through the city's Affordable Care Act exchange.[30]

The early results are promising. A researcher evaluating the Pay Equity Fund found "a significant correlation between immediate increases in [child care] employment levels in D.C. and the launch of the [Fund]."[31] At a time in 2022 when the child-care sector nationwide was down nearly 100,000 educators versus pre-pandemic levels and experiencing the crippling effects of staffing shortages, DC actually *gained* early educators. The human stories behind these numbers show why. The news site *DCist* quoted one assistant center teacher: "'It was at a point where had [the Pay Equity Fund check] not come, I probably would've had to put my two weeks in so that I could move in with my parents (in Florida),' Gladys says, holding back tears."[32]

It should be increasingly clear by now how difficult it is to say one cares about racial and gender equity and not forcefully support a strong child-care system—one that starts at birth with paid family leave.

Whither Paid Family Leave?

The first weeks and months of a child's life pose an extreme child-care challenge. Mothers are recovering from the truly heroic and physically taxing effort of birthing, infants are incredibly fragile, and this is a precious period for bonding between the newborn and their parents. Instead of looking toward formal or even informal child care, the clear answer—and direction of parental preference—is ensuring parents can be at home with their children during this time. Yet, oddly, we frequently act as if paid family leave is a separate policy area from child care. In fact, paid family leave is the first leg of the child-care marathon. And America puts up so, so many hurdles.

Not much needs to be said about the state of American paid family leave beyond the fact that the United States and Papua New Guinea are the only two countries in the *world* (other than a few tiny Pacific island nations) to not have any national paid maternity leave law.[33] In fact, most of our peer nations offer between six months and a year of such leave.

Once again, this is a place where racial dynamics intersect gender dynamics. Per the National Partnership for Women and Families, as of 2018, "only 25% of Latino workers and 43% of Black workers report having access to any paid or partially paid parental leave, compared to 50% of white workers."[34] In addition to negative impacts on the babies themselves, a lack of paid leave can have long-lasting consequences for mothers. For instance, many studies suggest a significant connection between the presence or absence of solid leave policies and rates of postpartum depression.[35]

We know, however, that addressing this first part of the child-care arc can head off these problems. The National Partnership notes that:

> [R]esearch from California's state paid leave program—the longest-running program in the country—finds that the state's program has increased parity in the duration of leave taken by white women and women of color, as well as in initiation of breastfeeding and other positive health outcomes across races. Before the state's program, Black women took, on average, just one week of maternity leave and white, non-Hispanic women took four weeks. After implementation, Black and white mothers took an average of seven weeks of leave.

Paid leave also addresses one of the thornier political issues around child care: Do we really want infants—by which I mean children between birth and their first birthday—in external child-care settings like centers?

First, it's worth noting that the vast majority of infants are *not* in these settings: While no data set exists, to my knowledge, that breaks out care settings for infants by month (in other words, 0–3 month olds, 3–6 month olds, and so on), we have a general picture of where children are during the first year of life. Federal data shows that as of 2019, nearly 60 percent of infants had no regular weekly nonparental care arrangement, meaning they were being cared for by some combination of a stay-at-home parent and irregular care (most likely from kin or friends).[36] Of the infants who are in regular nonparental care, only a third attend a center: Most have a relative caregiver, with another segment attending a home-based family child-care program.

Despite these facts, infants are frequently spotlighted by opponents of large-scale public child-care funding as an area of concern. As conservative scholars Katharine B. Stevens and Jenet Erickson have written, "we simply know too little about the effects of nonparental, group care on *children—especially infants and toddlers and those spending long hours in child care*" (emphasis theirs).[37] Although I disagree with Stevens and Ericksons' overall reading of the child-care evidence base, and their conflation of infants and toddlers, it's inarguable that research focused on infants in external child care—and the effects of having infants in external care on parents—is scarce.

I don't want to paint with an overly broad brush. There are certainly fair reasons why families may want or need to utilize external child care for infants: my wife and I did when she needed chemotherapy treatment for the brain cancer that was diagnosed while she was pregnant with our second daughter. Even in less extreme conditions, certain jobs or family circumstances simply do not lend themselves well to extended leave, and leave policies also need to be very strong if they are to meet the needs of single parents. Research may be limited, but what exists clearly indicates that high-quality infant care can lead to perfectly healthy child outcomes.[38] The point here is that the infant child-care question—which is often wielded as a culture-war cudgel against the whole enterprise of external child care—is first and foremost a paid-leave question.

Indeed, that is a major reason we don't know more about infants and child care. Normally, we can look to other countries that do a much more robust and rigorous job collecting data on their child-care systems. In most peer nations, however, the idea of an infant in a child-care center is largely ludicrous: They're almost all home with a parent. (I really mean almost all: In Canada, over 70 percent of employed mothers with children under the age of one are on parental leave, while 92 percent take advantage of some amount of paid leave.)[39] I once met a Finnish father at a Helsinki community center who was there with his fifteen-month-old son. The father mentioned that his wife had been home with the boy for the first year of life, and now he was on his six-month paternity leave, after which time the son would be attending an extremely low-cost, high-quality child-care program. Only 1 percent of Finnish children under the age of one are in formal child-care settings.[40]

Given the outsize impacts paid family leave has on women, we have to broaden our perspective to see paid leave as part and parcel of any good child-care system. We also have to extend our perspective on another axis to make sure stay-at-home parents are equally put on the path toward flourishing.

Stay-at-Home Parents, Redux

To take on the role of a stay-at-home parent is to accept a great deal of opportunity cost. We have already discussed the "motherhood penalty," but stay-at-home parents—again, overwhelmingly mothers (nothing against the fifth of stay-at-home parents who are dads, and who will also benefit from solving child care)—face extra challenges. While many if not most stay-at-home parents willingly accept these tradeoffs, their path does not need to be so difficult.

We spoke in the Family Values Case about the isolation and stress that stay-at-home parents face. If an aspect of equality is having fair opportunities to thrive—to enjoy one's family, follow one's passions, in essence fully realize one's right to "life, liberty, and the pursuit of happiness"—then choosing to stay home should not come at the expense of flourishing.

Moreover, not all stay-at-home parents are at home by preference. In many cases, financial concerns—of which child-care expenses are paramount—make it infeasible to return to the workforce. As one North Carolina woman said in a listening session led by a coalition of child-care groups, "I haven't been able to start work despite having graduated with my [master's degree in public health] and it breaks my heart because I love the program and I loved going to school. It's not been easy, and it's been a process of grieving because I don't know when I can get back to me. I love being a mother and his caregiver, but I feel like a part of me died, who I was up to the point of becoming a mother. That's not fair to me, personally."[41]

The pressures on and lack of support for stay-at-home parents can lead to their own inequities. For instance, a higher percentage of lower-income married mothers are at home compared to middle-income married mothers. One-third of stay-at-home parents live below the poverty line.[42] The conservative Institute for Family Studies has acknowledged that, "When children are in the picture, the high childcare costs often outweigh that (potential) second income. For these couples, it often makes more financial sense, given high childcare costs and her low potential earnings, to have someone stay at home, usually mom."[43]

At the same time, America's welfare system—especially since the welfare reform efforts of the 1990s—is set up to disadvantage and shame poor parents, and especially poor single mothers, who choose to stay home. Nearly every public assistance program for this group, from the Supplemental Nutrition Assistance Program (SNAP) to the Temporary Assistance for Needy Families (TANF) program, has a work requirement. As the writer Stephanie H. Murray has put it:

> This [welfare] system is rooted in a logic that anyone who recognizes the value of homemaking explicitly rejects: that a parent tending to a child full-time is lying fallow rather than actively engaged in important work; that a mother is of more use to society in any job than in caring for her child. And it actively undercuts a parent's ability to factor a child's needs into the quest for employment. By the logic of modern American family policy, any

sacrifice that a poor, single parent must make in the service of remaining employed is worth it.[44]

There is a racial dimension here as well. With loud echoes of history, journalist Lonnae O'Neal Parker has aptly noted that, "There has never been a national effort to keep Black women at home, caring sweetly for their children. They have always worked, and their work has never been a separate thing from their mothering."[45]

(A host of other policy changes that would help stay-at-home parents are beyond the scope of this book: For instance, unlike many peer nations, American stay-at-home parents do not receive caregiving credits toward Social Security, have limited retirement or health insurance options without their spouse, and are ineligible for the Social Security Disability Insurance Program despite the fact that their becoming disabled would have a massive impact on the entire household.[46] Stay-at-home parents also enjoy no specialized legal protections against discrimination when it comes to re-entering the workforce. Policymakers would do well to embrace a comprehensive agenda for supporting stay-at-home parents.)

A robust child-care system, then—particularly one that offers payments to stay-at-home parents—would advance gender equality for this group as well. It would not only make them better parents but help them thrive, give them the space to continue cultivating their own sense of self, and facilitate any desired return to the external labor force. It would also bring all parents under the same umbrella, and in the process strengthen a fraying American society.

Solidarity, Redux

Care, as I have indicated, has the potential to be a tie that binds because it is such a universal experience. In our fractious nation, child-care needs—though they can and do articulate more acutely for different groups—cross lines of race and class and gender and ideology. That opens the door for solidarity.

Such solidarity requires intentionality. Consider again the women's groups of the late nineteenth and early twentieth century. There were certainly deep racial divisions among the movement; early leaders like Elizabeth Cady Stanton, for all the good they did, also engaged in ugly, racist argumentation.[47] (These racial divisions would persist into the later waves of feminist movements.) Other women's groups attempted to be inclusive, in class if not always in race. In either case, as Theda Skopcol puts in, many of these groups and leaders "in their self-conception and public rhetoric, stressed solidarity between privileged and less privileged women, and honor for values of caring and nurturance."[48] Hence, the same groups that fought for women's suffrage and better maternal and infant health care were fighting for better working-class job conditions and for the end of child labor.

Note again the morally laden nature of this solidarity. It is often not enough to merely have material common cause. There must be an identity bond as well. That is how you get remarkable shows of solidarity like white Freedom Riders risking their lives during the civil rights movement, or Jewish leader Abraham Joshua Heschel literally linking arms with Martin Luther King, Jr. Although white allies were too few and far between and at times get outsize credit compared to the disenfranchised populations putting their lives on the line day after day, such episodes demonstrate the power of solidaristic movements.

Within child care, we are already starting to see some shifts along gender lines. While long coded as women's work, the current generation of fathers is far more active around child care than their own fathers (and an increasing number of fathers, though still a deep minority, are stay-at-home parents or single parents).[49] That has begun to extend into the political arena as well. As of 2023, there is finally a Congressional Dads Caucus.[50] Its founder, Rep. Jimmy Gomez of California, went viral that year when he wore his infant in a wrap on the floor of the House of Representatives as the House went through an arduous process of choosing a Speaker. Similarly, multimillionaire Alexis Ohanian, cofounder of the website Reddit and husband of tennis superstar Serena Williams, has been highly engaged in paid family leave efforts, including appearing in TV commercials as part of Dove's Men+Care campaign.[51]

Although some correctly pointed out that the attention Gomez gained highlighted the double standard for praising dads versus moms, the fact remains this is progress. In a country where more than two-thirds of Congresspeople and state legislators are male, and where it took until 2023 for women CEOs to outnumber CEOs named "John" within S&P 500 companies, men are going to need to be part of the fight.[52] (Also: Elect more women!) Given everything we've explored in this chapter, striving alongside women for better child care should be seen as non-negotiable: as essential a part of being a good partner as sharing in the day-to-day care of the children and family.

That said, much more needs to be done to rebuild a movement that reaches authentically across lines of race and gender as well as class and ideology. Though there have been strong efforts in recent years, the child-care sector is still dominated by a narrow view of what constitutes an effective system. This can be seen in the fact that major policy proposals tend to focus on formal licensed care settings, like child-care centers, largely to the exclusion of informal caregivers like family, friends, neighbors, or stay-at-home parents—despite the latter options being a disproportionate preference of certain population groups such as low-income families, rural families, and Latinos.

Similarly, traditional views of quality, as codified in state child-care Quality Rating and Improvement Systems (QRIS), have been roundly criticized for a lack of equity and can unintentionally make child care feel inaccessible for some. For instance, in 2022 a group of researchers led by the Children's Equity Project at Arizona State University published a report in which they asserted, "definitions of 'quality' have been sorely lacking attention to equity and to the unique experiences that affect children from historically marginalized communities . . . it is clear that our definition of quality and the instruments we use to measure it, are incomplete and insufficient."[53]

Access to child-care subsidy, too, is mired in bureaucracy and administrative burdens that ends up excluding many families of color. In addition to paperwork burdens (applications in many states, until recently, had to be filled out on paper and only in certain offices that could be difficult to reach), requirements can be onerous or not match families' lives on the ground. For example, a majority of states with high Latino populations require minimum weekly work hours in order to maintain child care aid, despite many of these parents working unpredictable, seasonal hours.[54]

Raising up a new movement centered around care that surmounts these divisions can be a powerful driver of positive change. As the author and public policy leader Annie-Marie Slaughter has written:

> Care is the crucible that can help reforge the sisterhood of the early feminist movement and expand and shape it into a much broader human coalition. Care can unite women up and down the income scale and across races and ethnicities. It can unite the experiences of heterosexual and

same-sex couples, older generations and younger ones. It can provide a common metric for the quality of single and married life, for couples and communities of different kinds.[55]

And, I would add: for men, too!

Conclusion

A good child-care system will advance a more equal America. It is a rare area of intervention that has the potential to reduce racial and gender inequities for multiple groups: parents, child-care providers, and children. And, as we have seen throughout the book, when you strengthen these groups, you strengthen entire communities and, in turn, the nation.

This is yet another reason why truly universal, free child care is such an important goal. There are many reasons why incremental improvements on the current system won't get us where we need to go, but lurking beneath nearly all of them is child care's racist, sexist DNA. Building off a legacy of exploitation, the current system was designed as, and remains to its core part of, what historian Sonya Michel explains as the "residual welfare state."[56] Michel says this model is "one that offers public support only as a last resort, when applicants implicitly concede that they are incapable of supporting themselves. A residual welfare state contrasts with a proactive or affirmative state that regards public provisions such as child care as a form of collective social good designed to achieve a consensual goal."

It seems unlikely that the nation can ever unwind child care in its current form out of the residual welfare state; the assumptions and programs that constitute the system are too tainted by discriminatory origins. Recall that child-care battles in the decades following Nixon's veto were largely fought (by both sides) on grounds of how to best integrate child care into the welfare system, not whether child-care assistance should be part of a last-resort safety net versus part of the national fabric.[57] At times, a bridge is so structurally deficient it simply needs to be replaced. That doesn't mean obliterating the existing system in one swoop—when replacing bridges, engineers often build the new one alongside the old—but it means acknowledging the necessity of a different approach using different materials.

The good news is that replacing our existing child-care system—and reforming the advocacy movements working to improve it—has the potential to better all of society. If gender and racial equality are centered, there is a significant opportunity to build solidarity that will fuel not just better child-care policy, but better family policy writ large.

> *Examples of "Racial and Gender Equity Case" Messages:*
> - "America has an ugly history of devaluing the care provided by people of color—especially Black people. Some of the first child-care providers were enslaved Black girls and women. We cannot build an equitable system off an inequitable foundation; we must move toward a new, universal child-care system."
> - "For women to have equal opportunities to thrive—regardless of whether they want to work outside the home or inside the home—the United States needs a robust child-care system. Anything less will continue to impose an unfair 'motherhood penalty' on American women."
> - "The child-care workforce is almost entirely women and disproportionately women of color. An effective child-care system can single-handedly move well over one million women into the middle class and, in doing so, strengthen their families and communities."
>
> *In a sentence:* Access to child care, as well as the child-care sector itself, is deeply influenced by racism and sexism; solving child care would be a major step forward for racial and gender equity.

Chapter 7
The Antipoverty Case

In Oregon, a group of Democratic Socialists and a group convened by liberal elected officials were fighting about how to best fix child care. This may sound like the setup to a *Portlandia* sketch, but it was the reality in Multnomah County (containing Portland and surrounds) in 2019.[1]

At issue was how bold the plan should be, how it should be funded, and how it should be passed. The two groups resolved their differences and moved forward with a powerful ballot measure: With a small tax on high-income families, the county would raise around $200 million annually at full implementation—more than some entire states spend on child care. The funds would be used to phase in a universal, free pre-K system for all four-year-olds and three-year-olds, with robust compensation for early educators and a set-aside for infant and toddler classrooms. In 2020, Multnomah voters approved the measure with a 64 percent majority.

The reason this story is relevant to the Antipoverty Case for child care is because of the *why* behind the campaign. I have interviewed many of the organizers involved in the Multnomah effort. The involvement from the Democratic Socialists was not primarily motivated by a desire to improve children's school readiness or improve the county economy (though those were nice consequences): It was an antipoverty play. One of the organizers explained to me that in the group's analysis of various barriers to Multnomah families' financial security and upward mobility, two issues flashed red: housing costs and child-care costs. While affordable housing continued to be a priority, they saw a clear lever that could be pulled in addressing child care.

The early results bear out the campaigners' logic. Although there have naturally been kinks to work out, priority for the free child-care slots has gone to low-income families, and many are benefitting. *The Oregonian* reported on one such mother, Irisbeth Martinez-Luna, whose daughter was able to access one of the first free spaces available. Martinez-Luna did not attend an early care and education program and never finished high school, but she sees the potential for her children now that cost is not a barrier: "'I want them to have it better than I did,' [Martinez-Luna] said, tearing up."[2]

As we will see in this chapter, creating a functional child-care system—particularly one that is free for families—is one of the best antipoverty measures the country could take.

Children and Poverty

For American families, the presence of young children is not just correlated with risks of poverty, it can be a direct *cause* of poverty. Consider the story of one mother, Kiarcia Shields. Journalists Brigid Schulte and Yuliya Panfil recounted Shields' experience in a 2024 op-ed:

> Before Kiarcia Schields and her four children were evicted from their home for the first time in August 2020, she saw it coming. The Covid-19 pandemic had shuttered her children's schools, child care, after-school programs and summer camps . . . What Schields couldn't have foreseen was how the continued lack of stable, affordable child care would launch her and her children—ages 10, five, four, and an infant—down a spiral of high-stress financial and housing instability.
>
> For more than three years, Schields, a college-educated nurse, has bounced between precarious and poorly paid temp jobs including catering, tax prep, sorting packages, and driving DoorDash with her baby strapped into his car seat.
>
> By the summer of 2023, with her savings depleted and car repossessed, Schields and her kids had been bouncing between a homeless shelter and cheap motel rooms. "I began having panic attacks. But I have to remain calm because at the end of the day, I have kids to raise," Schields explained. "Child care. That's my issue."[3]

Schulte and Panfil go on to cite research from Princeton University's Eviction Lab, where scholars for the first time linked 38 million eviction records to Census Bureau data in order to get a picture of who was being evicted.[4] The Eviction Lab, they write, reported startling findings: The population most at risk of eviction *are children under the age of five*. Harkening back to the Racial and Gender Equality Case, there is also a stark racial divide: "Even at higher income levels, the eviction rate for Black renters with children is more than double that of White renters with children. A staggering one in four Black infants and toddlers living in rental housing are in renter households threatened with an eviction each year."

Although child care is of course not the entire explanation for these deplorable figures—landlords may find children a nuisance, as they bring added scrutiny around health hazards such as lead and, frankly, children can be noisy and break things—it is a significant and underappreciated influence.[5] Child care pushes on family financial dynamics in several ways. First, unless the household is able to secure free care from a relative or friend, or nab one of the limited free slots in a program like Head Start, child care adds a new—frequently large—line item to a tight budget. As Schulte and Panfil note, "At one point, Schields was earning $800 a week, but paying more than $600 a week in child care costs."

These out-of-pocket expenses alone are a tremendous burden. In a 2017 paper, researchers at the University of New Hampshire found that among poor families that utilize paid child care, around one in three "are pushed into poverty by child care expenses. This represents an estimated 207,000 families."[6]

Second, as we have discussed, the constrained supply of child-care options means that families often have to take a slot wherever they can find one—convenient or not. That can impact parents' ability to get to work, which can be disastrous for poor parents given their frequent lack of job protections and leave policies. In 2024, *The New York Times* reported on the case of Shavon Johnson. Johnson, "who lives in public housing on the Lower East Side, is a recent widow who was fired in September from her job as a dog food cook, where she made $20 an hour. She said she was let go because she couldn't get to work on time and still drop her 4-year-old son, Dominique, off at [pre]school."[7]

Even when child-care challenges don't cause a family to descend into deep crisis, they can act like a sheet of ice, causing families to slip and stumble as they work hard to get on their feet and find solid ground. Sociologists Amanda Freeman and Lisa Dodson interviewed 250 low-income mothers, individually and in groups, and turned their research into the 2022 book, *Getting Me Cheap: How Low-Wage Work Traps Women and Girls in Poverty*.[8] They dedicate an entire chapter to child care, and the pair write:

> Problems finding and keeping childcare wove in and out of the stories women told us, blocking them from moving up in work and school. In fact, 60 percent of parents in community conversations in Georgia said they lost a job due to problems with childcare. Roughly seven in ten women in the lowest paid jobs in the United States are the breadwinners in their families,

so job loss may be catastrophic. We heard countless stories of jobs lost and college credits and programs left half-earned.

As we have begun to see, when child care goes awry, things can get very bad very quickly. Child care is so important to family stability and stress reduction, particularly for low-income families, that it is a protective factor against child abuse, the involvement of Child Protective Services—and even child death.[9] For example, a report from the Colorado Department of Human Services stated that "between 2013 and 2017, [the Colorado Child Fatality Prevention System] identified 223 child maltreatment deaths, which might have been prevented had quality, affordable child care been available to all families that needed it."[10]

Ostensibly, the country's public assistance programs for child care are supposed to aid these families. In reality, the lack of a universal child-care system has led to a bureaucratic and punitive kludge that helps very few people involved.

The Poor Legacy of Child Care as Welfare

Recall historian Sonya Michel's explanation that in the DNA of modern child-care assistance is the "residual welfare state," where help is offered reluctantly and for as short a time as possible. Michel has traced how child care was caught up in the broader welfare reform efforts of the 1980s and 1990s, and further expounds:

> In tethering child care subsidies to mandatory employment, lawmakers transformed what feminists had initially envisioned as an entitlement for all mothers—indeed, for all wage-earning parents—into a lever for punitive policy toward poor and low-income mothers. The policy was especially discriminatory toward those with low vocational skills, as child care, even with public subsidies, would take a huge chunk out of their paychecks. Perhaps most cruelly, the welfare reform legislation eliminated the previous regulation that had allowed recipients to rely on public assistance while pursuing training or education and thus improve their occupational prospects. Now, individual states had the option of prohibiting that use under the rubric of "Work First"—and many did.[11]

These policies translated to a painful reality for low-income parents. (Some of the worst parts of the law, known as the Child Care and Development

Block Grant Act, were improved upon in a 2014 reauthorization and via executive orders in the Obama and Biden administrations, but massive problems remain: With that origin, how could they not?) Freeman and Dodson report that,

> [M]others offered detailed accounts of problems accessing and relying on the current system of childcare "assistance." They reported filling out mountains of paperwork to apply, certify, and recertify qualifications for a voucher. Since the amount of the voucher is adjusted by income, moms would continuously report their earnings, which caused trouble when hours fluctuated as they often did. Fran, a single mother of two young children living in public housing in Boston, said, "It's hard to get hired when you are a parent, but I need to get a job first to get a voucher for her to go to daycare" in order to go to work.

(Fran's point was made dramatically in the hit Netflix show *Maid*, when Margaret Qualley's character Alex—a stand-in for Stephanie Land, author of the same-named memoir—is speaking to a social worker: "I need a job to prove that I need daycare in order to get a job. What kind of fuckery is that?!"[12])

Even if parents jump through all the hoops—and are lucky enough to find a provider nearby who accepts vouchers, which is voluntary—assistance is no guarantee. As a result of persistent underfunding, most states do not have enough funds to meet the needs of all eligible families. In fact, the Center for American Progress has shown that as of 2019, only one in nine eligible children nationwide actually received a subsidy voucher.[13] Similarly, Head Start and Early Head Start only serve a fraction of eligible families.

When low-income parents run out of options, they often resort to desperate measures to avoid destitution. Those measures can look like relying on low-quality, unlicensed, and/or illegally operating child-care programs—the latter of which can be outright dangerous—or even bringing a young child to work. Freeman and Dodson recount the story of Paula, a grocery worker at ShopRite, who "hid her five-year-old in the bread racks" behind the bakery counter.

The System Families Need

If tomorrow, all eligible families magically received subsidy vouchers and all existing providers agreed to accept those vouchers, many low-income families would be no better off. That's because the existing child-care system does an awful job offering care at the times it is actually needed, meaning it fails to meet a fraction of its poverty-fighting potential.

Many American working-class families have a parent who does not work a predictable, nine-to-five, Monday-through-Friday schedule. One can imagine the jobs that lead to needing care during nontraditional hours. While lawyers or finance managers may need a 6:30 AM drop-off or 6:30 PM pickup, they are not likely to need regular care at 9:00 PM or over the weekends. No, these are largely the households of low-wage employees, the janitors and health aides and restaurant servers who have little ability to stick to a traditional schedule.[14]

Among children who are in any kind of nonparental care (in other words, who don't have a stay-at-home parent), research from the Urban Institute found that 40 percent utilized some form of "nontraditional hours" care.[15] This is defined as care before 7 AM or after 6 PM on weekdays, or any time on weekends. The Urban Institute data confirms that the highest proportion of children needing care during nontraditional hours are poor: Fully half of kids living below the federal poverty line who use nonparental care are in this group.

While the most utilized nontraditional hours were early mornings (6 AM–7 AM) and evenings (6 PM–7 PM), a solid quarter of these children needed care as late as 9 PM–10 PM, and half were in care at some point during the weekend. The Urban Institute researchers report that 14 percent—nearly 700,000 children—need overnight care on weekdays.

Most of these children are cared for outside of traditional hours by a family member, friend, or neighbor. These arrangements can be fraught, especially if no grandparents are nearby: Freeman and Dodson record the experience of a mother who relied on her roommate, but at times the roommate became fed up and refused.

The answer is not necessarily to have all of these children in group care settings during nontraditional hours: Here, yet again, we see the importance of a comprehensive policy that supports informal caregivers, for instance by making it far easier for people like the roommate to be paid by the government for providing regular care.

That said, a fully funded system could bring many more nontraditional hours options for families. In Sweden, for instance, nearly half of municipalities offer publicly supported care options during these hours, including a series of "night nurseries."[16] The United States does have a smattering of such offerings, although they are few and far between and generally don't get much public funding.

What programs do exist can be incredibly impactful, however. As I wrote in a review of the 2021 documentary, *Through The Night*, which chronicles a 24-hour family child-care program in New York:

> The documentary takes viewers through the daily routines of Dee's Tots, where [Delores "Nunu" Hogan] and her husband Patrick work with children ranging from babies to one youth about to age out of subsidy eligibility upon turning thirteen. The title refers to the fact that Dee's is one of a growing number of 24-hour child care programs that serve children whose parent(s) work overnight; journalist Alissa Quart has described this phenomenon as "extreme [child]care." . . . Let's be clear: There is inarguably a specialized skill at work here, complex and valuable labor that is not easily replicated. Education is also certainly happening, as Nunu and Patrick ensure their school-aged charges complete their homework, while the little ones are frequently seen with books. But the interactions and informality border on familial, almost a form of village alloparenting. One can understand why some parents feel more comfortable with family child care over other settings.[17]

Nontraditional-hours care is not the only place that America's child-care system is misaligned with family needs. As we have seen throughout the book, cleaving early child care from school-aged child care has created an oddly fragmented system. Families with an elementary schooler and a toddler do not experience those care needs in two separate vacuums. Particularly for low-income families who operate with immense precarity thanks to America's unforgiving economy and weak safety net, a failure of care anywhere in the family system can be devastating. Sometimes, care needs crop up as problems in places that would be almost amusingly ironic if they didn't have such real human consequences: Freeman and Dodson record the stories of women unable to secure child care in order to attend the mandatory job trainings and other classes required to maintain their government child-care subsidy.

Child Care as Social Connection

There is another reason that child care helps alleviate poverty, and it may not be one that comes immediately to mind: Child-care programs are hubs that bring parents together, and—especially for mothers, to harken back to the Racial and Gender Equity Case—can be powerful settings for forging friendships and informal networks. Sociologist Mario Small explored this role in his award-winning, if dryly titled, book, *Unanticipated Gains: Origins of Network Inequality in Everyday Life*.[18]

Small looked specifically at child-care centers and found that they, "tend to be a remarkably effective broker for the mothers whose children they service. They broker both social and organizational ties, and their brokerage is associated with greater material and mental well-being."

These gains can be remarkable indeed. Small used data including a renowned set known as the Fragile Families and Child Wellbeing Study, which followed in exceptional depth around 5,000 children from major cities born between 1998 and 2000, with an oversampling of children born to unmarried mothers. In his analysis, Small found that among mothers who utilized centers, "about 60% made at least one friend, and more than 40% made three or more friends in centers."[19] (For what it is worth, my wife and I formed friendships at our daughters' child-care center that we maintain today despite now living halfway across the country.)

The friendships—as well as overall access to the networks that come with the territory of being part of an institution like a center—came in handy. Among both poor (average income: ~$29,000) and nonpoor mothers (average income: ~$61,000), center enrollment substantially reduced their likelihood of material hardship. In fact, compared to mothers not utilizing a center, the probability of having a housing-related hardship like not being able to make rent went down by more than *half* (from 8.8% to around 4%). The way this plays out in real life ranges from having friends to commiserate and share parenting tips with, to having friends who can provide emergency child care that can prevent a job loss or other crises. Cultivating these types of relational webs, sometimes fashioned as "social capital," have been found time and again to be a major antipoverty strategy.[20]

The advantages Small found were more than material: Whereas poor mothers who did not make friends at the center showed no change in their odds of depression, the poor mothers who did make friends had a more than 40 percent drop in risk.

(That all of these effects were present—and, in fact, often larger—for nonpoor mothers shows that child-care-as-social-capital could easily be part of several other Cases. It is situated here because it is an essential part of the antipoverty case, as these same low-income parents are the ones most often boxed out of access to formal child-care programs like centers. I would also be remiss not to note again that the too-common isolation of stay-at-home parents cries out for policy and cultural action.)

Parents also benefitted from being able to access information and services routed through child-care centers. As Small writes, based on his field work with New York City programs, "centers were nothing if not information banks for parents of young children." He notes:

> How to prevent eviction, stress, lead poisoning, or divorce; how to obtain health insurance, a good lawyer, a mortgage, or the child support payments to which one is entitled; or how to cut children's hair, to make sellable arts and crafts, or to get one's child into a good school—all of these were forms of information that parents acquired from external organizations through their centers.

This is not just the case for centers: As I wrote about *Through the Night*, "At a local parade, Nunu runs into a former attendee, now a young adult. The young woman appears to be having a hard time: 'I need to talk to you,' she tells Nunu, repeating herself. 'I really need to talk to you.'" A relational lens on child care emphasizes again why we need to support our child-care professionals with family-sustaining compensation that enables stable staffing levels and good working conditions. Not only does high staff turnover get in the way of relationship building, the stress of trying to hold a child-care program together with little more than baling wire can be hazardous: In the course of the documentary's filing, Nunu suffers a serious medical episode.

Small is clear, too, that there is variation among centers: Not all of them act as hubs or are interested in serving a networking role. But for many parents—and children—the social capital and solidarity inherent in child-care settings can be a figurative or literal lifeline, one whose impacts can echo for a long, long time.

Intergenerational Effects

Recall that when Lyndon Johnson announced the Head Start program, he invoked tropes of pathologized Black poverty: "Five- and six-year-old children are inheritors of poverty's curse and not its creators. Unless we act these children will pass it on to the next generation, like a family birthmark." Yet underneath the problematic rhetoric, Johnson was (knowingly or not) nodding to a broader idea that has since been borne out: Helping lift children and families out of poverty can have ripple effects across the decades.

First, who are America's poor? Policy analyst Matt Bruenig has shown that, using 2022 Census Bureau numbers, it may not be who you expect.[21] The largest percentage of those living under the Supplemental Poverty Measure threshold—in 2022, that was $34,518 for a two-adult, two-child household that rented their dwelling—are children, the elderly, and individuals who are disabled. Nearly one in ten are full-time caregivers, while 13 percent are fully employed. So, we can largely do away with the image of the lazy, "able-bodied" individual who is poor because they can't be bothered to work.

It is important to understand that poverty is not a static, binary state. It has been my observation that many people who have never experienced poverty imagine that one is either poor or not poor (I grew up in a middle-class household, and this was my view for a time as well). The reality is far more complex. In fact, far more people experience what experts call "transient poverty"—moving in and out of poverty—than experience "chronic poverty." One study by researchers at Stanford and Berkeley found, using data from the 2000s, that while 9 percent of children experienced chronic poverty, 21 percent experienced transient poverty.[22] Chronic poverty naturally poses the most risks to children and family flourishing, but the researchers note that transient poverty during "particularly important developmental windows" like childhood can have major impacts on health and well-being across the lifespan.

Understanding the nuances of America's poor helps illuminate the mechanisms of why child care is such an effective intergenerational antipoverty strategy. Consider the prevalence of transient poverty. The authors of the above study suggest that policies focused on transient poverty do not need the same level of intensity or duration at those focused on chronic poverty, but instead should "aim to reduce the impact of temporary income shocks at the household level, and to smooth income fluctuation over time."

A steady, universal, publicly funded child-care system is one such backstop. Without such a system, parents can be quickly thrust into a spiraling crisis where the loss of a job (the canonical "temporary income shock") leads to them being unable to pay for child care and thus forced to abandon a coveted slot or go further into debt. Instead, families could have a reliable source of care, social support, and the capacity needed to hunt for their next job.

It would avoid the "fuckery" of tethering child-care assistance so tightly to remaining employed—especially given that even in a strong economy, over a million individuals lose their jobs every month, often for company-related reasons entirely outside their control.[23]

What's more, such a system would help ensure that a college degree remains within reach for all who want it.

Child Care and College

For better or worse, attaining a college degree is still the most reliable path out of American poverty. As of 2019, 12 percent of those with only a high school diploma and no college coursework lived below the poverty line, compared to only 4 percent of those with a bachelor's degree.[24] Graduating college also unlocks access to many careers that an individual may find meaningful. While I do not think everyone must attend college—and we need to strengthen multiple pathways to meaningful careers, including community colleges and vocational programs, as well as ensuring those who do not attend college can still thrive—there can be no argument that college completion remains a key factor in life stability for many, many individuals.

Child care can either be a major barrier or major aid in that effort. Nearly four million college students are parents. In 2022, the think tank Education Trust and nonprofit Generation Hope released a report, "For Student Parents, The Biggest Hurdles to A Higher Education are Costs and Finding Child Care."[25] Although a modest federal program provides funds to colleges in order to help them offer child-care services, the report cites data showing that only about half of institutions do so, and "95% of on-campus child care centers have waiting lists." Student parents are then forced to turn to the general private-pay child-care marketplace, which as we have seen, is a wasteland of scarce slots and high fees (the latter of which is not helped by the fact many colleges do not factor child-care costs into financial aid awards).

The result is an untenable situation for many student parents: As the report notes, "there is no state in which a student parent can work 10 hours a week at the minimum wage and afford both tuition and child care at a public college or university." The lack of reliable child care also puts huge time pressure on these students. College students with children below the age of five are twice as likely to drop out as their counterparts without children; overall, between 2012 and 2017, around *half* of student parents failed to complete their degree within six years, compared to roughly a quarter of those without children who remained dependents of their own parents.[26]

Although there are college-specific policy responses—such as boosting overall financial aid or federal campus child-care funding—the real answer lies in creating a universal child-care system. Campus centers can be folded into such a system, while also giving student parents access to a bevy of high-quality options they may need to make school work for them. Just as importantly, those options should be free.

The Promise of Free Child Care

When child care is heavily subsidized—or, better yet, free—poverty rates go down. One study of member countries in the Organization for Economic Co-operation and Development (OECD) found that among young children who access early care and education services, child poverty rates were on average *halved* compared to a counterfactual where there were no child-care investments, with the effects understandably more pronounced in countries that put more into their systems.[27]

It is not difficult to see why. Consider again Shavon Johnson, the New York City widow who was fired because she couldn't juggle both getting her kid to child care and herself to her job. Her story takes a more upbeat turn:

> Now she is enrolled in a medical assistant program in the hopes of becoming a nurse—a goal she couldn't accomplish without the free day care program offered by Grand Street Settlement [a social service organization], which enables her to afford other necessities.
>
> "I would be homeless" if not for the program, she said.[28]

Similarly, in 2024 Jackie Mader of *The Hechinger Report* reported on a new set of child care centers in Hershey, Pennsylvania.[29] With funding from heirs to the Hershey fortune, the center is able to offer top-notch services with well-trained educators, a permanent nurse, parent resource center with coaches, and more. What makes the programs particularly notable is that they are zero-cost for any family making less than 300 percent of the federal poverty line ($77,460 for a three-person household, as of the article's publication). Mader recounts an interview with Tracey Orellana, the mother of two children at the center who works as an Amazon delivery driver. As you read, you will likely see connections between, at very least, the Antipoverty Case and the Parenting and Childhood Case:

> "We were juggling. We were juggling so much," said Orellana, who also has two school-age daughters. At the time, the family had incurred a mountain of debt and was struggling to afford basic needs like groceries. Now that the toddlers are in child care at no cost to their family, Orellana has been able to increase her work hours to full time, adding to her income and stability. The family is now able to afford food and has almost caught up with bills.
>
> The school "provides the opportunity to build a life for our kids and keep them out of whatever the situation may be, streets, poverty, keep them clothed, keep them fed, keep the electric on, the heat on," she said. Her daughters also have opportunities they wouldn't have at home, Orellana added, such as getting to ride bikes, play games and make new friends.
>
> "It gives them a childhood," Orellana said.

Of course, it is not scalable nor sustainable to expect nonprofit groups like Grand Street Settlement, or the largesse of philanthropists, to stand in the gap. (Appropriately, the headline of Mader's article is "Free child care exists in America—if you cross paths with the right philanthropist.") These can and should be implementation partners, but the core funding obligation falls to government. Evidence bears out how powerful such funding can be.

Drawing on natural experiments resulting from how Head Start funding was initially rolled out and allocated, in 2022 economists Andrew Barr and Chloe R. Gibbs released the first-ever study of *intergenerational* effects of this free child care and wraparound support.[30] Head Start offers an important viewing angle because unlike many early childhood studies that rely on very small samples (less than 150 children), with names you may have heard like Abecedarian and Perry Preschool, Head Start was rolled out at scale and provides thousands of data points. In short, Barr and Gibbs wanted to know: What is happening for the children of those children who attended Head Start in its early years?

The impacts they found are impressive, particularly when one takes into account the segregation effects around Head Start we discussed in the Racial and Gender Equity Case. Barr and Gibbs write that, "we find significant changes in both the second generation's home life (improved parenting behaviors) and early schooling (greater preschool participation). The changes lead to persistent developmental benefits and improved later-life well-being." Signals of that improved well-being included improved self-esteem and reduced grade repetition, and even a measurable impact on wages: an increase of up to 11 percent by age fifty, or more than $35,000 compared to similar children whose mothers did not attend Head Start.

Similarly, researcher Chris Herbst undertook a creative analysis of the children impacted by World War II Lanham Act centers. He found that Lanham Act spending was correlated with reduced high school dropout rates and increased college completion, employment, and earnings—effects that were detectable as late as the 1990 Census.[31] The benefits were most pronounced among low-income children.

If means-tested, suboptimal, or temporary versions of free child care can have these kinds of literally life-changing impacts, imagine the positive changes to American society if child care was free for everyone.

Conclusion

Poverty is a complex tree with deep roots in both policy and culture. As the prominent sociologist Matthew Desmond says in the prologue of his book, *Poverty, By America*, "Ending poverty will require new policies and renewed political movement to be sure. But it will also require that each of us, in our own way, become poverty abolitionists, unwinding ourselves from our neighbors' deprivation and refusing to live as unwitting enemies to the poor."[32]

Given what we have seen throughout this book, fighting for a universal child-care system can strike a victory both on policy grounds and on grounds of cross-class—indeed, cross-human—solidarity. Child care is a foundational and necessary, if insufficient, part of any comprehensive response to poverty and any comprehensive effort to ensure child and family flourishing. Its power is not merely in enabling work, though it does. Child care's power comes from knitting together young families, reducing isolation, offering support and slack in a country that too often offers only cold recriminations and the most reluctant of aid.

Importantly, child care's role in alleviating intergenerational poverty is most realized when it is not seen as part of a residual welfare state. The more we means-test, the more we get bogged down in administrative burden and dedicate immense resources to determining exactly who is deserving of help for how long, the more we lose the quintessence of child care as a societal weave. Recall the Patriotic Case: We owe parents our support not as a matter of a safety net catching them when they fall (or are pushed), but as recompense for the service they provide toward a healthy, prosperous, strong nation. America cannot reach its founding vision nor avoid its contemporary challenges if it casts down so many millions of families with young children, yet the potential if we do right by those families is colossal. By the same token, as we're about to see, America's safety and security also hang in the balance.

Examples of "Antipoverty Case" Messages:
- "A lack of child care is a direct risk factor for poverty, while access to child care can form the foundation for economic mobility. Child care should be at the core of any anti-poverty strategy."
- "Child care helps low-income families thrive through more than just enabling work. Child care programs have been shown to be vital sources of social connection and social capital, helping parents access needed resources and friendships. Enabling more families to get the child care they need and prefer can help reduce poverty and rebuild our social fabric."
- "Our current child care system is unable to, and will never be able to, meet the needs of low-income families. It was built with the DNA of wanting as few beneficiaries as possible for as little time as possible, and the system does not match the needs of those working nontraditional hours to keep the country running. A wholesale reform of child care into a universal, free system would slash poverty and spike flourishing."

In a sentence: Establishing a good child-care system, particularly one without loads of red tape, would be one of the strongest antipoverty measures America could take.

Chapter 8
The Security Case

The most unusual speech about child care I've ever heard came from the head of America's largest military shipbuilding company. Mike Petters is, to put it lightly, not what comes to mind when one thinks of a child-care champion. A bespectacled man with close-cropped, graying hair, Petters certainly looks the part of the former Navy submariner he is. After working his way through roles overseeing the construction of submarines and aircraft carriers, Petters served as CEO of Huntington Ingalls Industries (HII) from 2011 until 2022. You've probably never heard of HII, but it is a Fortune 500 company with massive shipbuilding complexes on the coasts of Virginia and Mississippi.

Yet on this day, Petters was not talking about defense contracts or naval operations. He was talking about child care. While I do not have the transcript of those specific remarks, it is a sign of Petters' belief in the power of early childhood that he has given a similar speech multiple times. In 2019, he spoke before a group of sectoral leaders at an Early Childhood Leadership Summit in New Orleans. Petters explained that more than workforce development and HII's bottom line, the reason he was focused on early childhood—"frankly, the reason we should *all* be interested in early education"—was national security.[1] To quote Petters at some length:

> The ships that we build in Mississippi and Virginia represent the best of America in every way.
>
> Think for a moment about the vision, the imagination, the technology, the skill, the will and the tens of millions of labor hours required to build Navy ships. Their hallowed purpose: never to sail on a mission of conquest, but always to keep the seas open and the world stable.
>
> Our fleet represents our commitment to invest in, believe in and prepare for the national security future of America. This is the very commitment we need to make for the future of our children.
>
> While the ships we design and build are engineering marvels, their power is not embedded in technology or weaponry. The power of our ships

Raising a Nation. Elliot Haspel, Oxford University Press. © Oxford University Press (2025).
DOI: 10.1093/oso/9780197799291.003.0009

will come from the young men and women—average age of 19—who will take them around the world, wherever needed.

A few years ago, I heard the then-Secretary of the Navy talk about the service's recruiting challenges. Look at the United States' population between the ages 18 and 25, he said.

Then take away anyone without a high school diploma . . . Take away anyone with physical fitness issues . . . Take away anyone with a criminal record . . . What you're left with is about 25 percent of the population.

That's the "talent pool" from which the Navy and other services are recruiting. When I heard that, I thought: That's who I'm recruiting too. But it gets worse.

More recent Pentagon surveys actually put the number at 20 percent. One in five . . . That is a staggering indictment.

The Pentagon's latest National Defense Strategy states that we are in a "near peer" competition with China and Russia. Think about going into a competition with only 20 percent of our capabilities to bear. That's something we should ALL be concerned about.

Now take those odds to an elementary school classroom. Only one in five students will ultimately be employable. The other four will face challenges that, frankly, we all will pay for.

The fact is: We have fallen desperately behind in teaching our children the most basic skill: the love of learning. Study after study shows that the most powerful and cost-effective way to make our children lifelong learners is to start them on that path before school—when they are 2 or 3 or 4 years old.

I might quibble with some of Petters' analysis, and I would certainly add that we have to consider children starting at birth and not at age two. But his point is well-taken: America's global competitiveness, national security, and even neighborhood security requires a strong, universal child-care system. That is true not only for children, but for servicemembers as well. This chapter will look at why.

Laying the Foundation

Petters is right that the foundation for later health, educational attainment, and overall well-being are laid from the beginnings of human development.

This may seem at odds with the Parenting and Childhood Case, but really it's more like viewing the same vista from a different vantage point.

Take health. Health reasons are the most common single cause for disqualification from military service. While there is limited evidence about child care and later health outcomes, what exists is optimistic. One policy brief noted that external child-care participation is linked to "improvements in blood pressure, reductions in smoking, and improved self-reported health in adolescence and adulthood. Other research finds that Head Start and model program participation reduces depression and disability rates in adolescence and early adulthood."[2]

Allowing that health has many influences, some strongly genetic, the mechanisms at play appear to be two-fold and two-generational. First, there are direct impacts on children. Attending a child-care program puts a child and their parents in contact with professionals who can encourage vaccinations and pediatric visits and can spot potential health concerns early. For lower-income children, these programs may also offer more consistent access to nutritious food.

Second, there are the effects on parents and households writ large. We've already explored these at length in the preceding chapters, but it is worth reiterating that good, affordable (or free) child care not only improves families' financial situation—and can be a bulwark against families falling into crises such as eviction or food insecurity, which bring acutely negative impacts on children's health and well-being—it also reduces stress and improves overall parenting. These supportive effects cannot help but improve child health.

That being said, it's clear that if the nation needs a potential universe of military members who have graduated high school with reasonable health, having a healthy child-care system is a crucial place to start.

Of course, eligibility to serve does not equate with a desire to serve. The reasons why individuals choose to pursue military service are nuanced, but surveys of servicemembers are clear that for large minorities (at least 40%) patriotism or a sense of duty are paramount—they see themselves embodying the "citizen-solider."[3] Therefore, the sense of civic pride that a strong child-care system supports, as discussed in the Patriotic Case, can also help build interest.

Then there's the question of what to do when those service members start having families.

Defense Department, Child-Care Provider

The Department of Defense (DOD) spends over $1 billion a year on child care for service members.[4] As of 2020, the DOD served around 200,000 children and employed 23,000 child-care staff, more than many small-to-medium sized states. For context, the $1 billion is equal to roughly one-eighth the amount the federal government spends annually on the Child Care and Development Block Grant, the main source of funding spread across all states and territories.

The rationale is straightforward. A 2023 Government Accountability Office (GAO) report on military child care starts off with the plain statement that "The Department of Defense views child care as essential to overall mission readiness, retention, and recruitment for the U.S. military."[5] Former Secretary of Defense Lloyd Austin went further, writing in a memo that, "The Department of Defense has a sacred obligation to take care of our service members and families. Doing so is a national security imperative. Our military families provide the strong foundation for our force, and we owe them our full support."[6]

Although child care is not free for service members, it is subsidized to the tune of about half the sticker price, and fees are set on an income-based sliding scale. For instance, as of 2023, those making between $61,000 and $71,000 a year pay $569 a month (a little under $7,000 a year) for full-time care.[7] Although this is far from ideal, it is a substantial reduction from what that family would pay in the wild.

The military also grasps three other facts we have touched on throughout the book: Parents want choices; care needs don't end at Kindergarten; and you can't provide decent child care with meager funding. To the first point, the DOD deeply subsidizes the costs for service members' children to attend community-based programs—including family child-care homes—as well as on-base centers. To the second, the DOD operates centers for school-aged children as well as young children. And third, the DOD invests in quality: All programs must be accredited by a national organization, all receive at least four unannounced annual inspections, and perhaps most importantly educators are not treated quite as much like disposable low-wage workers.

To be sure, DOD child-care educators are not paid amazingly well, but most start in the $18–$20 per hour range and, as federal government employees, are granted government benefits. In almost every case, the military is offering a better deal than child-care programs in the surrounding community.[8] DOD center directors can start at around $80,000 a year.

All of the above is only feasible because of the public money that is feeding the system.

Yet, it's not enough, which indicates just how much reform American child-care needs. The military child-care system is still badly underfunded, unable to maintain adequate supply or—even with a relatively stronger compensation package compared to the rest of the sector—adequate staffing. Consequently, it is plagued by long waitlists. As of 2023, there were more than 10,000 children on DOD waitlists, including over 2,500 in San Diego alone. As NBC News reported of one military family impacted by the lack of slots:

> Erin Williams has jumped out of airplanes, led a platoon in Afghanistan and earned an Ivy League degree with three young children at home. But the hardest thing to navigate in her military career is finding child care.
>
> "Child care is the only thing that has made me consider leaving military service," said Williams, an Army officer who is currently serving at Fort Campbell in Kentucky. "I've worked for awesome leaders, and I think I've done a good job leading, but the logistics and constant stress that come from child care is truly the hardest thing I've had to deal with."[9]

In response, the military has tried raising fees for families in order to offer higher educator wages, and offering deeply discounted or free child care for the kids of educators themselves. They have also tried asking for more money: The Pentagon requested from Congress a 10 percent increase in funding for child development programs between FY23 and FY24, boosting overall funding levels to nearly $1.8 billion; the Air Force alone requested a nearly 20 percent increase.[10] These measures have helped, but major struggles remain.

That this is the state of the nation's most invested-in child-care system throws the gap between current reality and needed reality into sharp relief. Incremental measures will not do. Half-measures will not do. The only solution is going to be a rather large, entirely warranted investment of public money into American child care: per the National Academies of Sciences, at least $175 billion a year (in 2024 dollars).[11]

This may all seem like a nice argument for investing public dollars in military child care but feel inapplicable to a broader case for universal child care. But the use case is not as narrow as it sounds: supplying and supporting America's armed services are an army (pun intended) of other parents.

The Military-Industrial-Child-Care Complex

What Dwight Eisenhower once termed the "military-industrial complex" is known in modern times as the "defense industrial base," or DIB. According to the Congressional Research Service, as of 2021, the domestic DIB—"those commercial, nonprofit, and public sector organizations and facilities that provide goods and services to DOD and are located in the United States"—constituted nearly 60,000 companies with a collective 1.1 million employees.[12] DOD spending on defense contracts alone totals nearly $400 billion year (in 2024 dollars), or 1.5 percent of the entire country's gross domestic product (GDP).

The DIB is a sprawling network. Contributing entities exist in all fifty states, and types of activities range from the manufacturing of metals, chemicals, and electronics, to scientific research, to waste management.[13] Many of the employees or would-be employees at these organizations are parents, which means they need child care. The lack thereof introduces vulnerabilities into the supply chain.

(There is a similar story for American intelligence services, by the way. Organizations like the National Security Agency (NSA) and Central Intelligence Agency have a rapidly aging workforce that needs replacing; more than half of NSA staff are eligible for retirement.[14] Particularly since intelligence agency headquarters are mainly located in high cost-of-living areas around Virginia and Washington, DC, child care absolutely plays a role in keeping these organizations functional.)

A further weakened DIB is about the last thing U.S. national security—or, frankly, global security—needs. In a 2024 report, "Rebuilding the Arsenal of Democracy," the Center for Strategic and International Studies issued this blunt assessment:

> The U.S. defense industrial base . . . lacks the capacity, responsiveness, flexibility, and surge capability to meet the U.S. military's production needs as China ramps up defense industrial production. Unless there are urgent changes, the United States risks weakening deterrence and undermining its warfighting capabilities against China and other competitors . . .
>
> . . . the U.S. defense industrial base continues to face a range of production challenges, including a lack of urgency in revitalizing the defense industrial ecosystem. The U.S. Department of Defense has taken some helpful steps to strengthen the industrial base, such as developing

a National Defense Industrial Strategy, increasing production for some weapons systems, and pushing for multiyear procurement. But there is still a shortfall of munitions and other weapons systems for a protracted war in such areas as the Indo-Pacific. Supply chain challenges also remain serious, and today's workforce is inadequate to meet the demands of the defense industrial base.[15]

This is an example of the nuance that gets lost when we make simplistic and vague arguments for child care on behalf of The Economy. As communications expert Anat Shenker-Osorio has pointed out, too often we treat The Economy as a kind of unknowable and ungovernable deity, as opposed to creating a values-laden story anchored in specific mechanisms of how it actually works.[16] Child care, as you can see, plays into the economic juggernaut that is the defense industrial base, but in doing so connects to the nation's ability to defend itself and be a force for good in the world.

When we pigeonhole child care as a private service, or as a mere support for business' bottom line, we artificially reduce child care's importance. One does not need to be compelled by, say, the Anti-Poverty Case to realize that national defense benefits every American—and is enough cause, in and of itself, to fund a robust child-care system.

Food Security, Too

Of course, America's national security is influenced by more than just the defense industrial base. For instance, the country needs to be able to feed itself. As the Department of Homeland Security has explained, "when large scale threats affect food and agriculture supplies, they become matters of national security. Many different threats to our food and agriculture sector exist, and any disruption to the supply chain can cause shortages at your local grocery store and limit the availability of food."[17] It might surprise you, then, to learn that child care has a significant influence on the iconic American farmers.

As I wrote in a summary of a 2024 study on the topic from researchers Florence Becot and Shoshanah Inwood:

> In the popular imagination, children are a boon for farms: they are a ready source of labor and, ideally, take over the family business. This is accurate, yet incomplete. Becot and Inwood explain: "[R]esearchers and

policy makers have overlooked the time, energy and resources that the households' social reproduction require. The caring of children is particularly demanding as children need to be fed, educated and emotionally supported. Care work happens simultaneously and in competition with meeting the farm enterprise production needs. As such care work affects the structure and trajectory of the farm enterprise."

. . . While the mere presence of young children has an understandable impact, the need to decrease resources going to the farm itself was particularly pronounced among families with child care challenges. [The study found] 46% of those without adequate child care reported making such reallocations, versus 23% of those who had decent child care options. Just 18% of farm families struggling with child care made no changes to their business at all. These moves have a predictable consequence on what the farm produces: "83% of respondents with childcare supply challenges report an impact on their farm productivity compared to 62% for those not reporting that challenge."[18]

Farmers need a functional child-care system, and the rest of us need farmers to have a functional child-care system. As Becot said in a different article, "the implication here is that child care not only impacts farm success for the families, but food availability for all."[19] The answer isn't to design a farmer-specific program, but to craft and fund a comprehensive policy that supports farmers alongside everyone else.

Moreover, since national security is inarguably a key area led by the federal government, not the states, the Security Case demonstrates again why the federal government should be taking a leading role in child-care funding—and why the federal government needs to be keeping an eye on population numbers.

Birth Rates, Redux

National security is hampered by low population. This is true, firstly, from a purely numerical standpoint. To expand Mike Petters' point, not only do we have a challenge in the percentage of young adults who qualify for military service, we have a challenge in the denominator: The sheer number of youths is declining. Whereas 4.32 million babies were born in the United States in 2007, there were 3.6 million born in 2023.

As a result of declining births and aging Baby Boomers, as of 2022 the median age in America was thirty-eight, up from thirty in 1980 (by contrast, a youthful country like Ghana has a median age of twenty). Yet the days of thirty-eight being the median age are soon going to start looking rosy: By 2040, even as the overall American population nears its projected peak, close to one in four Americans will be over the age of sixty-five.[20]

Too-low birth rates can also threaten security by piling added tension and urgency onto already challenging domestic and foreign issues. For instance, Russia has been contending with a rapidly shrinking and aging population, outpacing the demographic shifts of peer countries. Some experts have suggested that Vladimir Putin's decision to launch a war on Ukraine was at least partially motivated by a desire to bring millions of individuals into the Russian population.[21] Although no one is suggesting the United States is going to engage in wars of conquest to bolster its numbers, it is easy to see how low birth rates could intersect with hot-button topics like immigration, leading to civic and regional strife.

As previously mentioned in the Family Values Case, child-care policy cannot singlehandedly turn around birth rates or ensure that all can realize their desired family size; the influences on having children are multifactorial and involve a combination of policy and culture, to say nothing of individuals' relational and biological circumstances. A good child-care system can, however, help on the margins. And to reiterate public policy researcher Paul Constance's point, the difference between a birth rate of, say, 1.5 and 1.8 matters an awful lot. Then, to echo our earlier question, there's the matter of what happens once those children are born.

Global Competitiveness

In the broadest sense, America's position on the global stage influences its security. That position is deeply influenced by educational outcomes. With all of the caveats of overly focusing on the "investible child" and school readiness, it is worth sitting for a moment with the implications of correlations between early childhood experiences and educational attainment. This link takes on additional importance in modern times. In a 2022 *Foreign Affairs* article, a pair of researchers from the right-leaning American Enterprise Institute explained that:

Education is a crucial component of human capital and, by extension, of national might. A better-educated citizenry means a more productive economy and thus greater military potential . . . . Scholars and strategists have long understood that nations draw strength from their populations. Until recently, however, most have focused on head counts: numbers of people, broken down by age and sex, inhabiting different countries or alliances. But that simple approach makes little sense in a world where people from some countries have much greater economic potential than people from others. Switzerland has fewer residents than Burundi, for instance, but its GDP per capita is more than 90 times greater.

In an era when a single person's productivity in one country can be greater than that of 90 people in another, human productivity will increasingly affect the global balance of power. Productivity, in turn, is driven primarily by improvements in human capital—in health, knowledge, skills, and other intrinsically human factors. Rapid but sharply differential increases in human capital can open wide productivity gaps between countries, including between great powers, in just a few decades. One of the most important ingredients in human capital is education: more specifically, the sheer quantity of schooling received by national populations. Overwhelming evidence shows that more schooling means more productive potential at the national level, regardless of how high or low a nation's baseline level of educational attainment.[22]

Taking this argument to its logical conclusion, America has a serious interest in doing everything it can to enhance educational outcomes. Although school reform efforts have proven stubbornly difficult to implement at scale, the early years offer an enormous opportunity. Unlike America's K–12 school system, which groans under the inertial weight of 175 years of bureaucracy, inequitable funding formulas, and anachronistic foundations that get in the way of innovation (just try to shift from a model where all students move grades based on age to one where they can shift around based on mastery of the material, or try to modernize the high school course progression!), the early care and education field is far more open to evolution.[23]

Moreover, in-school influences are a minority of what generates educational attainment. Depending on the study one looks at, if you consider the educational outcomes of two demographically similar students, school effects like teacher quality account for, at best, a third of the difference.[24]

This does not mean schools aren't vitally important—I am a former fourth grade teacher!—of course they are; and the impact of teachers on students' self-perception, interests, and networks aren't captured in attainment statistics. What it means is that family and neighborhood effects loom large, as does access to quality early education.

Of those, family economic stability may be the single largest factor. As of 2020, nearly 60 percent of youth in the highest income quartile, and 40 percent of youth in the second-highest quartile, received a bachelor's degree by age twenty-four.[25] That contrasts with 25 percent and 15 percent, respectively, in the two lowest quartiles. (Racism, and structural factors that create barriers to lower-income students attending and completing college, are of course also heavily at play.)[26]

As we have seen over and over throughout the book, this shows that child care, too, looms large. If one cares about America's global competitiveness, and the security consequences thereof, one must care about moving toward a universal child-care system that supports families in all their diversity.

Neighborhood Security

All of this discussion about national security and global competitiveness can feel a bit abstract, so it is important to note that the security implications of child care also go down to the very local level.

We saw in the Community Case chapter how child care can directly impact the number of first responders like police officers, as well as their response times. The need is so significant that in 2024, a rare bipartisan coalition of Congresspeople introduced the "Providing Child Care for Police Officers Act."[27] The legislation would direct $24 million a year for five years to help local law enforcement agencies in easing the child-care burden on officers. It is supported by both police management and police unions. In announcing the legislation, U.S. Senator Kirsten Gillibrand asserted that, "Offering child care services is a powerful tool to attract and retain new talent, and it's an essential way to promote public safety while maintaining a stable law enforcement workforce."[28]

(Of course, the profession-specific nature of such a proposal shows the strangeness of both relying on employers and not having a universal approach. Why a discrete funding stream for police officers and not firefighters? The farmers we were discussing earlier? How about emergency medical technicians, nurses, teachers, sanitation workers? The incoherence is startling, but, in the context of this chapter, not the main point.)

Police staffing is not the only way in which child care influences crime rates and a general feeling of neighborhood safety and togetherness.

Numerous studies suggest high-quality early childhood experiences are correlated with a lower likelihood of criminal behavior later in life, but I will not be spending time on them other than to note their existence.[29] Criminogenic influences are incredibly complex and deeply connected to systemic and structural factors—often implicitly or explicitly tinged with racism—that lead to poverty and a lack of opportunity. To consider toddlers with a lens of whether or not they will engage in theft or violent crime when they are adolescents or adults is a too-narrow view that makes dangerous assumptions and can quickly slide into pathologizing children.

That said, the presence of child-care programs themselves may prove a protective factor against neighborhood crime. Although there is limited and mixed empirical research around the question, research does suggest this can be the case for elementary schools. For instance, one study concluded that "the presence of elementary schools is associated with decrease in burglary at the block level."[30] Why might this be? Even mechanisms as simple as adults having a reason to be out and about in public—such as doing drop-off, pick-up, and school activities—can mitigate crime by putting more pairs of eyes on the streets, contributing to what criminologists call "passive surveillance."

Perhaps more impactfully, a trio of crime researchers offers that, "elementary schools, with their relatively higher rates of parent participation and lower student to teacher ratios, may promote the formation of collective efficacy."[31] In this context, collective efficacy is defined as "the process of activating or converting social ties among neighborhood residents in order to achieve collective goals, such as public order or the control of crime."[32]

There are strong reasons to suspect that child-care programs also contribute to both passive surveillance and collective efficacy. Recall the research of Mario Small, who found that child-care programs frequently catalyzed the formation of friendships, trusted relationships, and wider social networks.[33] More broadly, child-care centers fall into the category of what sociologist Eric Klinenberg calls social infrastructure—"the physical conditions that determine whether social capital develops." In his book, *Palaces to the People: How Social Infrastructure Can Help Fight Inequality, Polarization, and the Decline of Civic Life*, Klinenberg notes that, "when social infrastructure is robust, it fosters contact, mutual support, and collaboration among friends; when degraded, it inhibits social activity, leaving families and individuals to fend for themselves."[34]

Notably, the ways in which schools—and, as I am positing here, child-care programs—improve neighborhood security and vibrancy is yet another reason these services benefit even those without children. Although we have discussed many ways those without children need a society with a robust number of children, we haven't yet touched on a deeply self-interested consequence: property values. In America, wealth and financial equity is frequently tied up in property ownership; therefore, safe and desirable neighborhoods improve the property values for all residents.[35]

When a lack of public funding causes local child-care programs to close up shop, and also leads to market consolidation by less community-rooted corporate chains (most of which are owned by private equity firms with a short-term profit motive), there is a plausible knock-on effect on neighborhood safety and overall quality. Consider again the precipitous drop in family child-care programs, with the United States losing half the supply—nearly 100,000 individual home-based providers!—between 2005 and 2017, and likely many more since.[36] We do not often consider the ripple effects of these closures, because as Klinenberg writes, "the components of social infrastructure rarely crash as completely or as visibly as a fallen bridge or a downed electrical line, and their breakdowns don't result in immediate systemic failures." But, he warns, "When the social infrastructure gets degraded, the consequences are unmistakable."

Conclusion

It is a pernicious legacy of the marketization of child care, and the narrowing of its perceived role to primarily one of work enabler, that we miss the ways in which child care impacts both the smallest and broadest aspects of national prosperity, day-to-day life, and even global politics. The Security Case illuminates just how foolish such a shift has been. Speaking of foolishness, here again we see how child care is very much a concern for every resident, whether or not they have children, and quite frankly whether or not they choose to look beyond their own self-interest. From a standpoint of military readiness, global educational competitiveness, or neighborhood safety, child care is inextricable from American strength and security.

Examples of "Security Case" Messages
- "A universal child-care system will strengthen national defense not only by ensuring America can recruit and retain military service members, but by shoring up the entire defense industrial base."
- "America is safer and stronger when it is globally competitive. That means having high levels of educational attainment, which is deeply connected to having a good child care system."
- "Child care programs, like elementary schools, can enhance neighborhood safety by strengthening social ties and putting more eyes on the streets. Having an abundance of child care will raise property values and the overall vibrancy of neighborhoods."

In a sentence: America's national security, neighborhood security, and global competitiveness are all tied up in questions of child care; to continue neglecting child care is to weaken the nation.

Chapter 9
The Economic Case

This entire book is in some ways a corrective to overreliance on the Economic Case for child care. As I have pointed out since the Introduction, full-throated economic arguments for child care have been made for more than a quarter-century, and their origins go back much farther. That said, there is danger of swinging the pendulum too far: The economic case is both real and can be an effective arrow in the quiver. Throwing it out would be as misguided as allowing it to dominate. The key is properly positioning the Economic Case. That involves showing all angles—the benefits to the economy go far beyond improving a business' bottom line, and in fact fuel American innovation and entrepreneurship—and making it clear that the role of employers is to maintain family-friendly workplaces while fighting for and paying into a universal system via taxation.

Before properly positioning the Economic Case, though, let's review the common arguments.

A Brief Recap

Child care impacts the economy most directly because of how it affects the labor force. When there are accessible and affordable child-care options, there will be a larger labor force because parents—especially mothers—can fully participate; employees will be less distracted and miss less work; and businesses will have to expend less energy and money on recruitment and training because turnover will be reduced. Rolled together, this means that companies get more production while households gain more income, which in turn stimulates the great economic flywheel.

This chain is emphatically true. Across high-income nations, there is a strong correlation between rising maternal labor force participation and gross domestic product (GDP).[1] One study suggested that major child-care investments along the lines of the Build Back Better Act could generate well over $100 billion annually when looking at reduced business

Raising a Nation. Elliot Haspel, Oxford University Press. © Oxford University Press (2025).
DOI: 10.1093/oso/9780197799291.003.0010

losses, increased parental income, and improved economic output from the child-care sector itself.[2] The U.S. Chamber of Commerce Foundation has reported that states like Arizona and Florida drop billions of dollars in potential economic activity every year due to inadequate child care.[3]

(I also want to recap here that economic metrics like GDP almost entirely ignore home-based work such as child care provided by stay-at-home parents, as well as the tradeoffs that come when a parent decides to take on outside employment. Further, the logic of the labor force part of the Economic Case does not require *high-quality* child-care options, only minimally adequate ones.)

Almost no one disputes the economic benefits of child care, and as noted, versions of this argument have been put forward by presidents like Donald Trump and Joe Biden, governors and legislators of both parties, economic institutions like the U.S. Department of Treasury and the Federal Reserve, progressive and conservative advocates, and nearly every researcher in every country who has ever looked into the question.

That said, in a post-pandemic world marked by high levels of remote work, the tether between child-care access and maternal labor force participation rates is decoupling dramatically, which is a big problem if the rhetorical eggs have been put into that particular basket. Despite all the chaos the child-care system is experiencing, as of this writing in 2024 maternal labor force participation is at an all-time high.[4] In fact, mothers of children under the age of five were the *fastest* group of women to exceed pre-pandemic participation rates.

That fact certainly doesn't suggest that child care is unnecessary as a work support—many mothers, as we have seen, are scrabbling up the hill of paid employment despite inadequate child care and suffering all the cuts and gashes to their well-being that come along with that stressful path.[5] Take the story of one Seattle mother, Skye Henley. Seattle's National Public Radio affiliate reported in 2024 of Henley, an interior designer: "She and her husband can't afford child care for their two youngest children, so she works from home, often early in the morning and late into the night. Henley worries about the 'hours of TV time' her kids get while when she and her husband are tied up with work . . . What Henley and many other women in her position have realized is that working from home is not a substitute for affordable, accessible child care."[6] Yet as far as labor statistics go, Henley simply shows up as contributing to the maternal labor force participation rate.

Moreover, some women are still absolutely dropping out of the labor force and/or working fewer hours or at a worse job than in a counterfactual where universal child care was in place. Despite being at a historic high, the U.S. maternal labor force participation rate is several percentage points below many peer nations; particularly as Baby Boomers age out, we will likely need more mothers in the workforce than we currently have. This statistical decoupling does suggest, however, that the traditional economic argument for child care is arguably weaker than it used to be, and certainly easier for opponents to attack.

The second piece of the Economic Case surrounds the children, and specifically the "investible child" idea. Given that solid child care stabilizes families and provides positive foundational experiences that help children in school and help them make positive choices, then we should expect to see more children emerging as young adults prepared to fully engage in career and consumption. The evidence here is less ironclad—in general, it is difficult to predict what will influence child outcomes because humans are complicated, there are innumerable factors at play, and two kids receiving the exact same inputs will reliably have different results—but as we have seen, there are certainly positive correlations.[7]

I submit that these two pillars are thus likely true, but they also form an incomplete picture.

Nuancing the Economic Case

One problem with the standard Economic Case is that the "return on investment" calculations frequently fail to consider the costs of a *good* child-care system. In fact, leaning into economic impacts gives credence to what I have termed the "minimum viable child care fallacy."[8] Simply put, if the main reason to have a child-care system is so that parents can work and businesses can maximize their productivity, then there's no cause to create a well-funded, well-functioning system. Such a system would actually be the wrong policy target; all you need is a minimally adequate number of slots. It doesn't matter if some parents can't access care because, like inventory shrinkage companies bake into their budget projections, the return on trying to ensure universal access to high-quality programs isn't worth the squeeze. It doesn't matter if child-care staff turn over at an alarming rate; so long as there is a warm body in the room, the parent can still make it to their job on time.[9] (This may sound a bit extreme given the child-focused part of the Case, but the history of child care tells us such leanings are real.)

I've mentioned that an expert working group estimated $175 billion (in 2024 dollars) is needed for a widely affordable system with abundant supply, well-compensated educators making middle-class salaries and benefits, facilities to be proud of, and so on.[10] Yet that group's model only included the birth-to-five years, only included licensed centers and family childcare settings, and still involved significant parent co-pays at higher income levels. By my calculations, a more holistic system that makes care universally free or nearly free and that fully includes school-aged child care, FFN caregivers, and stay-at-home parents likely runs in the ballpark of $250 to $300 billion a year. Although such a system may produce increased economic activity somewhere in that ballpark—what I am proposing is actually far more generous than what was in Build Back Better—that does not mean the government will be taking back that much in annual tax revenues.

This is where we need to expand the Case in order to avoid the minimum viable child-care fallacy. No one has ever tried to quantify the cumulative economic effects of better social connectivity; reduced crime and medical failures as a result of better staffed public services; healthier faith communities; more stable families that are more likely to stay in their communities and meet their desired family size; better marriages and better parenting that increases children's well-being and reduces rates of mental health challenges; a stronger democracy; improved racial and gender equity; lower poverty rates and better health among parents, kids, and caregivers; safer neighborhoods and a more robust defense industrial base; and, as we see in the next section, boosted entrepreneurship and innovation. To name a few!

I'm not sure the true economic impact of a universal child-care system *is* quantifiable. The threads of impact are too myriad and too subtly woven into nearly every part of life. What we can say is that if our nation's economic output is related to the health, well-being, and self-determination of its residents, then child care has a figuratively and perhaps literally incalculable return on investment.

That said, it is worth going back to Anat Shenker-Osorio's point that the Economy is a construct with knowable workings, not an abstraction. One particular part of the American economy fuels much of the nation's success: cutting-edge innovation.

Entrepreneurs and Economic Dynamism

Entrepreneurship and innovation are key to American economic dominance.[11] Consider tech: Despite Europe having a combined population that doubles that of the United States, as of 2023 the United States had double the number of "unicorns"—startups valued at over $1 billion—and roughly the same number of startups overall.[12] It is no surprise that so many global brands, in just about every industry imaginable, have their roots in America's entrepreneurial economy. The six largest metro areas in the nation—those based around New York City, Los Angeles, Chicago, Dallas, Washington, DC, and San Francisco, also known as hotbeds of business startups—produce a quarter of the national GDP and would, combined, constitute the third-largest economy in the world.[13]

Innovative businesses not only create jobs and stimulate consumer spending, they often improve productivity across the board. The work of powerhouses like Microsoft and Intel have changed the way entire industries function. Even companies that aren't such modern household names shape much of the world around us. Alcoa is a major manufacturer of aluminum products, some of which were used by the Wright Brothers and many of which are now critical components of airplanes and other aerospace engineering marvels.

Yet America's economic dynamism is not as healthy as it could be. In 2019, four business scholars wrote in the *Harvard Business Review*: "Is American innovation sputtering? The data suggests so: Productivity growth in the United States, which is powered by innovation, has been decelerating. Total factor productivity grew substantially in the middle of the 20th century, but started slowing in 1970. This slow growth continues today, with productivity lower than it was more than 100 years ago."[14]

The authors point to several possible explanations for this slowdown, including it simply being harder to find new ideas to a pullback in corporate research spending. One solution the authors propose is increasing the odds of breakthroughs by "nurtur[ing] scientific entrepreneurial talent." Although the article does not mention child care, it is easy to see how we could increase the pipeline of potential researchers by helping more student parents complete college, and helping parents who so desire step fully into innovation-focused careers.

Beyond technical innovation, the economy is strongest when small businesses are humming alongside corporate giants. Per a 2019 report commissioned by the U.S. Small Business Administration, small businesses—independent companies with less than 500 employees—account for nearly 44 percent of GDP.[15] These small businesses often make up the lifeblood of communities' commercial corridors, complementing big box stores and chains by adding a local flair: They are the unique coffee shops and restaurants and game stores, the place to go for used outdoor gear, the garden center that hosts weekly workshops. They can also be important hubs of social activity by acting as "third spaces," or a gathering spot other than home and work.

Yet child care gets in the way of entrepreneurship, especially for women. In a 2024 survey of small business owners by the advocacy group Small Business Majority, nearly 60 percent reported a lack of affordable, quality child care for their own children was an "impediment" to starting and/or growing their business.[16] A similar number said that employee work absences due to child care breakdowns negatively impacted their operations. One of the owners surveyed was Emilie Aries, the owner of a leadership development and career services firm in Denver focused on helping women. Aries recounted that,

> I'm a small business owner and employer with a two-year-old who's in daycare, so I know first-hand that when your childcare situation falls apart, your entire life falls apart. My ability to grow my own small business and create jobs in Colorado is dependent on access to affordable, high-quality childcare. Due to a change in my childcare situation last year, I was nearly forced to close my business.

In the end, after "weeks of calling dozens of child care providers," Aries was able to secure a slot, which "saved her business." Not all small business owners are so lucky: A quarter of those surveyed had to shut down their operation "due to childcare issues." Small business owners overwhelmingly want to see more federal funding for child care.[17]

America needs female entrepreneurs. Between 2012 and 2019, women-owned firms grew nearly 17 percent while men-owned firms grew a shade over 5 percent.[18] Many of these companies are injecting needed jobs and innovation into rural communities. As a statement from the United WE National Commission on Childcare and Women's Entrepreneurship puts it, "the dynamism of the American economy depends on entrepreneurs' ability to create jobs, build new products, establish businesses, and drive innovation ... Women entrepreneurs, in particular, stand to gain from solutions to the market failure that is childcare in America."[19]

What then, the question arises, is the role of businesses in achieving those solutions?

The Role of Employers

It is tempting to think that employers should simply offer child-care benefits to their employees. These might look like an on-site child-care center or a child-care stipend. After all, it's good for the bottom line, and child care is a work enabler. Especially in the absence of a publicly funded system, why not ask employers to step up?

In the first half of the 2020s, employer-sponsored child-care benefits are in vogue across the political spectrum. States from Iowa to New York have set aside tens of millions in taxpayer dollars to incentivize employer child-care benefits, while the Biden administration required semiconductor manufacturers to detail a plan for employee child-care assistance in order to access CHIPS Act funding.[20]

Yet centering employers fails on multiple grounds. The thesis running through this book is that child care is far more than a mere work enabler; it is an essential thread in America's social—and, yes, economic—fabric. We do not, for instance, ask employers to subsidize elementary education for employees' children, nor to run an on-site elementary school. As I concluded in a 2024 report for the think tank New America's Better Life Lab:

> Employer-sponsored child care benefits carry an inherent tension. They do help—sometimes tremendously—the small circle of recipients. Many employers are unimpeachably sincere in their intentions to support employees. Yet there is a real tradeoff against the philosophical and practical efforts being made to build an inclusive, fair, high-quality, publicly funded system that works for all involved. It is arguably like taking painkillers for cancer. They can ease the pain for a while, but the body gets sicker, and the temptation to overly rely on painkillers only grows ...
>
> ... Employers might have a role in an idealized child care system. It is my contention that whatever direct role they play must be subordinate to their

active support of a publicly funded system. Employers are not a sustainable core solution for the problem of child care. This is not their fault; on philosophical and practical grounds, employers are misaligned with the child care needs of American families, child care educators, and children. Public or social goods are simply not delivered through the employer-employee relationship. Rights are not conferred via fringe benefits. Any current or future efforts to promote employer-sponsored child care must reckon with these tensions if we are to have any hope of achieving a nation with a healthy, prosperous economy and healthy, prosperous families.[21]

Note that none of this means on-site child-care programs are bad. They can be excellent options, convenient for workers and for keeping children close at hand. Such programs, however, can and should be part of a universal publicly funded system, one option among many, which is how they are positioned in many peer nations. France, for instance, has one of the better-regarded child-care systems in the world, and around 10 percent of their child-care centers are connected to places of employment.[22] These centers are primarily funded through the public system, and are regulated and cost the same as community-based programs, so employees can freely choose what works best for them.

When I speak of practical concerns and tradeoffs, I mean that in addition to ceding the values-laden ground on which a real child-care system might be built, running child care through employers risks replicating the worst parts of the American health insurance system. Any such system is irredeemably unfair (benefits flow mostly to high-income workers, frontline workers receive limited support, and part-time and gig workers are generally excluded entirely); causes job lock (an inability to freely move between jobs due to fear of losing benefits, and in this case, one's child losing their beloved caregiver); introduces volatility (companies can and do change their minds about offering child-care benefits); fails to build a sustainable system (employer benefits do not add substantial new money into the mix, and tend to build the economic and political power of private-equity-backed for-profit child-care chains); and extracts a political opportunity cost (allowing elected officials to claim a win without doing the hard work of funding a comprehensive and inclusive system).

In fact, the history of American health insurance proves a cautionary tale. As I have explained, "We've been at this crossroads before, with health care. During World War II, companies began offering health insurance as a perk. This was done to get around wage caps established in 1942 to prevent the economy from going haywire as companies competed for the suddenly shrunken labor force. Coming out of the war, President Harry Truman proposed a national health-insurance system akin to what would become the U.K.'s National Health Service. The plan failed under opposition not just from business interests but from several major labor unions that had become invested in the idea of employer-sponsored insurance—a decision whose effects the country still feels today."[23]

Even if all of the above were not true, employers are strikingly unlikely to ever be the source of a scalable solution. Our child-care-starved nation has turned its lonely eyes toward employers for a very long time. The Clinton White House event that led off the book's Introduction was actually a late entrant to the conversation. Back in 1988—as in, prior to the fall of the Berlin Wall—the national Child Care Action Campaign held an event titled, "Child Care: The Bottom Line" where they advanced the economic case and called for more business engagement, and then produced a monograph with the same title. The preface states, in all italics for emphasis:

Our economy is weakened by our failure to respond to the needs of families. In order to improve productivity, increase competitiveness, and make the investment in human capital necessary to sustain economic growth, all sectors of our economy must make a significant investment in child care.[24]

That same year, Utah's *Deseret News* ran an article headlined, "The bottom line for business: Quality child care makes sense."[25] The article, reporting on a teleconference for business executives hosted by Utah's PBS television affiliate and the American Express credit card company, noted that: "National and local panelists agreed that both governments and businesses must work together to solve the child care crisis—not only to help the working parents, but to give their children the love and education they need so they can become the productive employees and parents of tomorrow."

If that language sounds familiar, it may be because it is almost word-for-word the argument being made in the modern era by leaders of both political parties. Recall that in 2017, the U.S. Chamber of Commerce Foundation produced the report, "Workforce of Today, Workforce of Tomorrow: The Business Case for High-Quality Child Care."[26] Truly, there is nothing new under the sun.

I would not suggest that companies currently offering child-care benefits cease to do so with no alternative system in place, but it is important that we position employers properly in the way we talk about child care.

Leveraging Business' Political Muscle

In 2023, Vermont passed an impressive child-care reform bill known as Act 76. The legislation is pumping over $120 million a year into the small state's child-care system, massively expanding the percentage of families eligible for fee reductions while increasing the funding flowing to child-care programs themselves. Already, Vermont programs are raising their capacity as parent payments fall. As a group of fifteen child-care directors wrote in May of 2024, "We are already seeing the results of all this new funding: Our programs are expanding, increasing compensation for our staff, and in some instances, offering health insurance and other employee benefits for the first time. In some of our communities, we are even seeing new programs open to meet the demand for quality child care."[27]

What's notable about Act 76 is how it pays for these permanent funding increases. Vermont was the first state in the country to fund child care primarily with a small payroll tax: 0.44 percent, three-quarters of which is paid for by the employer. You might expect this proposal to cause an outcry from the business community, and it did—but not in the direction you think.

Business owner after business owner—from the owners of local restaurants to some of the state's largest employers—came before the Vermont Senate's Economic Development Committee and told legislators to tax them.[28] Take for instance the testimony of Brian Leffler, the owner of Instrumart, a Burlington-area company that supplies industrial and laboratory instruments. He told the Committee:

> We have 70 employees. When people ask me what my job is I tell them I take care of 70 families. Vermonters still care about their neighbors, and we have a strong sense of community. We are not going to solve this issue on an individual level. As a businessperson I do not view addressing the child care crisis as an expense, it is an investment. It will help all facets of our state. We need to pull together and solve this issue for everyone. We will get back more than we invest. It is time to make this investment and address the child care crisis.

Vermont's experience is an example of how business can actively step up to help pass child-care reform. And make no mistake, business interests generally wield far more political power than any child-care advocacy group. One study reviewed the political contributions of 400,000 corporate leaders at 15,000 of the largest U.S. companies. It found that "the corporate leaders... gave 19% of the total dollar amount recorded by the [Federal Election Commission] between 1999 and 2018. While less than 1% of all Americans donated during that period, 40.5% of corporate execs did."[29]

Too often, however, businesses talk out of both sides of their mouths on child care. They may say the right things and then, like the U.S. Chamber of Commerce and National Association of Manufacturers, turn around and spend six-to-seven figures opposing the Build Back Better Act. Indeed, business interests regularly oppose tax measures or items that would make it easier for states or the federal government to raise new revenue. For instance, the Chamber put up a TV ad targeting Senator Joe Manchin of West Virginia, the key swing vote, which included West Virginians "thanking" Manchin for "standing up for my family," "fighting for my business," and so on, with a call to action at the end urging West Virginia voters to contact Manchin's office and tell him to oppose Build Back Better.[30] How putting the kibosh on $400 billion worth of child-care investments helps West Virginia families or businesses remains unexplained.

Even within child care itself, private-equity-backed for-profit chains—companies like KinderCare and Primrose—have quietly opposed child-care bills that come with conditions attached to public funding that threaten a profit-maximizing business model.[31] For instance, when the Massachusetts Senate passed a child-care bill in 2024 that involved $475 million in grants for child-care programs, they included profiteering restrictions on large for-profit chains. These guardrails included requiring chains to dedicate a certain percentage of the money to educator pay, and capping the total amount any one chain could receive. The chains' lobbying group attempted to have the restrictions stripped out.[32] Similarly, *The New York Times* has reported that the same lobbying group worked behind the scenes against Build Back Better, and several chain executives showered Manchin's campaign coffers with donations the month after he killed the legislation.[33] (One private-equity expert, Brendan Ballou, writes that "quite simply, Congress works for few constituencies harder than it works for private equity.")[34]

Private equity has a long history of negative impacts in human services ranging from nursing homes to autism support programs, with the results frequently being lower-quality products, worse-treated employees, and a higher risk of sectoral collapse.³⁵ The very fact private equity is a major player in child care speaks to the danger of overly casting child care as a service that should reside in the business environment. As Elizabeth Leiwant, a child-care advocate in Massachusetts, has mused, "How would you feel if I told you that, say, Morgan Stanley owned your child's elementary school?"³⁶ In fact, there is a symbiosis between large for-profit child-care chains and business attempts to provide child care as a fringe benefit: the two chains that dominate operations of on-site child-care programs are KinderCare (owned by a Swiss private-equity firm from 2015 until late 2024, and now traded on the stock market) and Bright Horizons (previously owned by the private-equity firm Bain Capital, made famous by Mitt Romney, and now traded on the stock market).

The growing market share of corporate for-profit chains also threatens the benefits we've explored around child-care programs' role as community assets and connectors and sources of solidarity. As the writer Noelle Bodick has mused, corporate child care can create an environment of "unsocialization":

> Grandparents live far away, friends aren't having kids, a nanny is too morally perilous and too risky. The impersonal mechanisms of a corporate center enable one to fulfill one's obligations to those in charge of your child's care through simple online payment. Escaping feelings of dependence and intimacy, even more than an exaggerated respect for a professional setting of putative experts and focus-grouped art projects, comes to define the appeal of these programs. Altogether, corporate day care reverses the natural order of human allegiances: you can't trust in fickle individuals, but you can trust in LLCs, vast systems, corporate oversight and the cameras.³⁷

So if the Economic Case is to be advanced, it must be done in such a way as to hold employers to account. If businesses care about child care, then they should—must, if indeed sincere—be prepared to leverage their political influence toward a universal system. They should—must, if indeed sincere—be willing to say, "tax me, this is well worth my contributions." If they want to offer direct benefits to their employees, they should—must, if indeed sincere—do so in a way that bolsters rather than detracts from community-based programs. Corporations and business groups who refuse to join the fight for a comprehensive system either do not understand what child care is all about, or they do not actually believe in the cause.

Employers can show their true colors in another way: how they treat employees who are parents more broadly.

Family-Friendly Workplaces

As we've discussed, although this is a book about child care, child care is not the only area that influences the well-being of parents and children, nor the ripple effects of that well-being on communities and the nation writ large. Working conditions for all employees—parents and nonparents alike—matter greatly, but we will focus here on the impacts on families with children.

Perhaps the most consequential choice made by employers is around wages. Although the lowest-paid employees have seen long-needed wage gains in the post-pandemic labor market, millions remain trapped in jobs that do not offer a family-sustaining salary nor a credible path toward such a salary. As author and political thinker Michael Lind wrote in his 2023 book, *Hell To Pay: How the Suppression of Wages is Destroying America*, "the United States . . . remains a world leader in one area—creating bad jobs with low wages and inadequate hours and no union representation."[38]

Lind asserts that a combination of policy choices, particularly around weakening labor unions and offshoring jobs, has led to many employers taking maximum advantage of their workers. Indeed, in a competitive marketplace under a neoliberal world order, it takes a literally extraordinary company to do well by its employees. (Lind and others have pointed out that the only reason employers can pay such miserly wages is by leaning on the public welfare system, deeply flawed as it may be, rather than paying their fair share. As he writes, "Today in the United States employers are allowed to pay poverty wages—wages too low for millions of workers and their families to live on. To make up the gap between what workers earn and what their families need to survive, the American taxpayer has been forced to pay the bill.")

At the risk of stating the obvious, wages matter enormously for family health and well-being. Although money is not a panacea, having a reasonable—and, as we will discuss in a moment, predictable—flow of income is positively correlated with just about every child and adult outcome we care about. Physical health, mental health, learning, creativity, social connectivity, civic engagement, plain old happiness: go down the line, and there's a link to wages. And, for as long as we have a pay-to-play child-care system, wages matter for being able to secure child care, too!

Thus, the first role of employers should be to ensure all employees are making enough money to support themselves and their families. Whatever other noise an employer may make around child care, if they are persistently paying poverty wages to frontline workers, their commitment to children and families is as hollow—and as well-intentioned—as the Trojan Horse. (This also goes for the large, investor-backed for-profit child-care chains.)

So, too, with predictable scheduling. Danny Schneider is the director of Harvard University's Shift Project. Alongside his colleague Kristen Harknett, Schneider has surveyed over 200,000 shift workers at 150 of the largest U.S. service sector companies such as Amazon and Walmart. In an interview with Sam Pressler, a human flourishing researcher and author of the *Connective Tissue* newsletter, Schneider explained:

> About two-thirds of [surveyed] workers get less than two weeks' notice of schedules. About 20 percent of workers have experienced on-call shifts. Workers frequently have shifts canceled at the last minute. Two-thirds of workers have had at least one last-minute timing change to their schedule. So this predictable uncertainty is a reality of life for these workers.
>
> At a fundamental level, this arrhythmia makes it very difficult for workers to make commitments in their personal lives and to uphold regular obligations and routines. This uncertainty is also enormously stressful and taxing in a way that significantly reduces bandwidth. I'll give you one example of how some of this plays out. We've written a lot about how parental exposure to unstable and unpredictable scheduling affects kids. We find that comparing among the children of hourly service sector workers, those whose parents have more unstable and unpredictable schedules end up in more fractured and informal childcare arrangements. Parents report being able to spend less time with their kids helping with homework or having family meals when they have more unstable schedules. All of this matters for child wellbeing. What's really stark here is that we can well imagine that parents' first commitments are to their kids. So, if we see these negative consequences for parenting, then that should warn us that

exposure to such scheduling practices are [sic] likely to have even more pronounced effects on workers' ability to engage with their communities and cultivate other relationships."[39]

Scheduling predictability is, again, a choice. Companies can choose to forgo marginal gains from just-in-time scheduling (some research suggests any gains are offset by the strain added onto the workforce). Similarly, they can choose to support predictive scheduling laws which have been enacted in Oregon and a handful of cities around the nation, but which regularly come up against opposition from business groups. One such opposing group, the National Retail Federation, represents many of the big employers that the Shift Project has looked into, such as Walmart, Target, and Macy's.[40] An employer cannot be a child-care champion while trying to beat back laws that make the child-care landscape vastly easier for parents to navigate.

A final way that employers reveal themselves is with their paid-leave policies. Paid family leave, as we have discussed, is the first stretch of the child-care marathon. A national paid-leave law is surely the best solution, but as of this writing such a law is not close to being enacted, and only thirteen states have paid-leave laws. This is a place where employers can step up both with their advocacy and with direct provision. Unlike employer benefits around regular child-care arrangements or health insurance, paid leave has fundamentally different characteristics. For instance, there is no "job lock" with paid leave, given its time-limited nature, and it is a benefit easy to apply across the board as opposed to only for high-earning employees.

Yet despite this, there are rank inequities in who has access to paid family leave. Per the Bureau of Labor Statistics (BLS), only around a quarter of private sector employees were offered paid family leave in 2023.[41] The Center for American Progress has analyzed the BLS data and concluded, "Many industries also have paid family leave coverage rates that are notably lower than that of the private sector workforce as a whole, including construction (16%), leisure and hospitality (8%), accommodation and food service (7%), and transportation and warehouse work (9%)."[42]

Paid leave is not only needed when a newborn arrives. Children get sick, and child-care providers—particularly when there is a single provider, as with a family child-care program or relative—also get sick or otherwise become temporarily unavailable. Yet the average sick day bank for private sector employees is seven days a year, and very few have access to a separate bank of dependent care leave, meaning that they have to sacrifice the ability to take time when they themselves fall ill.[43]

Wages, predictable scheduling, paid leave: employers, especially large corporations, have many levers to pull to help their parent employees with child care. To adapt a quote from Maya Angelou: When companies show you who they are, believe them.

Conclusion

Child care is essential to the American economy. A strong child-care system helps the business bottom line, fuels innovation and entrepreneurship, and keeps workers more stably connected to their source of income. A vibrant economy leads to a more prosperous nation; tide, meet boats.

All of the above is true. It is a useful argument, especially for those lawmakers (usually older men, if we're being honest) who hear the phrase child care and think of a squishy, low-priority social issue. For members of the Republican party in particular, the Economic Case has given them an angle of approach that can avoid cultural clashes about the role of government with regards to families while accepting the need to raise new tax revenue. As a 2024 Associated Press article headline read, "More Republicans back spending on child care, saying it's an economic issue."[44] That said, as we have seen since the beginning of the book, it's not just the GOP: both parties have grabbed the Economic Case by the horns and are riding it as far as it will go.

Yet recall the words of sociologist and advocate Susan Prentice: "Economic reframing displaces the justice-based rationale for childcare . . . The business case for child care builds an ideological/conceptual bridge to contemporary wealth production, not to social transformation." When we put the Economic Case front and center, it drowns out the other eight Cases that preceded this one and leaves no room for the vital final one to follow. It can actually let businesses off the hook of doing the hard work of creating truly family-friendly workplaces and fully contributing to the social contract. To extend Prentice's metaphor, the bridge built by overreliance on the business case does not lead anywhere that is likely to win the level of public funding needed for a truly effective child-care system. Therefore, we must wield the Economic Case carefully and thoughtfully: always, always,

always reinforcing the need for employers to utilize their political influence to advance universal child care.

At stake is no less than the American Dream.

Examples of "Economic Case" Messages:
- "Child care is good for business productivity, but it's more than that: A strong child care system sparks American innovation and entrepreneurship and small business ownership; it is essential for a dynamic economy."
- "If businesses truly care about their employees, they won't just provide a child-care benefit for a few at HQ. They need to use their political and financial muscle to fight for universal child-care policies."
- "Employers can help employees with child care without offering an on-site center. Making sure that their employees have family-sustaining wages, predictable schedules, and solid paid leave are all key ways for employers to show their commitment to workers and their families."

In a sentence: Child care absolutely boosts the economy, including through helping small businesses and innovators, and the best role for employers is to use their political muscle to move America toward a universal publicly funded system.

Chapter 10
The American Dream Case

It may surprise you to learn that the American Dream, as originally conceived, was not primarily about getting rich. In modern times, the concept has taken on a largely material or financial flavor: Anyone, we suggest, can strive toward a full bank account, one ideally overflowing. As the singer Lorde (perhaps with New Zealander perceptiveness) mocked in her 2013 hit *Royals*, "But everybody's like/Cristal, Maybach, diamonds on your timepiece/Jet planes, islands, tigers on a gold leash." Yet the term is supposed to imply a much more expansive concept. Sarah Churchwell, an author and cultural critic, writes of the man who in the 1930s first popularized the phrase, historian James Truslow Adams:

> Adams concluded that America had lost its way by prizing material success above all other values: Indeed, it had started to treat money as a value, instead of merely as a means to produce or measure value.
>
> For Adams, worshipping material success was not the definition of the American dream: It was, by contrast, the failure of "the American dream of a better, richer, and happier life for all our citizens of every rank." Adams did not mean 'richer' materially, but spiritually; he distinguished the American dream from dreams of prosperity. It was, he declared, "not a dream of motor cars and high wages merely, but a dream of social order in which each man and each woman shall be able to attain to the fullest stature of which they are innately capable, and be recognized by others for what they are, regardless of the fortuitous circumstances of birth or position."[1]

We have seen throughout this book all the ways in which child care supports components of human flourishing: It can reduce poverty and strengthen the ties that bind, secure our communities, and enhance our family lives. In this chapter, we will harmonize the Cases to show that child care undergirds what it means to be American: Child care is, quite simply, essential to the true American Dream.

Human Flourishing, Redux

What does it mean to "attain to the fullest stature of which" one is capable? I read the phrase as suggestive of human flourishing. Recall the domains of flourishing posited by Harvard's Human Flourishing Project:[2]

- Happiness and Life Satisfaction
- Mental and Physical Health
- Meaning and Purpose
- Character and Virtue
- Close Social Relationships
- [Cross-cutting enabling factor] Financial and Material Stability

Considering all the Cases we have explored in the book, I hope the connections are clear. Child care has direct and causal impacts on stress levels, mental health, physical health, social connectivity, quality time spent with loved ones, and so on down the list. You can likely imagine how each Case maps onto one or more of the flourishing domains. In its negative formulation, the lack of good child-care options drags down flourishing like cement shoes; when a fully realized asset, child care acts as a ballast allowing flourishing to rise.

A flourishing perspective offers perhaps the sharpest relief against the narrowness of treating child care as mere economic infrastructure, similar to roads or bridges. This is, as we saw in the previous chapter, inarguably one function. But roads and bridges do not (generally speaking) play into the ability to build and maintain close social relationships, to cultivate virtue, to explore and live out a meaningful life full of love and laughter. No, child care is much more than infrastructure: It is a critical part of our social fabric. It also, in the final read, is a critical part of family freedom—and therefore the American Dream.

Family Freedoms

Life is, of course, full of tradeoffs. You can go to college after high school or start a full-time job. You can have a child in your early twenties (or sooner) or wait until your early thirties (or later). There is no single right choice, and one must be prepared to absorb the opportunity costs—the price of the road not taken.

America's lack of a decent child-care system, however, artificially imposes an enormous opportunity cost for the socially necessary act of having children. We have seen stories of these costs: parents forced out of careers they found meaningful, parents forced to move away from their beloved communities, parents unable to pursue an innovative business or social improvement idea, parents forced to have less children than they want because the fees are unbearable. In short, we are seeing a denial of freedom and self-determination, two cornerstones of the American experiment.

Self-determination rests between two types of freedom: freedom *to* and freedom *from*. Citing the great social theorist Isaiah Berlin, a pair of scholars clarify that, "*Freedom from* consists in the absence of obstacles or constraints to one's own action. By contrast, *freedom to* identifies the possibility to autonomously determine and achieve individual or collective purposes."[3] As an adult American, one enjoys (ostensibly) a freedom from government discrimination as well as a freedom to vote. We may be far from fully realizing these ideals, but they are American ideals.

Given all of the ways in which child care shapes the choice set for families, I would argue the lack of a comprehensive system negatively impacts freedom. Parents deserve the freedom to set down roots in their community and the freedom to realize their desired family size. They deserve the freedom to care for their own children. They also deserve freedom from backbreaking child-care costs and scarcity that restrict care-work setups, as well as freedom from differential access to care based purely on income and geography.

The opportunity costs extend far beyond the years in which the children are young. Because child-care costs generally land in parents' relative youth, the logic of compound interest is harsh. Take around $10,000 a year for five years (and if you have multiple children, eight, or ten, or more) starting when you're thirty, and stick that into a simple stock index fund. Based on historical averages, by the time you're fifty you'll have made hundreds of thousands of dollars. Or, use that money as part of a down payment for a house. Or, max out a retirement contribution that your employer will match. Or, seed a small business. Instead, a 2024 poll commissioned by the Institute for Women's Policy Research found that nearly one in five households with a child under the age of thirteen had delayed a major life purchase or tapped into emergency savings to cover care needs.[4] One in ten had tapped into retirement accounts or refinanced their homes.

Thus, the current situation actually siphons power and decision-making authority from parents. To paraphrase the economist Kathryn Anne Edwards, in a misguided attempt to keep government away from the family, America has allowed the callous market to dictate how parents raise their children and live their lives.[5] The only winners are rich corporate interests.

Again, it is worth saying that these opportunity costs are a policy imposition. Certainly, if you choose to spend $10,000 a year for five years taking extravagant overseas vacations, you will elicit little sympathy if you are forced to drain retirement funds to make ends meet. Child care is emphatically not that. It goes back to the fundamental question of what and who child care is for, and the ways in which healthy families enrich all of society. And—setting aside for a moment the consequences of family instability and stress—none of this gets into the opportunity costs and loss of freedom that are absorbed by children.

In this respect, child care should be a right, just as public education is a right. All families in America have a right to free K–12 schooling per all fifty state constitutions—a freedom to attend and a freedom from exclusion. No parent is required to come up with the nearly $14,000 a year average per-student expenditure. The connection between schooling and freedom, and all the societal ripple effects thereof, was seen as so important that Congress made inclusion of such a right a de facto requirement for Confederate states' readmission to the Union.[6] This right both conveys a remedy (you can sue the state if they do not make a slot available or try to charge you tuition) and conveys a sense of societal value.

The question of whether something is a right has strong valence when it comes to how the issue is seen by voters. For instance, contested language around rights underlies many of the great healthcare debates that America has undertaken for the last eighty years. As journalist Jonathan Cohn has noted in his book on the subject, such a question can also reveal differences in principle that cut through much of the political noise: he cites a moment in the second presidential debate between then-Senator Barack Obama and the late Senator John McCain, where the moderator posed the question: "Is health care in America a privilege, a right, or a [personal] responsibility?"[7] We would do well to ask the same of child care.

It is not absurd to apply a rights-based framework to child care. Other countries do, and not just Nordic nations with the population of South Carolina. In 2013, Germany passed a law that conveyed a legal right to a slot in a child-care program for all families with children between the ages of one and primary school entry.[8] (Prior to the age of one, sensibly, German parents are covered by a robust paid family leave policy.) The law also provided for cash stipends to parents who chose to stay home with their young children; that national provision was later struck down by Germany's high court, but it has been taken up instead on a province-by-province basis.[9] The German reforms are especially notable because the country has a history, like the U.S., of strong traditional gender norms around care. While the German system is not perfect, it shows that rapid policy and cultural shifts regarding child care are possible.

Indeed, if child care is seen as attached to freedom, then that further elevates the need for wholesale reform—and the need for a truly universal and inclusive system.

A Path for All

Individuals have different talents, skills, predilections, and preferences. Science tells us that these are influenced by a complex interplay of nurture (the environment in which one is raised) and nature (genetics). One reason America is so divided is because we have a system in which flourishing is largely reserved for the few: those who are affluent, largely mediated by the ability to decipher school, get a college degree, and move into a so-called white-collar career—all of which is easier to accomplish if you share majority identity traits. If one wants a comfortable life and did not inherit wealth, the only option is navigating the treacherous path of social mobility: a warped version of Adams' American Dream.

The story we explicitly or implicitly tell assigns moral valence to the upper class ("winners") and working class ("losers"), entirely ignoring factors of structural advantage/disadvantage, pure circumstantial luck, and what behavioral geneticist Kathryn Paige Harden calls "the genetic lottery." This is not to suggest there is no role for individual effort; of course there is. But to put it plainly, two individuals in America can exert precisely the same amount of hard work, sweat, and tears, and end up with two entirely different outcomes. Such unfairness opens the door for populist demagogues to position themselves as champions of those on the wrong end of the equation.

Instead of denigrating those who might follow such demagogues, we can change the variables. Political philosopher Michael Sandel has written that:

Breaking down barriers is a good thing. No one should be held back by poverty or prejudice. But a good society cannot be premised only on the promise of escape.

Focusing only, or mainly, on rising does little to cultivate the social bonds and civic attachments that democracy requires. Even a society more successful than ours at providing upward mobility would need to find ways to enable those who do not rise to flourish in place, and to see themselves as members of a common project. Our failure to do so makes life hard for those who lack meritocratic credentials and makes them doubt that they belong.

It is often assumed that the only alternative to equality of opportunity is a sterile, oppressive equality of results. But there is another alternative: a broad equality of condition that enables those who do not achieve great wealth or prestigious positions to live lives of decency and dignity—developing and exercising their abilities in work that wins social esteem, sharing in a widely diffused culture of learning, and deliberating with their fellow citizens about public affairs.[10]

The current child-care system is deeply unfair. The truly wealthy do not have to contend with the same sacrifices, stress, and opportunity costs as everyone else: They are the only ones able to handle sky-high fees, and their spending capacity is attractive enough to send child-care owners scrambling to make offerings available. Yet the unfairness goes beyond the two-tiered system present in so much of life where the rich can simply buy their way out of struggle. Not everyone—even among married, two-parent households—has a viable option to stay home and care for the children if that's their preference. One's access to licensed child care is also determined by geography. Rural areas and poor areas have less; upper-middle-class suburbs have more.

Consider the behavior of large corporate child-care chains, which control an increasing percentage of the child-care system and most of which are owned by private-equity firms.[11] An analysis I led of the five largest chains across seven states found that in every case, the median household income surrounding chain sites was significantly higher than the state median income.[12] The surrounding median income for franchises like Goddard and Primrose exceeded $100,000. There is state variation, too: Washington State and Missouri have similarly sized populations (Washington's is about 20% larger), yet Washington has nearly three times the number of chain sites, likely owing to the affluence of the Seattle region. Although I do not think more for-profit chain activity is desirable—in fact, the involvement of private-equity firms is deeply alarming and calls for policymaker action—it's clear we have a nation of child-care haves and have-nots.

Universal child care, then, has the potential to be a key component of that equality of condition. We have seen throughout this book how good child care can help individuals and couples stay in their beloved hometowns, realize their desired family size, and participate fully in the democratic process. We have seen how good child care can reduce stress and open doors—not doors that necessarily lead to the next income bracket (though they may), but to a more stable life full of laughter and love. Such a child-care system is a strike toward regaining a nation defined more by what unites us than by what divides us. It is also a strike toward regaining a nation defined more by human relationships than an endless pursuit of wealth. As the esteemed labor activist Ai-Jen Poo has written: "Care is something we do; it's something we want; it's something we can improve. But more than anything, it's the solution to the personal and economic challenges we face in this country. It doesn't just heal or comfort people individually; it really is going to save us all."[13]

Valuing Care

Recall the Salzburg Global Seminar's statement that "Every individual will need care at some point in their lives; every individual will give care at some point in their lives. Care for self and others is fundamental to building and maintaining social relations and its value to individuals, families and societies is truly incalculable." Yet this is not how care is generally treated in American society (or most of the Anglosphere, for that matter).

Instead, as Tim Jackson, Director of the U.K.'s Centre for the Understanding of Sustainable Prosperity, has asserted: "In the so-called social contract of neoliberal economics, wages follow productivity. Because care takes time, care workers are condemned to pitiful wages, insecure jobs, impossible working conditions and—pandemic aside—the lowest ranks in the status game played out in modern society. Capitalism condemns care, not accidentally, not inadvertently, but systematically."[14]

To harken back to the Gender and Racial Equality Case, care is of course also deeply gendered. Female caregivers are at best, per scholar Emma Dowling, "valorized but not valued."[15] They are commonly subjected to an impossible double bind of expectations, particularly when it comes to child care, while fathers like myself can get plaudits for doing the basic meat-and-potatoes work of parenting.

That said, I have written elsewhere that if you want to distill the essential problem of considering care only within an economic context, step away from children and look to the elderly. Here, there is no "investible child" case to fall back upon: "A dementia-stricken 85-year-old is no longer producing, and will never again produce, anything of significant economic value. Yet it is clear to most that we would be morally impoverished, indeed give up a bit of our national soul, to simply cast that person aside."[16]

Centering care opens the door to a new way of seeing the social contract. As journalist Elissa Strauss explained in her 2024 book, *When You Care: The Unexpected Magic of Caring for Others*, there is an underacknowledged field of philosophy known as "care ethics."[17] Care rumbles under the surface of our American social foundations—there is an implied dependence on one another even in the Declaration of Independence—but because it is submerged, it is rarely appreciated. Strauss writes:

> Care is as fundamental to the good life as justice, but it's rarely presented in fundamental terms.
>
> For [philosopher] Eva Feder Kittay... and others, this blind spot is one of the root causes of why we don't have real care infrastructure in the United States, and why we don't value caregivers. Our society and institutions were built around the idea of ensuring our equality and protecting our independence. Both are noble values, even if they have yet to be delivered to all. But as a culture, we fail to acknowledge those times we aren't equal, like when we are young, old, or impaired in some fashion. Nor do we do much to acknowledge the times when we aren't independent, the norm for the many of us who spend the beginning and end of our lives depending on another, and much of the middle being depended on.
>
> ...Cultivation [of a caring society] can look like better government policies supporting caregivers, which, besides giving them some financial and practical relief, tell them that their efforts are acknowledged and valued, that what they do matters. It also requires a culture shift that takes us away from seeing humans as a collective of individuals and instead as a collective of relationships.

The creation of a strong child-care system—particularly one that supports all types of care, including parental care, and that ensures educators in external programs receive family-sustaining compensation—is thus actually quite a radical act. It would be nothing less than a statement, and arguably a recapturing, of national values.

The implications of allowing free-market individualism to swamp relational care are wide-reaching. In 2024, the left-leaning Roosevelt Institute think tank published a paper by a trio of scholars and activists with the wordy but meaningful title, "The Cultural Contradictions of Neoliberalism: The Longing for an Alternative Order and the Future of Multiracial Democracy in an Age of Authoritarianism." The authors write that neoliberalism has,

> eroded community care networks and public care systems, further adding to the crisis of isolation . . . the hyperindividualistic and competitive orientation of neoliberalism, paired with its concrete policy agenda, has had downstream effects on how we relate to and care for one another, fundamentally warping our outlook on humanity and our sense of responsibility to one another.[18]

As a response to this relational wreckage, they contend, individuals are increasingly grasping for ways to cope, turning variously to options such as authoritarian-minded leaders and rageful politics-as-identity; conspiracy theories; the detachment offered by hard drugs; or in too many cases the ultimate detachment of suicide.

I cannot emphasize this point enough: reducing care to its instrumental value for work or school readiness hides the sheer weightiness of the issue. Child care can form one pillar of a redefined social order, an order that leans on the best virtues of the American project and points toward a renewed future with a shared promise of widespread flourishing.

What is America For?

The philosopher Roman Krznaric writes that a *telos*, the ancient Greek word for an ultimate goal or purpose, "functions as a compass for our thoughts and actions, helping us make choices among a sea of possibilities."[19] The United States lacks a strong national *telos*. While we most commonly think about life's purpose on an individual scale, Krznaric adds, "the astronomer Carl Sagan argued that whole societies should also adopt a *telos* to guide them—what he called 'a long-term goal and a sacred project.'"

The societal hole where a *telos* should be poses a vital threat, not so different from a hole in the human heart. Journalist Elizabeth Bruenig wrote poignantly after the massacre at Robb Elementary School in Uvalde, Texas, that, "the nature of the problem, as best I can tell, is that American life isn't about what is good but is rather about nothing at all (which is, at least, broadly inoffensive and inclusive of most tastes and creeds) or about violence itself." The result is a soft nihilism: If there's nothing larger to strive for, why strive at all?

The absence of purpose is eating away not only our national soul, but the well-being of generations. In December 2022, researchers at Harvard's Making Caring Common Project commissioned a nationally representative survey of young adults aged eighteen to twenty-five. They found fully 58 percent reported feeling little to no "purpose or meaning in life" over the previous thirty days.[20] One respondent said, "I have no purpose or meaning in life. I just go to work, do my mundane job, go home, prepare for the next day, scroll on my phone, and repeat." More than half of those experiencing a crisis of purpose also reported symptoms of anxiety and depression, over twice the rate of their counterparts who were secure in their purpose.

Collective care can be our sacred project. It is an ennobling and enabling factor, one that allows us to reconnect with the best parts of ourselves and, in doing so, reconnect with one another. As we have seen, good child care—and care more broadly—stands opposed to hypercapitalism, to constant comparison, to intensive parenting, to both the rat race and the rug rat race. Properly positioning care in society allows all residents, parents and nonparents alike, to embrace the role of "citizen-caregiver," striving for policies and a culture where every child and family has the support they need. And when America begins to dust itself off from decades of bitter rancor and division, sniping and strife, so, too, will the nation reclaim its role as a shining city on the hill.

Examples of "American Dream Case" Messages:
- "Good child care is essential to the American Dream—it offers families the self-determination and well-being they need to flourish. Without child care, too many hardworking individuals are not able to achieve their self-defined potential, and the very future of the nation will be in peril."
- "A strong child-care system can help us move beyond an unfair, winner-takes-all society. By centering care and relationships, we can

Continued

Continued

> rebuild social connections and better meet America's promise to be a place where everyone has a fair shot at success."
> - "The American Dream means that one can live a dignified, thriving life regardless of the circumstances of one's birth. Child care helps make sure that Dream is open to everyone."
>
> *In a sentence:* A good child-care system will broaden American freedom and opportunity, and can even start to knit a divided country back together.

Conclusion

The Child-Care System America Needs and Parents Deserve

I envision a very different Rose Garden scene to the one that opened this book. A president will be there, yes. But this time they will be signing a bill designed not to cement child care as economic infrastructure, but one that finally honors child care as an elemental part of America's national fabric and national values.

You may have noticed that throughout this book, I have only intimated at what I see as an ideal child-care system. That's because my entire thesis is built around the idea that we need to lead with values first and policy specifics second. This is a particular challenge for those on my side of the political aisle. As explained by the authors of the Roosevelt Institute paper on neoliberal alternatives, Shahrzad Shama, Deepak Bhargava, and Harry Hanbury, "policy is not a master turnkey of politics, and by relying too much on policy, progressives have narrowed the terrain of engagement," and largely ceded the ground of culture and mass popular engagement.

Elsewhere, the three have shown that even when political victories put money in the pockets of voters, as the expanded child tax credit did during the pandemic years, policies garner meager lasting support absent a larger, values-laden story into which such policies fit. The trio write that, "policies that deliver economic benefit without speaking to, reinforcing, and constructing a social identity are likely to have little political impact."[1]

With a book-length treatment now in hand on how child care can speak to, reinforce, and construct a social identity, we can turn to the question of what an effective child-care system may look like.

After all, policy design matters a great deal. For one, a policy vision can be the source of "sticky" messaging that ties values-based frames to a concrete proposal. As importantly, policy defines how money is distributed, who is eligible, how one proves eligibility (if needed), what quality and accountability measures are in place, and so forth.

There are innumerable examples of badly designed policy, even if passed with the best of intentions. To use an international child-care example, in 1997 Quebec embarked on an ambitious reform plan, but the province only gave itself until 2000 to have a low-cost slot available to every child under the age of five—despite starting with capacity for only 15 percent of those children. As a group of Canadian researchers later concluded, "In the simplest terms, Quebec tried to do too much too fast. It ended up taking short cuts that harmed the development of the child care system," including reliance on questionable for-profit providers, inadequately qualified educators, and shoddy facilities.[2] The flaw wasn't with the idea—and the newer iteration of the Canadian model has been going much better—but with the design.

My "first principles" of child-care policy design are as follows:

- *Universality:* As an essential part of the nation's social fabric, child care should be available to all families for free at the point of service. That means a minimum of friction: no means-tests or activity tests for access. The poorest or richest American families should be able to benefit from the system (with the rich paying more in taxes on the back end).
- *Inclusive Options*: To honor the diversity of family needs and preferences, an ideal child-care system should fully and fairly ensure a diversity of viable options. Families should be supported in accessing licensed child care (secular or faith-based centers, family child-care programs, etc.), utilizing a family, friend, or neighbor caregiver, or having a stay-at-home parent. The format and mechanisms of such support will vary, because different settings require different levels of funding, but enough support should be in place to create a truly pluralistic system.
- *Comprehensiveness*: Understanding how families experience care needs, an ideal child-care system should extend at least up through elementary school. Before- and after-school care, as well as summer care, should be fully included in the system. On the other end, strong paid parental leave—ideally at least six months—should be considered the first part of the child-care arc. There should also be an end to the artificial segmentation of child-care provision: Pre-K, for instance, should be folded into a comprehensive system as one piece of the whole.
- *Supply-side and demand-side balance*: The practicalities of a universal, inclusive, comprehensive child-care system require that funding

flows both directly to providers and also into the hands of parents. Supply-side funding to providers ensures sustainability and stability, and allows them to raise educator salaries and invest in their facilities. Enough direct funding can accomplish access goals by also allowing providers to reduce their fees to zero while incentivizing the expansion of supply. At the same time, supply-side funding does not map well onto informal child-care provision such as that delivered by family, friend, or neighbor caregivers or stay-at-home parents. In those cases, direct cash assistance to families is the most promising path.

- *Quality via caregivers*: The most important factor determining quality in any child-care setting is the relationship between the caregiver and the child. Therefore, paramount importance should be placed on ensuring America's caregivers and child-care educators are stable and do not frequently churn, are minimally stressed, and have the support they need and deserve. This begins with wages: All child-care educators should receive a family-sustaining wage (i.e., not just a living wage, but one that enables family flourishing) with robust benefits. This can be accomplished via states establishing salary scales and directly funding programs to meet them, as is currently done in Washington, DC and several peer nations. Families using informal care or a stay-at-home parent should be eligible for a monthly stipend. Training and certification is, of course, important for licensed formal care settings, given that the group care of unrelated children calls for skills above and different than those required for care of one to two kin (although training support should be offered on a voluntary basis to informal caregivers), but should be considered secondary to caregiver stability.

- *Cultural supports*: Policy can bolster cultural supports for child care through decisions around funding, zoning, community planning, and so forth. The ability of child-care programs to open in and near housing developments; the presence of drop-in child-care centers with workshops or social events for parents or grandparents; stroller-friendly sidewalks and access to public transportation; safe, largely pedestrianized streets near schools and child-care programs; ample, high-quality parks and playgrounds (outdoor and indoor); organized, subsidized babysitting services; all of these elements contribute to communities where families with young children are welcome and have what they need to build a life where they can flourish.

These principles are not the same as legislative language: naturally, local contexts must be considered. That said, if America were to create a child-care system anchored in these principles—and anchored in the national values we have talked about throughout the book—the future for American families would look much, much brighter.

***

What needs to happen to take us from the mire to the mountaintop?

The first step is changing how we talk about child care. The language used—and mental models evoked by language—shapes how child care is perceived by the public.

As things stand, even would-be champions default into economic language that emphasizes child care as a work support. For instance, President Biden's Commerce Secretary Gina Raimondo declared multiple times in public settings that child care is an economic issue and not a social issue, going so far as to say, "Anyone who thinks child care is social policy is deeply misguided and doesn't know how to run a business."[3] This is, to put it lightly, unhelpful.

Instead, we need to be framing child care as crucial to the American experiment, an inextricable element of our freedom and prosperity. As my colleague Caroline Cassidy, a communications expert, has noted, "Narrative change is fundamentally about creating an alternative future, not just problem solving or having the loudest voice."[4] Each Case, for all its particularities, has that alternative future as its taproot: a vision of the good life that centers care, connection, and flourishing.

Moreover, research suggests narrative change requires pulling on three different levers at once: mass culture, mass media, and mass movements.[5] To that end, a whole-of-society response is required, intentionally embracing different Cases for different audiences while always starting and ending with the overarching values frame around what and who child care is for. Change will not occur with a small group of individuals who already agree with one another continuing to meet and say how much they agree. We need to engage the great public influencers, not just politicians and journalists, but groups from celebrities and athletes and social media gurus to clergy and healthcare professionals and schoolteachers and labor unions to passionate affinity groups like yogis and gamers. Similarly, depictions of child care on television and in movies needs to come into alignment; there are nascent efforts to push the entertainment industry in this direction from organizations like the think tank New America's Better Life Lab, and they could do with reinforcements.[6]

Day-to-day relational conversations matter as well, which is where movement-building comes in. How a group of grandparents sitting around a bridge table or at the neighborhood pool talks about their children's search for child care is as important for shifting mindsets as any rally outside the state capitol (not that these are mutually exclusive). Those in the child-care battle should always remember that the median American voter is not themselves a parent struggling with child care. As the writer Matthew Yglesias has half-joked, those wanting to do well in politics should have a Post-It on their computer: "The median voter is a 50-something white person who didn't go to college and lives in an unfashionable suburb."[7]

While we are changing the narrative, we also need to be developing that sticky, popular policy proposal, so that once people are on board with the *why*, they can get on board with the *what*. Currently, major national and state child-care proposals tend to be kludgy means-tested complexities pegged around the standard of no one other than the rich paying more than 7 percent of their income on child care. Even if 7 percent weren't an arbitrary number—it is drawn from a well-intentioned effort in 2016 to reduce copays for families receiving subsidy assistance so they were in line with the average all American families were paying—it's an awkward one.[8] (Quick: What's 7 percent of your income?). Similarly, as we've discussed, stay-at-home parents and school-aged child care are almost entirely excluded from current legislation.

Thus, we need to move toward a new generation of child-care proposals, ones that are simple, comprehensive, inclusive, and narratively powerful. This is far easier said than done, but make no mistake, it is doable. In fact, child-care champions, and those funding child-care champions, must insist it be done.

***

A colleague asked me recently what I thought was the biggest challenge preventing the United States from achieving the child-care system it needs. Clearly, my first answer is values framing. Secondary answers include gender norms and reactionary politics and strategic failures of movement-building. But there is also an atmospheric problem that reliably restricts forward momentum, like an electrical storm keeping planes grounded: the inescapable fact that a real child-care system—a child-care guarantee—is *expensive*.

As I've said, $175 billion a year is table stakes. But a clear-eyed assessment of a system built off the principles described here yields a sum more in the range of $250 to $300 billion a year. (Remember: The United States spends over $800 billion a year on both K–12 education and Medicaid, and close to a trillion on Medicare.) I can, have, and will continue to argue that such an outlay is well worth the cost: that, in fact, what it costs us in lost family flourishing, family formation, community vibrancy and safety, social connectivity and solidarity—and yes, economic dynamism—means we can hardly afford *not* to invest such sums.

There are many number of ways to pay for child care, though it is not my purpose here to propose a specific package, and legislators tend to find the money when they want to pass something. For instance, the 2017 Tax Cuts and Jobs Act, whose benefits flowed with vast disproportionality to the rich, is estimated by the Congressional Budget Office to cost $1.9 *trillion* over ten years.[9] Making the tax code fairer—including requiring corporations to start paying into a child-care system they do, by any analysis, benefit from—would surely be a good place to start.

However, a bloodless and utilitarian economic argument will never get us there. The most ambitious federal child-care proposal on the table as of this writing, Rep. Ro Khanna's Child Care for America Act, would outlay around $100 billion a year. While this would of course be transformative for many families, even that funding level would only be a waypoint (what Khanna correctly describes as a "down payment") on the path toward a fully functional system.

Yet we are not so far from the necessary support as it might seem. There are already hints that child care is a political winner. For instance, in 2020 seven child-care measures were on ballots nationwide, six in cities/counties and one, in Colorado, statewide. The locations ranged from the initiative in ultraprogressive Multnomah County (Portland), Oregon to one in deep-red Escambia County in the Florida Panhandle. All seven passed.[10] One 2024 poll found that voter support for tax increases on wealthy individuals and corporations jumped more than 10 percent when voters were told the new revenues would fuel care policies.[11]

Indeed, although there are certainly hardliners who resist any government intervention and remain uneasy with the whole idea of working mothers, child care is not an overly intense partisan issue. In 2022, Republican Senators Tim Scott and Richard Burr introduced a child-care bill that, while imperfect, echoed many of the priorities we have been discussing.[12] The legislation would have made child care free for every American family making less than 75 percent of the state median income, and called for child-care programs to receive public funding so they could pay their educators enough to maintain a quality service. The bill attracted thirteen Republican cosponsors, meaning there would have been a filibuster-proof majority had they joined with all the Democrats. The rub was that zero dollars were attached, making it seem like the mother of all unfunded mandates, so the legislation stalled. Still, to have that many Republicans on the record backing those underlying concepts is remarkable.

So the potential is there. But we will not make the necessary strides until and unless we push child care out of its pigeonhole. Child care is more than a work support. Child-care educators are more than the workforce behind the workforce. The return on investment does not end at the water's edge of the Economy. Child care resonates with the deepest and most sacred of American values: freedom, self-determination, family, community. It is a core part of our ongoing fight for equality and fairness. It is inextricably wrapped up in questions of American prosperity, safety, and strength. A good child-care system helps bring the American Dream to life and helps bring the nation into the light: a society centered around the wealth of relationships and human flourishing.

In short, this is no longer 1998, and it is certainly no longer 1971. If we can marshal strong values-based framing and a strong vision for an alternative child-care future alongside a strong policy proposal, we may well open new doors for child, family, community, and national prosperity.

Acknowledgments

I've been writing this book for years prior to a word of the manuscript being typed. Conversations with child-care advocates and policy wonks, academics, child-care educators, parents, politicos, journalists, and more have all fed into how I see child care and the need to reposition it within the American context. There are far too many contributors to name, but know that I am immensely grateful to all of you for the passion, dedication, and expertise you daily bring to bear.

That said, the presence of this book owes a special debt of gratitude to certain individuals. Steven Morales, Katie Albitz, Patrick T. Brown, Casey Stockstill, Anna Danziger Halperin, Eva Colen, Jessica Calarco, and Rebecca Gale all reviewed chapters or talked through ideas with me. Jason Amirhadji provided a sounding board and, as needed, encouragement or pushback.

Joe Waters not only reviewed the work but has, through the think tank Capita, provided an avenue for me to advance next-generation child-care policy and messaging while pushing me to anchor in the bigger picture of human flourishing. To the whole team at Capita—Caroline, Erika, Michael, Ankita, Ivana, Elise, Amy—thank you.

Linda Shockley, Marisa Busch, and *Early Learning Nation* have given me a journalistic home, and capacious room to run, so that I can explore many of the concepts that appear in these pages. Brigid Schulte and the staff at New America's Better Life Lab have similarly shown a consistent willingness to consider new ideas and help me fulfill the role of friendly gadfly within the child-care sector.

My agent, Laura Usselman, has been a stalwart source of partnership and advice, always open to reviewing ideas and angles with her keen eye. I couldn't ask for a better champion.

Julia Steer at Oxford University Press has been an enthusiastic booster despite the fact we were originally connected around an entirely different book project. Thank you for taking a chance on this idea.

Finally, any book, but especially a book about child care, does not come into being without one's family. Alma and Esther have given me a firsthand look into the joys and challenges of parenting in modern America—I am so glad I get to be your dad. Grandparents Abe, Diane, Les, and Lisa offered support when I needed to hole up and bang out chapters. And Melissa, your clear sense of purpose is perhaps only matched by your unyielding support: Thank you for journeying with me. There's no one I'd rather write a book alongside.

Endnotes

Introduction

1. Clinton, William J. "Remarks by the President on Child Care, The Rose Garden." *The White House*, 23 April 1998, https://clintonwhitehouse6.archives.gov/1998/04/1998-04-23-remarks-by-president-at-child-care-event.html.
2. Obama, Barack. "Remarks of President Barack Obama—State of the Union Address." *The White House*, 20 Jan. 2015, https://obamawhitehouse.archives.gov/the-press-office/2015/01/20/remarks-president-state-union-address-january-20-2015.
3. Trump, Donald J. "Remarks by President Trump at the White House Summit on Child Care and Paid Leave." *The White House*, 12 Dec. 2019, https://trumpwhitehouse.archives.gov/briefings-statements/remarks-president-trump-white-house-summit-child-care-paid-leave/.
4. e.g., Rowe, Mary Potter, and Husby, Ralph D. "Economics of Child Care: Costs, Needs, and Issues." In *Child Care—Who Cares? Foreign and Domestic Infant and Early Childhood Development Policies*, edited by Pamela Roby, 98–123. New York: Basic Books, 1973.
5. National Academies of Sciences, Engineering, and Medicine. *Transforming the Financing of Early Care and Education*. 2018. The National Academies Press. https://doi.org/10.17226/24984.
6. Lowrey, Annie. "The Reason Child Care Is So Hard to Afford." *The Atlantic*, 1 Oct. 2022, www.theatlantic.com/ideas/archive/2022/10/us-child-care-market-broken-expensive/671603/.
7. Hayhoe, Katharine. *Saving Us: A Climate Scientist's Case for Hope and Healing in a Divided World*. New York: Simon & Schuster, 2021.
8. Levi, Margaret, host. "A Social Science of Caregiving." Center for Advanced Study in the Behavioral Sciences (Stanford University) podcast, episode 70. 26 Feb. 2024, https://casbs.stanford.edu/podcast#social-science-caregiving.
9. Ruggles, Steven. "Patriarchy, Power, and Pay: The Transformation of American Families, 1800–2015." *Demography*, vol. 52, no. 6, 28 Oct. 2015, pp. 1797–1823, www.ncbi.nlm.nih.gov/pmc/articles/PMC5068828/, https://doi.org/10.1007/s13524-015-0440-z.
10. Michel, Sonya. *Children's Interests/Mothers' Rights: The Shaping of America's Child Care Policy*. New Haven and London: Yale University Press, 2000.
11. Bailey, Martha J., and DiPrete, Thomas A. "Five Decades of Remarkable but Slowing Change in U.S. Women's Economic and Social Status and Political Participation." *RSF: The Russell Sage Foundation Journal of the Social Sciences*, vol. 2, no. 4, 2016, p. 1, https://doi.org/10.7758/rsf.2016.2.4.01.
12. Prentice, Susan. "High Stakes: The 'Investable' Child and the Economic Reframing of Childcare." *Signs: Journal of Women in Culture and Society*, vol. 34, no. 3, March 2009, pp. 687–710, https://doi.org/10.1086/593711.
13. Pal, Leslie A. *Beyond Policy Analysis: Public Issue Management in Turbulent Times*. (5th edition). Nelson Higher Education, 2014.
14. Foreman, Matt. "Winning Marriage Equality." *Washington Monthly*, 22 June 2016, https://philanthropy.washingtonmonthly.com/portfolio_page/winning-marriage-equality/.
15. Haspel, Elliot. "Why Are Child Care Programs Open When Schools Are Not?" *The New York Times*, 7 Aug. 2020, www.nytimes.com/2020/08/04/parenting/schools-day-care-children-divide.html.
16. Cui, Jiashan, et al. "Early Childhood Program Participation: 2019" U.S. Department of Education, National Center for Education Statistics (NCES 2020–075REV), Table 1. May 2021, https://nces.ed.gov/pubs2020/2020075REV.pdf.
17. Afterschool Alliance. "America After 3pm: Demand Grows, Opportunity Shrinks." 2020, https://afterschoolalliance.org/documents/AA3PM-2020/AA3PM-National-Report.pdf.

18. American Camp Association. "Breakthrough Study from American Camp Association Outlines the Benefits of Camp Experience." 18 April 2023, https://www.acacamps.org/news/press-release/breakthrough-study-outlines-benefits-camp-experience.
19. "Child-to-Provider Ratio Standard and Group Size." *Child Care Technical Assistance Network*, Administration for Children and Families, 2011, https://childcareta.acf.hhs.gov/sites/default/files/547_1305_ratiosgroupsize_2011.pdf.
20. Nguyen, Janet. "Why Is Child Care So Expensive When Child Care Providers Are Paid So Little? Let's Do the Math." Marketplace, 7 Dec. 2023, www.marketplace.org/2023/12/07/why-is-child-care-so-expensive-when-child-care-providers-are-paid-so-little-lets-do-the-math/.
21. U.S. Bureau of Labor Statistics. "Occupational Employment and Wages, May 2023 (39–9011 Childcare Workers)." May 2023, https://www.bls.gov/oes/current/oes399011.htm.
22. Davis, Elizabeth E., and Sojourner, Aaron. "Increasing Federal Investment in Children's Early Care and Education to Raise Quality, Access, and Affordability." The Hamilton Project. 12 May 2021, https://www.hamiltonproject.org/publication/policy-proposal/increasing-federal-investment-in-childrens-early-care-and-education-to-raise-quality-access-and-affordability/.
23. Helland, E., and Tabarrok, H. "Why Are the Prices So Damn High: Education, Health, and the Baumol Effect." Mercatus Center at George Mason University. May 2019, https://www.mercatus.org/students/research/books/why-are-prices-so-damn-high.
24. Palmer, Annie. "Amazon Adding 250,000 Workers for the Holidays and Bumping Average Pay." CNBC, 19 Sept. 2023, www.cnbc.com/2023/09/19/amazon-adding-250000-workers-for-the-holidays-and-bumping-average-pay.html.
25. Baumol, William J. *The Cost Disease: Why Computers Get Cheaper and Health Care Doesn't*. New Haven and London: Yale University Press, 2012.
26. Waters, Joe. "Towards a National Children and Family Policy." *Capita*, 15 Feb. 2021, https://www.capita.org/capita-ideas/2021/2/15/towards-a-national-children-and-family-policy.
27. Elder, Laurel, and Greene, Steven. *The Politics of Parenthood: Causes and Consequences of the Politicization and Polarization of the American Family*. Albany: State University of New York Press, 2012.
28. VanderWeele, Tyler J. "On the Promotion of Human Flourishing." *Proceedings of the National Academy of Sciences*, vol. 114, no. 31, 1 Aug. 2017, pp. 8148–8156, www.pnas.org/content/114/31/8148#ref-8, https://doi.org/10.1073/pnas.1702996114.
29. Kennedy, Robert F. Remarks at the University of Kansas. 18 March 1968, https://www.jfklibrary.org/learn/about-jfk/the-kennedy-family/robert-f-kennedy/robert-f-kennedy-speeches/remarks-at-the-university-of-kansas-march-18-1968.

Chapter 1

1. Kiesling, Lydia. "Paid Child Care for Working Mothers? All It Took Was a World War." *The New York Times*, 2 Oct. 2019, www.nytimes.com/2019/10/02/us/paid-childcare-working-mothers-wwii.html.
2. Stoltzfus, Emilie. "Child Care: The Federal Role During World War II." *Congressional Research Service*, 29 June 2000, https://crsreports.congress.gov/product/pdf/RS/RS20615/9.
3. Stoltzfus, Emilie. *Citizen, Mother, Worker: Debating Public Responsibility for Child Care after the Second World War*. Chapel Hill: University of North Carolina Press, 2003.
4. Riley, Susan E. "Caring for Rosie's Children: Federal Child Care Policies in the World War II Era." *Polity*, vol. 26, no. 4, June 1994, pp. 655–675, https://doi.org/10.2307/3235099.
5. Dratch, Howard. "The Politics of Child Care in the 1940s." *Science & Society*, vol. 38, no. 2, 1974, pp. 167–204. JSTOR, http://www.jstor.org/stable/40401779. Accessed 1 Dec. 2023.
6. "My Day by Eleanor Roosevelt, September 8, 1945." Www2.Gwu.edu, www2.gwu.edu/~erpapers/myday/displaydoc.cfm?_y=1945&_f=md000125.
7. Fousekis, Natalie M. *Demanding Child Care: Women's Activism and the Politics of Welfare, 1940–1971*. Amazon (1st edition). Urbana: University of Illinois Press, 3 Aug. 2011.
8. Hass, Steven. "Daycare is Expensive" *The Humboldt Jungle*. Uploaded to Instagram by @stevenhaasinstaa, 23 Feb. 2024, https://www.instagram.com/reel/C3scSrBgWwq/?igsh=NjZiM2M3MzIxNA%3D%3D.
9. Johnson, J., et al., 2000. "Necessary Compromises: How Parents, Employers and Children's Advocates View Child Care Today." Public Agenda Foundation.
10. Roth, William. The Politics of Daycare: The Comprehensive Child Development Act of 1971. Discussion Papers 369–376. Distributed by ERIC Clearinghouse, 1976.

11. Schulte, Brigid. *Overwhelmed: Work, Love, and Play When No One Has the Time*. New York: Sarah Crichton Books, Farrar, Straus and Giroux, 2014.
12. e.g., Iati, Marisa. "For D.C.-Area Parents, Registering for Summer Camp Is a Brutal Scramble." *The Washington Post*, 16 March 2024, https://www.washingtonpost.com/dc-md-va/2024/03/16/summer-camps-dc/.
13. Anderson, Dylan. "'Fingers Crossed': Child Care Still a Crisis in Routt County." *Steamboat Pilot*, 17 April 2022, https://www.steamboatpilot.com/news/fingers-crossed-child-care-still-a-crisis-in-routt-county/; Cardenas, Rebecca. "Dozens of parents wait overnight to secure daycare spot." CNN Regional, 21 May 2022, https://localnews8.com/cnn-regional/2022/05/21/dozens-of-parents-wait-overnight-to-secure-daycare-spot/.
14. Boots, Michelle Theriault. "Parents with Kids Enrolled in Anchorage Child Care Are Being Turned Away Because There's Not Enough Staff." *Anchorage Daily News*, 16 June 2024, https://www.adn.com/alaska-news/education/2024/06/16/parents-with-kids-enrolled-in-anchorage-childcare-are-being-turned-away-because-theres-not-enough-staff/.
15. Prentice, Susan. "High Stakes: The 'Investable' Child and the Economic Reframing of Childcare." *Signs: Journal of Women in Culture and Society*, vol. 34, no. 3, March 2009, pp. 687–710, https://doi.org/10.1086/593711.
16. Levitsky, Sandra R. *Caring for Our Own*. New York: Oxford University Press, USA, 2014.
17. Skocpol, Theda. "Lessons from History: Building a Movement for America's Children." Washington DC and Santa Monica, CA: The Children's Partnership, 1997.
18. Dukich, Tamara. "Women's Organizing after Suffrage: The Women's Joint Congressional Committee and the Sheppard-Towner Act." *Newcomb College Institute Research on Women, Gender, & Feminism* (Tulane University), Vol. 1, Iss. 2. 15 July 2014, https://journals.tulane.edu/NAJ/article/view/200/138.
19. Suskind, Dana, and Lydia Denworth. *Parent Nation: Unlocking Every Child's Potential, Fulfilling Society's Promise*. New York: Dutton, 2022.
20. Suddath, Claire. "How Child Care Become the Most Broken Business in America." Bloomberg News, 18 Nov. 2021, https://www.bloomberg.com/news/features/2021-11-18/biden-s-build-back-better-wants-to-save-america-s-child-care-business.
21. Eichner, Maxine. *The Free-Market Family: How the Market Crushed the American Dream (and How It Can Be Restored)*. New York: Oxford University Press, 2020.
22. Orsekes, Naomi, and Conway, Erik M. *The Big Myth: How American Business Taught Us to Loathe Government and Love the Free Market*. Bloomsbury Publishing, 21 Feb. 2023.
23. "What Sort of World For Them?" *McCall's* 1958-08: Vol 85 Iss 11, p. 9. Gruner + Jahr USA Publishing, 1 Aug. 1958, archive.org/details/sim_rosie_1958-08_85_11/page/90/mode/2up.
24. Cooper, Melinda. *Family Values: Between Neoliberalism and the New Social Conservatism*. Brooklyn, NY: Zone Books, 2019.
25. Perlstein, Rick. *Reaganland: America's Right Turn 1976–1980*. Simon & Schuster, 2020.
26. Delano Roosevelt, Franklin. Address Accepting the Presidential Nomination at the Democratic National Convention in Chicago. 2 July 1932.
27. Cooper, Melinda. *Family Values: Between Neoliberalism and the New Social Conservatism*. Brooklyn, NY: Zone Books, 2019.
28. Bellah, Robert N., et al. *Habits of the Heart: Individualism and Commitment in American Life*. Berkeley, Los Angeles, London: University of California Press, 2008.
29. Kobes Du Mez, Kristin. *Jesus and John Wayne: How White Evangelicals Corrupted a Faith and Fractured a Nation*. New York: Liveright Publishing Corporation, A Division of W.W. Norton & Company, 2020.
30. Eichner, Maxine. *The Free-Market Family: How the Market Crushed the American Dream (and How It Can Be Restored)*. New York: Oxford University Press, 2020.
31. Riviera, Gloria. "Birth of a Broken System." No One Is Coming to Save Us (Lemonada Media), 20 May 2021, lemonadamedia.com/podcast/2-birth-of-a-broken-system/.
32. Halperin Danziger, Anna. "Education or Welfare?" *American and British Child Care Policy*, 1965–2004. 1 Jan. 2018, https://doi.org/10.7916/d81k0t6t.
33. Blank, Helen. "Helen Blank Oral History, Interviewed by Deborah Phillips." *Smith College Libraries*. 1 May 2023, https://findingaids.smith.edu/repositories/2/resources/1713.
34. Ruggles, Steven. "Patriarchy, Power, and Pay: The Transformation of American Families, 1800–2015." *Demography* vol. 52, iss. 6 (2015): 1797–1823. doi:10.1007/s13524-015-0440-z.

35. Hipple, Steven F. "Labor Force Participation: What Has Happened since the Peak?: Monthly Labor Review: U.S. Bureau of Labor Statistics." Bls.gov, 27 Sept. 2016, www.bls.gov/opub/mlr/2016/article/labor-force-participation-what-has-happened-since-the-peak.htm.
36. Lelyveld, Joseph. "IN AMERICA; Drive-in Day Care." *The New York Times*, 5 June 1977, timesmachine.nytimes.com/timesmachine/1977/06/05/140075582.html?pageNumber=411.
37. Palley, E., and Shdaimah, C. *In Our Hands: The Struggle for U.S. Child Care Policy*. New York: NYU Press, 2014.
38. Milkie, Melissa A., et al. "What Kind of War? 'Mommy Wars' Discourse in U.S. And Canadian News, 1989–2013." *Sociological Inquiry*, vol. 86, no. 1, 14 Dec. 2015, pp. 51–78, https://doi.org/10.1111/soin.12100.
39. Ibid.
40. Grose, Jessica. "Opinion | the Child Care Crisis Has Been 'Urgent' since '86. Just Ask Cosmo." *The New York Times*, 7 Dec. 2022, www.nytimes.com/2022/12/07/opinion/child-care.html.
41. Levitsky, Sandra R. *Caring for Our Own*. New York: Oxford University Press, USA, 2014.
42. Garbes, Angela. *Essential Labor: Mothering as Social Change*. HarperCollins, 2022.
43. Salzburg Global Seminar. "A World United for Care: A Salzburg Call to Transform Care and Caregiving." www.salzburgglobal.org/news/latest-news/article/a-world-united-for-care-a-salzburg-call-to-transform-care-and-caregiving.
44. Corbin, Ian, and Waters, Joe. "Building a Moral Renaissance in 2023." *Newsweek*, 28 Dec. 2022, www.newsweek.com/building-moral-renaissance-2023-opinion-1765125.
45. Zigler, E., et al. *The Tragedy of Child Care in America*. New Haven, CT: Yale University Press, 2009.
46. Teh, Cheryl. "Sen. Ron Johnson Says It's Not 'Society's Responsibility' to Care for 'Other People's Children' While Arguing against Child-Care Subsidies for Working Parents." *Business Insider*, 26 Jan. 2022, www.businessinsider.com/ron-johnson-not-societys-responsibility-care-for-other-peoples-children-2022-1.
47. Mayer, Eric. "Gov. Noem on Child Care: Not Government's Role." KELOLAND.com, 18 Dec. 2023, www.keloland.com/keloland-com-original/gov-noem-on-child-care-not-governments-role/.
48. Skocpol, Theda. *Lessons from History: Building a Movement for America's Children*. Washington, DC and Santa Monica, CA: The Children's Partnership, 1997.

Chapter 2

1. Burke, Edmund, 1729–1797. Reflections on the Revolution in France.
2. Parker, Qweyonoh. "Readers Write: Child Care, Legislature, RFK Jr., Uber and Lyft, Israel and Hamas." *Star Tribune*, 14 March 2024, https://www.startribune.com/readers-write-child-care-legislature-rfk-jr-uber-lyft-israel-hamas/600351309/.
3. Owens, Victoria, and Smith, Linda. "The Illusion of Parent Choice: Lessons Learned from BPC's Parent Survey Series." Bipartisan Policy Center, May 2023, https://bipartisanpolicy.org/download/?file=/wp-content/uploads/2023/05/BPC_ECI-Parent-Report_R04.pdf.
4. Arnade, Chris. *Dignity: Seeking Respect in Back Row America*. New York: Sentinel, 2019.
5. Ojeda, Christopher. "Depression and Political Participation∗." *Social Science Quarterly*, vol. 96, no. 5, 9 June 2015, pp. 1226–1243, https://doi.org/10.1111/ssqu.12173.
6. Gill, Tim. *Urban Playground: How Child-Friendly Planning and Design Can Save Cities*. Routledge, 2021.
7. Blackwell, Angela. "The Curb-Cut Effect." *Stanford Social Innovation Review*. Ssir.org, 2017, ssir.org/articles/entry/the_curb_cut_effect.
8. Gill, Tim. *Urban Playground: How Child-Friendly Planning and Design Can Save Cities*. Routledge, 2021.
9. Bipartisan Policy Center. "Child Care in Rural America—What Have We Learned?" Bipartisanpolicy.org, bipartisanpolicy.org/event/child-care-in-rural-america-what-have-we-learned/.
10. Couture, Ray. "Lack of Child Care Forces Out Families." *Valley News*, 31 Oct. 2022, www.vnews.com/Woodstock-committee-aims-to-increase-access-to-child-care-47194876.
11. The Kansas Sampler Foundation & Office of Rural Prosperity. "Kansas Power Up and Go." May 2021, https://kansassampler.org/images/assets/PUG_FinalReport_05-21_2.pdf.

12. Gunderson, Dan. "Rural Town Tries Innovative Solution to Child Care Crisis." *MPR News*, 14 Dec. 2022, www.mprnews.org/story/2022/12/14/rural-town-tries-innovative-solution-to-child-care-crisis.
13. Roberts, David. "Young Families Typically Leave Cities for the Suburbs. Here's How to Keep Them Downtown." *Vox*, 21 June 2017, www.vox.com/2017/6/21/15815524/toderian-families-cities.
14. British Columbia Ministry of Education and Child Care. "B.C. Reaches Milestone in Newly Funded Child Care Spaces." 2 May 2022, https://news.gov.bc.ca/releases/2022ECC0035-000689.
15. Greenblatt, Alan. "Do Cities Need Kids?" *Governing*, 26 Jan. 2015, www.governing.com/archive/gov-seattle-kids-gentrification-series.html.
16. Huddleston, Scott. "SAISD Board Approves Controversial School Closure Plan after Contentious Debate." *San Antonio Express-News*, 14 Nov. 2023, www.expressnews.com/news/education/article/school-closures-approved-saisd-18484015.php.
17. "The Forum." Unify Montrose, 28 June 2023, www.unifymontrose.org/initiatives/nr8e8pfz56tsh4optb1qyw4nxmr4zp.
18. Rieck, Dana. "St. Louis County Aims to Be 2nd Police Department in US with Subsidized Day Care." STLtoday.com, 23 Dec. 2023, www.stltoday.com/news/local/crime-courts/st-louis-county-aims-to-be-2nd-police-department-in-us-with-subsidized-day-care.
19. U.S. Bureau of Labor Statistics. "Registered Nurses: Occupational Outlook Handbook: U.S. Bureau of Labor Statistics." Bls.gov, 18 April 2022, www.bls.gov/ooh/healthcare/registered-nurses.htm.
20. Guyer, Sherrie Page. "We're Facing a Massive Nursing Shortage. On Site Childcare Is the Answer." *Newsweek*, 11 Nov. 2022, www.newsweek.com/were-facing-massive-nursing-shortage-site-childcare-answer-opinion-1757998.
21. Dean, Erin. "Doctor Parents and Childcare: The Untold Toll Revealed." *BMJ*, vol. 384, 2024, p. q128 doi:10.1136/bmj.q128.
22. Gale, Rebecca. "More Hospitals Are Offering Child Care. But They Shouldn't Have To." STAT, 30 May 2023, www.statnews.com/2023/05/30/hospitals-child-care-health-workers/.
23. Haddad, Lisa M, et al. "Nursing Shortage." National Library of Medicine, StatPearls Publishing, 13 Feb. 2023, www.ncbi.nlm.nih.gov/books/NBK493175/.
24. Davis, Jim, et al. The Great Dechurching. *Zondervan*, 22 Aug. 2023.
25. Elsdon, Mark. *Gone for Good?: Negotiating the Coming Wave of Church Property Transition*. William B. Eerdmans Publishing Company, 2024.
26. Lewis, Andy. "Some Positive Benefits Churches Bring to Communities." Ethics and Religious Liberty Commission of the Southern Baptist Convention. May 2015.
27. Lindsay, Drew. "What Philanthropy and Nonprofits Lose as Religion Fades." *Chronicle of Philanthropy*, 12 Dec. 2023, https://www.philanthropy.com/article/what-philanthropy-and-nonprofits-lose-as-religion-fades.
28. Morgan, Kimberly, and Steenland, Sally. "The Challenge of Faith: Bringing Spiritual Sustenance to Busy Lives." In *The Shriver Report: A Woman's Nation Changes Everything*. Center for American Progress. 16 Oct. 2009, https://www.americanprogress.org/press/the-shriver-report-a-womans-nation-changes-everything/.
29. Workman, Simon. "Where Does Your Child Care Dollar Go?" Center for American Progress, 14 Feb. 2018, www.americanprogress.org/article/child-care-dollar-go/.
30. Morris, Suzann, and Smith, Linda. "Examining the Role of Faith-Based Child Care." Bipartisan Policy Center, May 2021, https://bipartisanpolicy.org/download/?file=/wp-content/uploads/2021/06/ECI-Faith-Based-Brief_RV2-1-1.pdf.
31. Hoover, Sydney. "Brunswick Families Scrambling for Childcare after Preschool Closes." *Wilmington StarNews*, 18 March 2022, www.starnewsonline.com/story/news/2022/03/17/brunswick-families-struggle-finding-daycare-leland-preschool-closes/9442400002/.
32. Mayer, Erik, and Volk, Kelli. "Good Shepherd Lutheran Closing Child Care Center." KELOLAND.com, 30 Oct. 2023, www.keloland.com/news/local-news/good-shepherd-lutheran-closing-child-care-center/.
33. Kustanowitz, Esther. "EarlyJ Initiative Looks to Tackle Jewish Early Childhood Education, First in the Bay Area, Then Beyond." *EJewish Philanthropy*, 28 June 2023, ejewishphilanthropy.com/earlyj-initiative-looks-to-tackle-jewish-early-childhood-education-first-in-the-bay-area-then-beyond/.

34. McNeel, Bekah. "The Solution to Unused Church Space Might Be Toddlers." *Sojourners*, 11 July 2023, sojo.net/articles/solution-unused-church-space-might-be-toddlers.
35. Norgren, Jill. "In Search of a National Child Care Policy: Background and Prospects." *The Western Political Quarterly*, vol. 34, no. 1, March 1981, p. 127, https://doi.org/10.2307/447895.
36. Capita and The Aspen Institute. "Flourishing Children, Healthy Communities, and a Stronger Nation: The U.S. Early Years Climate Action Plan." Oct. 2023, https://earlyyearsclimateplan.us/.
37. Kisner, Kathy, et al. "Millennial Connections: Findings from ZERO TO THREE's 2018 Parent Survey." ZERO TO THREE. 2018, https://www.zerotothree.org/resource/millennial-connections-executive-summary.
38. "Make a Circle." Bradwell, Jen, and Boekelheide, Todd. Center for Independent Documentary, 2024.
39. Carrazana, Chabeli. "The Death of a Day Care: When a Child Care Center Closes, an Entire Community Is Affected." *The 19th*, 31 Aug. 2023, https://19thnews.org/2023/08/child-care-centers-closing-pandemic-era-funding-communities/.
40. National Center on Early Childhood Quality Assurance (U.S. Administration for Children and Families), Addressing the Decreasing Number of Family Child Care Providers in the United States. May 2020, https://childcareta.acf.hhs.gov/resource/addressing-decreasing-number-family-child-care-providers-united-states.
41. Cosslett, Rhiannon Lucy. "Why Should I Pay for You to Have a Child?" This Is the State of the Debate on Childcare Right Now." *The Guardian*, 18 Oct. 2022, www.theguardian.com/commentisfree/2022/oct/18/pay-child-uk-childcare.

Chapter 3

1. Novak, Michael. "The Family Out of Favor." *Harper's Magazine*, 1 April 1976, pp. 37–46.
2. Neece, C. L., Green, S. A., & Baker, B. L. (2012). "Parenting Stress and Child Behavior Problems: A Transactional Relationship Across Time." *American Journal on Intellectual and Developmental Disabilities*, vol. 117, no.1, p. 48, https://doi.org/10.1352/1944-7558-117.1.48.
3. Remarks by Secretary of the Treasury Janet L. Yellen on Shortages in the Child Care System, 15 Sept. 2021, https://home.treasury.gov/news/press-releases/jy0355.
4. Carrazana, Chabeli. "Day Care Waitlists Are so Long, Moms Are Quitting Their Jobs or Choosing to Stop Having Kids." *The 19th*, 30 March 2023, 19thnews.org/2023/03/day-care-waitlists-child-care-strain-parenting/.
5. Dickens, Mollie, and Hutner, Lucy. "Opinion | The Stress of Finding Child Care is Hurting Parents' Health." *The New York Times*. 16 Jan 2024, https://www.nytimes.com/2024/01/16/opinion/child-care-parenting-stress.html.
6. Harris Poll. "Examining Evolving Sentiment on Dual Career Households in the United States." 1 May 2024, https://theharrispoll.com/briefs/dual-career-households/.
7. Yamauchi, Chikako. "The Availability of Child Care Centers, Perceived Search Costs and Parental Life Satisfaction." *Review of Economics of the Household*, vol. 8, no. 2, 25 Oct. 2009, pp. 231–253, https://doi.org/10.1007/s11150-009-9071-8.
8. Bigras, Nathalie, et al. "Parental Stress and Daycare Attendance. Does Daycare Quality and Parental Satisfaction with Daycare Moderate the Relation between Family Income and Stress Level among Parents of Four Years Old Children?" *Procedia—Social and Behavioral Sciences*, vol. 55, Oct. 2012, pp. 894–901, https://doi.org/10.1016/j.sbspro.2012.09.578.
9. Bodick, Nicole. "Blighted Horizons." *The Point Magazine*, 23 May 2024, https://thepointmag.com/examined-life/blighted-horizons/.
10. Landivar, Liana Christin, Graf, Nikki L., and Rayo, Giorleny Altamirano. "Childcare Prices in Local Areas: Initial Findings from the National Database of Childcare Prices." Women's Bureau Issue Brief. U.S. Department of Labor, January 2023.
11. Tate, Emily. "Child Care Programs See Closures, Resignations and Tuition Hikes after Federal Funding Expires." *The 19th*, 30 Nov. 2023, 19thnews.org/2023/11/child-care-programs-closures-resignations-tuition-funding/.
12. Malik, Rasheed. "The Build Back Better Act Substantially Expands Child Care Assistance." Center for American Progress, 2 Dec. 2021, www.americanprogress.org/article/the-build-back-better-act-substantially-expands-child-care-assistance/.

13. Murray, Stephanie H. "Why Parents Struggle so Much in the World's Richest Country." *The Atlantic*, 5 Jan. 2024, www.theatlantic.com/family/archive/2024/01/america-failed-parents-rich-countries-raising-kids/677023/.
14. Riviera, Gloria. "Good Childcare *Can* Work." No One is Coming to Save Us (Lemonada Media), 27 May 2021, lemonadamedia.com/podcast/2-birth-of-a-broken-system/.
15. Guendelsberger, Emily. *On the Clock*. Little, Brown, 2019.
16. Schneider, Daniel, and Harknett, Kristen. "Close to the Edge: Service Workers and Their Children at the Front Lines of a Crisis." William T. Grant Foundation, 2 April 2020, wtgrantfoundation.org/close-to-the-edge-service-workers-and-their-children-at-the-front-lines-of-a-crisis.
17. Nickelsburg, Monica. "The Second Shift: Child Care Crisis Forces Families into Grueling Schedules." www.kuow.org, 27 Nov. 2023, www.kuow.org/stories/the-second-shift-child-care-crisis-forces-families-into-grueling-schedules.
18. Calarco, Jessica. *Holding It Together: How Women Became America's Safety Net*. New York: Penguin Random House, 2024.
19. Kearney, Melissa S. *The Two-Parent Privilege*. Chicago: University of Chicago Press, 2023.
20. Marcil, Lucy E., et al. "Women's Experiences of the Effect of Financial Strain on Parenting and Mental Health." *Journal of Obstetric, Gynecologic & Neonatal Nursing*, vol. 49, no. 6, Aug. 2020, https://doi.org/10.1016/j.jogn.2020.07.002.
21. Idstad, M., Torvik, F.A., Borren, I., et al. "Mental Distress Predicts Divorce Over 16 Years: The HUNT Study." *BMC Public Health*, vol.15, no. 320, 2015, https://doi.org/10.1186/s12889-015-1662-0.
22. Saunders, Lindsey K. "Having a Baby in America Should Be Easier." *Pittsburgh Post-Gazette*, 15 Feb. 2024, www.post-gazette.com/opinion/Op-Ed/2024/02/15/children-baby-birth-america-cost/stories/202402150070.
23. Lebrun-Harris, Lydie A., et al. "Five-Year Trends in US Children's Health and Well-Being, 2016–2020." *JAMA Pediatrics*, vol. 176, no. 7, 14 March 2022, https://doi.org/10.1001/jamapediatrics.2022.0056.
24. Murthy, Vivek. "Our Epidemic of Loneliness and Isolation: The U.S. Surgeon General's Advisory on the Healing Effects of Social Connection and Community." Office of the U.S. Surgeon General, 2023.
25. Kent, Ana Hernández. "Single Mothers Face Difficulties with Slim Financial Cushions." *Federal Reserve Bank of St. Louis*, 9 May 2022, https://www.stlouisfed.org/on-the-economy/2022/may/single-mothers-slim-financial-cushions.
26. Vega, Tanzina. "The Financial Fragility of Single Parents Who Need Child Care." *The Boston Globe*, 20 Mar 2023, https://www.bostonglobe.com/2023/03/20/opinion/financial-fragility-single-parents-who-need-child-care/.
27. Ranji, U., Rosenzweig, C., and Gomez, I. "Executive Summary: 2017 Kaiser Women's Health Survey Kaiser Family Foundation." *Women's Health Policy*, 2018, https://files.kff.org/attachment/Executive-Summary-2017-Kaiser-Womens-Health-Survey.
28. Fort Worth Star-Telegram. "Lack of Child Care Forced Her to Delay Cancer Treatment. Then This Dallas Group Stepped In." 20 Nov. 2022, https://tarrant.tx.networkofcare.org/kids/news-article-detail.aspx?id=139501.
29. Johnson, Anna D., and Padilla, Christina M. "Childcare Instability and Maternal Depressive Symptoms: Exploring New Avenues for Supporting Maternal Mental Health." *Academic Pediatrics*, vol. 19, no. 1, Jan. 2019, pp. 18–26, https://doi.org/10.1016/j.acap.2018.05.006.
30. Greco, Ivana. "Supporting American Homemakers." American Compass, 2023, americancompass.org/rebuilding-american-capitalism/supportive-communities/supporting-american-homemakers/.
31. Greco, Ivana, and Haspel, Elliot. "Invisible Labor, Visible Needs: Making Family Policy Work for Stay-At-Home (and All) Parents." *Capita*, 15 Oct. 2024, https://capita.org/publication/invisible-labor-visible-needs/.
32. Chaparro, J., Sojourner, A. and Wiswall, M. J. "Early Childhood Care and Cognitive Development" NBER Working Paper No. 26,813, Feb. 2020, JEL No. J13.
33. Mother/Untitled. American Mothers on Pause (Proof Insights). 2023, https://www.motheruntitled.com/americanmothersonpause.
34. Calarco, Jessica. *Holding It Together: How Women Became America's Safety Net*. New York: Penguin Random House, 2024.

35. Robbins, Katherine Gallagher, and Mason, Jessica. "Women's Unpaid Caregiving Is Worth More than $625 Billion—and It Could Cost More." National Partnership for Women & Families, 14 Aug. 2023, nationalpartnership.org/womens-unpaid-caregiving-worth-more-than-625-billion/.
36. Build Initiative. "State Scan of Family, Friend, and Neighbor (FFN) Policies and Supports." Aug. 2023, https://buildinitiative.org/resource-library/state-scan-of-family-friend-and-neighbor-ffn-policies-and-supports/.
37. Cohen, Rachel M. "Rent Control For Child Care?" *Vox.* 21 May 2024, https://www.vox.com/24145136/can-lawmakers-cap-out-of-pocket-child-care-costs.
38. Hazan, Moshe, et al. "Why Did Rich Families Increase Their Fertility? Inequality and Marketization of Child Care." Federal Reserve Bank of St. Louis, Working Papers, vol. 2018, no. 022, 2018, https://doi.org/10.20955/wp.2018.022.
39. Seligson, Hannah. "The Three-Seat Strollers." *The New York Times*, 9 April 2014, https://www.nytimes.com/2014/04/10/fashion/The-Growing-Three-Child-Household-in-Manhattan.html.
40. Hazan, Moshe, et al. "Why Did Rich Families Increase Their Fertility? Inequality and Marketization of Child Care." Federal Reserve Bank of St. Louis, Working Papers, vol. 2018, no. 022, 2018, https://doi.org/10.20955/wp.2018.022.
41. Zoabi, Hosny, and Hazan, Moshe. "Highly Educated Women No Longer Have Fewer Kids." CEPR, 11 Dec. 2015, cepr.org/voxeu/columns/highly-educated-women-no-longer-have-fewer-kids.
42. Cain Miller, Claire. "Americans Are Having Fewer Babies. They Told Us Why." *The New York Times*, 5 July 2018, www.nytimes.com/2018/07/05/upshot/americans-are-having-fewer-babies-they-told-us-why.html.
43. Brown, Anna. "Growing Share of Childless Adults in U.S. Don't Expect to Ever Have Children." *Pew Research Center*, 19 Nov. 2021, www.pewresearch.org/short-reads/2021/11/19/growing-share-of-childless-adults-in-u-s-dont-expect-to-ever-have-children/.
44. Goldstein, Dana. "Why You Can't Find Child Care: 100,000 Workers Are Missing." *The New York Times*, 13 Oct. 2022, www.nytimes.com/2022/10/13/us/child-care-worker-shortage.html.
45. American Compass. "2021 Home Building Survey." Feb. 2021, https://americancompass.org/wp-content/uploads/2022/10/American-Compass_2021-Home-Building-Survey_Final.pdf.
46. Stone, Lyman. "How Big Is the Fertility Gap in America?" In a State of Migration, 5 Oct. 2017, medium.com/migration-issues/how-big-is-the-fertility-gap-in-america-fd205e9d1a35.
47. Pregnant Then Screwed. "6 in 10 Women Who Have Had an Abortion Claim Childcare Costs Influenced Their Decision." 8 July 2022, pregnantthenscrewed.com/6-in-10-women-who-have-had-an-abortion-claim-childcare-costs-influenced-their-decision/.
48. Longman, Philip. *The Empty Cradle: How Falling Birthrates Threaten World Prosperity and What to Do about It.* 14 April 2004.
49. Vespa, Jonathan, Medina, Lauren, and Armstrong, David M., "Demographic Turning Points for the United States: Population Projections for 2020 to 2060," Current Population Reports, P25-1144, U.S. Census Bureau, 2020.
50. Berg, Anastasia, and Wiseman, Rachel. *What Are Children For?: On Ambivalence and Choice.* St. Martin's Press, 2024.
51. Doepke, Matthias, et al. "The Economics of Fertility: A New Era." *National Bureau of Economic Research (Working Paper 29,948)*, April 2022, https://doi.org/10.3386/w29948.
52. Flowers, Anna Claire, et al. "Childcare Regulation and the Fertility Gap." *Social Science Research Network*, 20 May 2024, https://papers.ssrn.com/sol3/papers.cfm?abstract_id=4834635.
53. Constance, Paul. "The Heresy of Decline." *Long Now*, 6 March 2023, longnow.org/ideas/the-heresy-of-decline/.

Chapter 4

1. Skocpol, Theda. *Protecting Soldiers and Mothers: The Political Origins of Social Policy in the United States.* Cambridge, MA: Harvard University Press, 1992.
2. Kelley, Florence. *Some Ethical Gains, Through Legislation.* New York: Macmillan, 1905.

3. Skocpol, Theda. *Protecting Soldiers and Mothers: The Political Origins of Social Policy in the United States*. Cambridge, MA: Harvard University Press, 1992.
4. Thomas, Leigh. "France to Reform Parental Leave after Births Hit Post-War Low." *Reuters*. 17 Jan. 2024, https://www.reuters.com/world/europe/france-sees-collapse-births-lowest-since-world-war-two-2024-01-16/.
5. Pieter Vanhuysse, et al. "Taxing Reproduction: The Full Transfer Cost of Rearing Children in Europe." *Royal Society Open Science*, vol. 10, no. 10, 1 Oct. 2023, https://doi.org/10.1098/rsos.230759. Accessed 23 Feb. 2024.
6. Folbre, Nancy. "Children as Public Goods." *American Economic Review*, vol. 84, no. 2, 1994, pp. 86–90.
7. Folbre, Nancy. *For Love and Money: Care Provision in the United States*. New York: Russell Sage Foundation, 2012.
8. Quart, Alissa. *Bootstrapped: Liberating Ourselves from the American Dream*. HarperCollins, 2023.
9. Cahan, Emily. *Past Caring: A History of U.S. Preschool Care and Education for the Poor, 1820–1965*. National Center for Children in Poverty (Columbia University), 1989.
10. Ibid.
11. Beatty, Barbara. "A Commonwealth for Children." Speech to the PreK Now Conference, 15 Nov. 2006, http://www.strategiesforchildren.org/doc_research/06_BeattySpeech.pdf.
12. Krauss, Allison, et al. "The State of Preschool 2022." *National Institute for Early Education Research (Rutgers University)*, 2023, https://nieer.org/sites/default/files/2023-09/yb2022_fullreport.pdf.
13. Grossman, Allyson Sherman. "Working Mothers and Their Children." U.S. Bureau of Labor Statistics, May 1981, https://www.bls.gov/opub/mlr/1981/05/rpt3full.pdf.
14. Black, Derek W. "Freedom, Democracy, and the Right to Education." 116 Northwestern University Law Review. 1031, 2022, https://scholarlycommons.law.northwestern.edu/nulr/vol116/iss4/3.
15. Levitsky, Sandra. "Public Pre-School Expanded Kids' Entitlement to Childcare, but Not Women's Entitlement to Gender Equality." Gender Policy Report (University of Minnesota), 13 May 2019, genderpolicyreport.umn.edu/public-pre-school-expanded-kids-entitlement-to-childcare-but-not-womens-entitlement-to-gender-equality/.
16. Beatty, Barbara. "A Commonwealth for Children." Speech to the PreK Now Conference, 15 Nov. 2006, http://www.strategiesforchildren.org/doc_research/06_BeattySpeech.pdf.
17. Vote Mama Foundation. "Politics of Parenthood: Representation in the 118th Congress." 2023 and Vote Mama Foundation. "Politics of Parenthood: Representation in State Legislatures 2022." 2022, https://www.votemamafoundation.org/reports.
18. Gale, Rebecca. "Want Better Policies? Elect More Moms." *Marie Claire*, 7 Nov. 2022, https://www.marieclaire.com/politics/mothers-in-state-legislatures-paid-leave-child-care/.
19. Bryant, Lisa, and Hellwege, Julia Marin. "Working Moms Represent: Fighting For Family Friendly Policies in Congress." Presented at Visions in Methodology Conference, 16–18 May 2016, https://visionsinmethodology.org/wp-content/uploads/sites/4/2016/05/Bryant_Hellwege_VIM_2016.pdf.
20. Covert, Bryce. "This Is What Happens When Childcare Is Free." *The New Republic*, 25 Oct. 2023, newrepublic.com/article/175647/free-childcare-pandemic-programs-economy.
21. Cools, Angela. "Parents, Infants, and Voter Turnout: Evidence from the United States." *Quarterly Journal of Political Science*, vol. 17, no. 1, 2022, https://doi.org/10.1561/100.00020072.
22. David, Arnold. *The Effect of Children on Voter Turnout*. Berkeley: University of California Press, 6 May 2013, https://www.econ.berkeley.edu/sites/default/files/David%20Arnold%20thesis.pdf.
23. Clemens, Austin, et al. "Evidence from the 2020 Election Shows How to Close the Income Voting Divide." *Washington Center for Equitable Growth*. 8 July 2021, https://equitablegrowth.org/evidence-from-the-2020-election-shows-how-to-close-the-income-voting-divide/.
24. Putnam, Robert D. *Our Kids: The American Dream in Crisis*. New York: Simon & Schuster Paperbacks, 2015.
25. Astuto, Jennifer, and Ruck, Martin D. "Early Childhood as a Foundation for Civic Engagement." In *Handbook of Research on Civic Engagement in Youth*, edited by L.R. Sherrod, J. Torney-Purta and C.A. Flanagan, John Wiley & Sons, Inc., 2010. https://doi.org/10.1002/9780470767603.ch10.

26. Wessler, Rachel. "From Circletime to Civics: Involve Our Youngest Learners in Civic Engagement." Albert Shanker Institute, 3 Nov. 2022, www.shankerinstitute.org/blog/circletime-civics-involve-our-youngest-learners-civic-engagement.
27. Klinenberg, Eric. *Palaces for the People: How Social Infrastructure Can Help Fight Inequality, Polarization, and the Decline of Civic Life.* New York: Broadway Books, 2018.
28. Brenan, Megan. "Extreme Pride in Being American Remains near Record Low." Gallup.com, 29 June 2023, news.gallup.com/poll/507980/extreme-pride-american-remains-near-record-low.aspx.
29. Fetterolf, Janell, and Kramer, Stephanie. "Americans Are Less Likely Than Others Around the World to Feel Close to People in their Country or Community." *Pew Research Center,* 8 May 2024, https://www.pewresearch.org/short-reads/2024/05/08/americans-are-less-likely-than-others-around-the-world-to-feel-close-to-people-in-their-country-or-community/.
30. Weiss, Joanna. "'A Truer Reality Beyond Reality': Hannah Arendt's Warning About How Totalitarianism Takes Root." *Politico Magazine,* 19 May 2024, https://www.politico.com/news/magazine/2024/05/19/mag-weiss-samantharosehill-q-a-00158439.
31. Smith, Noah. "Try Patriotism." *Noahpinion,* 1 April 2024, https://www.noahpinion.blog/p/try-patriotism-ab3.
32. Public Religion Research Institute staff. "Competing Visions of America: An Evolving Identity or a Culture under Attack? Findings from the 2021 American Values Survey." PRRI, 1 Nov. 2021, www.prri.org/research/competing-visions-of-america-an-evolving-identity-or-a-culture-under-attack/.

Chapter 5

1. Mintz, Steven. *Huck's Raft: A History of American Childhood.* Cambridge, MA: Belknap Press of Harvard University Press, 2004.
2. King, Wilma. *Stolen Childhood: Slave Youth in Nineteenth-Century America.* Indiana University Press, 2011.
3. Zelizer, Viviana A. *Pricing the Priceless Child: The Changing Social Value of Children.* Princeton, NJ: Princeton University Press, 1994.
4. Russell, Hilary. "Training, Restraining and Sustaining: Infant and Child Care in the Late Nineteenth Century." *Material Culture Review,* vol. 21, Jan. 1985, https://journals.lib.unb.ca/index.php/MCR/article/view/17242.
5. Shonkoff, Jack. "Re-Envisioning Early Childhood Policy and Practice in a World of Striking Inequality and Uncertainty." Harvard Center on the Developing Child, Jan. 2022, https://developingchild.harvard.edu/re-envisioning-ecd/.
6. Stevens, Katharine B. "Workforce of Today, Workforce of Tomorrow: The Business Case for High-Quality Child Care." *U.S. Chamber of Commerce Foundation.* 21 June 2017.
7. Prentice, Susan. "High Stakes: The 'Investable' Child and the Economic Reframing of Childcare." *Signs: Journal of Women in Culture and Society,* vol. 34, no. 3, March 2009, pp. 687–710, https://doi.org/10.1086/593711.
8. Evers-Hillstrom, Karl. "Chamber of Commerce Warns Moderate Democrats against Voting for Reconciliation." *The Hill,* 22 Sept. 2021, thehill.com/business-a-lobbying/business-a-lobbying/573353-chamber-of-commerce-warns-moderate-democrats-against/.
9. Bandelj, Nina, and Spiegel, Michelle. "Pricing the Priceless Child 2.0: Children as Human Capital Investment." *Theory and Society,* 8 Dec. 2022, https://doi.org/10.1007/s11186-022-09508-x.
10. McGee, Nikki. "New Report: Majority of Kids in Illinois Not Ready for Kindergarten." WICS, 8 Nov. 2019, newschannel20.com/news/local/new-report-majority-of-kids-in-illinois-not-ready-for-kindergarten.
11. Salzbank, Lena. "Is Your Child Kindergarten Ready? 43 Percent of Students Are Not, according to State Data." WPEC, 11 March 2021, cbs12.com/news/local/is-your-kid-kindergarten-ready-43-percent-of-students-are-not-according-to-state-data.
12. Haspel, Elliot. "Early Childhood Policy Meets Early Childhood Science, Part I: On School Readiness." Early Learning Nation. 21 April 2020, https://earlylearningnation.com/2020/04/early-childhood-policy-meets-early-childhood-science-part-i-on-school-readiness/.
13. Mader, Jackie. "Behind the Findings of the Tennessee Pre-K Study." *The Hechinger Report,* 2 Feb. 2022, hechingerreport.org/behind-the-findings-of-the-tennessee-pre-k-study-that-found-negative-effects-for-graduates/.

14. WSJ Editorial Board. "Opinion | the Evidence on 'Free' Pre-K." *The Wall Street Journal*, 31 Jan. 2022, www.wsj.com/articles/the-evidence-on-free-pre-k-vanderbilt-study-build-back-better-11643656440.
15. Whitaker, Anamarie A., Burchinal, Margaret, et al. *Why Are Preschool Programs Becoming Less Effective?*" (EdWorkingPaper: 23-885) Annenberg Institute at Brown University, 2023, https://doi.org/10.26300/smqa-n695.
16. Rhode Island Kids Count. "Findings from the National School Readiness Indicators Initiative." Feb 2005, https://assets.aecf.org/m/resourcedoc/RIKC-GettingReady-2005.pdf.
17. Keleher, Lori. "Integral Human Development." *Routledge Handbook of Development Ethics*, 16 July 2018, pp. 29–34, https://doi.org/10.4324/9781315626796-4.
18. VanderWeele, Tyler J. "On the Promotion of Human Flourishing." *Proceedings of the National Academy of Sciences*, vol. 114, no. 31, 1 Aug. 2017, pp. 8148–8156, www.pnas.org/content/114/31/8148#ref-8, https://doi.org/10.1073/pnas.1702996114.
19. Henderson, Rob K. *Troubled: A Memoir of Foster Care, Family, and Social Class*. Swift Press, 2024.
20. Gopnik, Alison. *The Gardener and the Carpenter: What the New Science of Child Development Tells Us about the Relationship between Parents and Children*. New York: Farrar, Straus and Giroux, 2016.
21. Haspel, Elliot. "How to Quit Intensive Parenting." *The Atlantic*, 10 May 2022, www.theatlantic.com/family/archive/2022/05/intensive-helicopter-parent-anxiety/629683/.
22. Mullainathan, Sendhil and Shafir, Eldar. *Scarcity: Why Having Too Little Means So Much*. New York: Times Books, Henry Holt and Company, 2013.
23. Khan, Nisa, and Won, Grace. "How Summer Camp for Kids Got So Complicated (and Expensive)." *KQED*, 5 July 2023, www.kqed.org/news/11954995/how-summer-camp-for-kids-got-so-complicated-and-expensive.
24. Redford, Jeremy, Burns, Stephanie, and Hall, Jane L. "The Summer After Kindergarten: Children's Experiences by Socioeconomic Characteristics." May 2018. National Center for Education Statistics (U.S. Department of Education), https://nces.ed.gov/pubs2018/2018160.pdf.
25. Petersen, Anne Helen. "The Past and Potential Future of the Summer Care Scramble." *Culture Study*, 20 March 2022, annehelen.substack.com/p/the-past-and-potential-future-of.
26. Gale, Rebecca. "When Summer Camp Doesn't Work for Your Kid." *TIME*, 3 June 2023, time.com/6284396/when-summer-camp-doesnt-work-for-your-kid/.
27. Haspel, Elliot. "The Summer-Camp Feeding Frenzy Has Already Begun." *The Atlantic*, 26 Jan. 2023, www.theatlantic.com/family/archive/2023/01/summer-day-camps-activities-childcare/672837/.
28. Haspel, Elliot. "How to Quit Intensive Parenting." *The Atlantic*, 10 May 2022, www.theatlantic.com/family/archive/2022/05/intensive-helicopter-parent-anxiety/629683/.
29. Ramey, Garey, and Ramey, Valerie A. "The Rug Rat Race." *National Bureau of Economic Research*, 22 March 2010, https://doi.org/10.3386/w15284.
30. Fraiberg, Selma. *The Magic Years*. Scribner Book Company, 1959.
31. Kisner, Kathy, et al. "Millennial Connections: Findings from ZERO TO THREE's 2018 Parent Survey." ZERO TO THREE. 2018, https://www.zerotothree.org/resource/millennial-connections-executive-summary.
32. Mendes, Elizabeth, Saad, Lydia and McGeeney, Kyley. "Stay-At-Home Moms Report More Depression, Sadness, Anger." Gallup, Inc. 18 May 2012, news.gallup.com/poll/154685/stay-home-moms-report-depression-sadness-anger.aspx.
33. Frech, Adrianne, and Damaske, Sarah. "The Relationships between Mothers' Work Pathways and Physical and Mental Health." *Journal of Health and Social Behavior*, vol. 53, no. 4, 2012, pp. 396–412, www.ncbi.nlm.nih.gov/pmc/articles/PMC4120870/, https://doi.org/10.1177/0022146512453929.
34. Ryan, Rachael, et al. "Parenting and Child Mental Health." *London Journal of Primary Care*, vol. 9, no. 6, 10 Aug. 2017, pp. 86–94, www.ncbi.nlm.nih.gov/pmc/articles/PMC5694794/, https://doi.org/10.1080/17571472.2017.1361630.
35. Chaparro, J., Sojourner, A., and Wiswall, M.J. "Early Childhood Care and Cognitive Development" NBER Working Paper No. 26,813, Feb. 2020, JEL No. J13.
36. Capita and The Aspen Institute. "Flourishing Children, Healthy Communities, and a Stronger Nation: The U.S. Early Years Climate Action Plan." Oct. 2023, https://earlyyearsclimateplan.us/.

37. Early Childhood Scientific Council on Equity and the Environment. (2023). *Extreme Heat Affects Early Childhood Development and Health: Working Paper No. 1*. Retrieved from www.developingchild.harvard.edu.
38. EPA. 2023. Climate Change and Children's Health and Well-Being in the United States. U.S. Environmental Protection Agency, EPA 430-R-23-001.
39. Haspel, Elliot. "Climate Change Is Forcing Us Indoors—and Childhood Will Never Be The Same." *The Washington Post*, 23 July 2021, https://www.washingtonpost.com/outlook/2021/07/23/climate-change-childhood/.
40. Johnson, Ron. "School Streets Programs Surging In Some Cities But Others Have More Homework To Do." *Momentum Magazine*. 3 Mar 2023, https://momentummag.com/school-streets-programs/.

Chapter 6

1. Graves, Fatima Goss. "The Roots of Our Child Care Crisis Are in the Legacy of Slavery." *The Hill*, 21 June 2021, thehill.com/changing-america/opinion/559457-the-roots-of-our-child-care-crisis-are-in-the-legacy-of-slavery/.
2. Douglass, Frederick. *Narrative of the Life of Frederick Douglass, an American Slave*. Dover Publications, 1995.
3. Graves, Fatima Goss. "The Roots of Our Child Care Crisis Are in the Legacy of Slavery." *The Hill*, 21 June 2021, thehill.com/changing-america/opinion/559457-the-roots-of-our-child-care-crisis-are-in-the-legacy-of-slavery/.
4. Mintz, Steven. *Huck's Raft: A History of American Childhood*. Cambridge, MA: Belknap Press of Harvard University Press, 2004.
5. Stockstill, Casey. *False Starts: The Segregated Lives of Preschoolers*. New York: NYU Press, 2023.
6. Williams, Rachel E. "Uncovering the Role of Early Childhood in Black Women's Clubs Work towards Racial and Gender Justice." *Center for the Study of Child Care Employment*, 15 Sept. 2022, cscce.berkeley.edu/publications/brief/the-role-of-early-childhood-in-black-womens-clubs-work/.
7. Cahan, Emily. *Past Caring: A History of U.S. Preschool Care and Education for the Poor, 1820–1965*. National Center for Children in Poverty (Columbia University), 1989.
8. Michel, Sonya. *Children's Interests/Mothers' Rights: The Shaping of America's Child Care Policy*. New Haven and London: Yale University Press, 2000.
9. Roth, William. "The Politics of Daycare: The Comprehensive Child Development Act of 1971." Dec. 1976, University of Wisconsin-Madison, Institute for Research on Poverty, https://www.irp.wisc.edu/publications/dps/pdfs/dp36976.pdf.
10. Greenberg, Erica, and Monarrez, Tomas. *Segregated from the Start: Comparing Segregation in Early Childhood and K–12 Education*. The Urban Institute. 1 Oct. 2019, https://www.urban.org/features/segregated-start.
11. Babbs Hollett, K., and Frankenberg, E. "A Critical Analysis of Racial Disparities in ECE Subsidy Funding." *Education Policy Analysis Archives*, vol. 30, Feb. 2022, p. 14, doi:10.14507/epaa.30.7003.
12. Ibid.
13. Stockstill, Casey. *False Starts: The Segregated Lives of Preschoolers*. New York: NYU Press, 2023.
14. Administration for Children and Families, U.S. Department of Health and Human Services. "Head Start Program Facts: Fiscal Year 2022." https://eclkc.ohs.acf.hhs.gov/data-ongoing-monitoring/article/head-start-program-facts-fiscal-year-2022.
15. The Century Foundation. "The Benefits of Socioeconomically and Racially Integrated Schools and Classrooms." 29 April 2019, https://tcf.org/content/facts/the-benefits-of-socioeconomically-and-racially-integrated-schools-and-classrooms/.
16. Rothstein, Richard. *The Color of Law: A Forgotten History of How Our Government Segregated America*. New York and London: Liveright Publishing Corporation, A Division of W.W. Norton & Company, 2017.
17. Cain Miller, Claire. "The Motherhood Penalty vs. the Fatherhood Bonus." *The New York Times*, 6 Sept. 2014, www.nytimes.com/2014/09/07/upshot/a-child-helps-your-career-if-youre-a-man.html.
18. Calarco, Jessica. *Holding It Together: How Women Became America's Safety Net*. New York: Penguin Random House, 2024.

19. Valle-Gutierrez, Laura. "New Data Demonstrates Mothers' Retirement Insecurity." The Century Foundation. 26 April 2023, https://tcf.org/content/report/new-data-demonstrates-mothers-retirement-insecurity/#easy-footnote-bottom-8-52680.
20. Harrington Conner, Dana. "Financial Freedom: Women, Money, and Domestic Abuse," *Wm. & Mary J. Women & L*, vol. 20, 2014, p. 339, https://scholarship.law.wm.edu/wmjowl/vol20/iss2/4.
21. Wiens, Jason, and Kumar, Michelle. "Working Mothers Want to Start and Grow Businesses—but Barriers Exist | Bipartisan Policy Center." Bipartisan Policy Center, 9 June 2022, bipartisanpolicy.org/blog/working-mothers-want-to-start-and-grow-businesses-but-barriers-exist/.
22. Ruppanner, Leah. *Motherlands: How States Push Mothers Out of Employment*. Temple University Press, 2020.
23. Evans, Alice. "Does it really matter if female labor force participation is miscounted?" *The Brookings Institution*, 15 July 2022, https://www.brookings.edu/articles/does-it-really-matter-if-female-labor-force-participation-is-miscounted/.
24. Smith, Linda, et al. "Characteristics of the Child Care Workforce." Bipartisan Policy Center, 8 Feb. 2021, https://bipartisanpolicy.org/blog/characteristics-of-the-child-care-workforce.
25. Cohn, D'Vera, et al. "After Decades of Decline, A Rise in Stay-at-Home Mothers." *Pew Research Center*, 8 April 2014, https://www.pewresearch.org/social-trends/2014/04/08/after-decades-of-decline-a-rise-in-stay-at-home-mothers.
26. Butcher, Kristin, et al. "The Labor Market for Childcare Workers." *Federal Reserve Bank of Chicago*, June 2024, https://www.chicagofed.org/publications/chicago-fed-insights/2024/childcare-labor-market.
27. Fisher, Philip. "Child Care Providers Experience High Levels of Anxiety and Depression." RAPID Survey (Stanford Center on Early Childhood). May 2024, https://rapidsurveyproject.com/our-research/child-care-providers-experience-high-levels-of-anxiety-and-depression.
28. McMillian, Tonia. "COMMENTARY: We Must Take Better Care of Our Home-Based Child Care Providers." *EdSource*, 9 April 2024, edsource.org/2024/we-must-take-better-care-of-our-home-based-child-care-providers/709363.
29. Rummler, Orion. "Washington, D.C., Offers Financial Relief to Local Child Care Workers." *The 19th*, 20 Sept. 2022, 19thnews.org/2022/09/child-care-workers-washington-dc-payments/.
30. Anbar-Shaheen, Ruqiyyah. "DC Announces Free Health Insurance for Child Care Workers and their Families." *Under 3 DC*. 20 Sept. 2022, https://under3dc.org/healthcareforchildcareworkers/.
31. Schochet, Owen. "Jobs in the Balance: The Early Employment Impacts of Washington, DC's Early Childhood Educator Pay Equity Fund." *Mathematica*, Sept. 2023, https://www.mathematica.org/publications/jobs-in-the-balance-the-early-employment-impacts-of-washington-dcs-early-childhood-educator-pay.
32. Berman, Emily. "D.C. Is Giving Preschool Teachers a Pay Bump. Here's How It's Making a Difference to Them." *DCist*, 14 March 2023, dcist.com/story/23/03/14/d-c-is-giving-preschool-teachers-a-pay-bump-heres-how-its-making-a-difference-to-them/.
33. Miller, Claire Cain. "The World 'Has Found a Way to Do This': The U.S. Lags on Paid Leave." *The New York Times*, 25 Oct. 2021, www.nytimes.com/2021/10/25/upshot/paid-leave-democrats.html.
34. National Partnership for Women and Families. "Paid Family and Medical Leave: A Racial Justice Issue—And Opportunity." Aug. 2018, https://nationalpartnership.org/wp-content/uploads/2023/02/Paid-Family-and-Medical-Leave-A-Racial-Justice-Issue-and-Opportunity.pdf.
35. Hidalgo-Padilla, Liliana, et al. "Association between Maternity Leave Policies and Postpartum Depression: A Systematic Review." *Archives of Women's Mental Health*, 17 July 2023, https://doi.org/10.1007/s00737-023-01350-z.
36. Cui, Jiashan and Natzke, Luke. Early Childhood Program Participation: 2019 (NCES 2020-075REV). May 2021. National Center for Education Statistics, Institute of Education Sciences, U.S. Department of Education, https://nces.ed.gov/pubs2020/2020075REV.pdf.
37. Stevens, Katharine B., and Erickson, Jenet. *Universal Child Care: A Risky Experiment with Our Nation's Children*. Institute for Family Studies, 27 April 2021, ifstudies.org/blog/universal-child-care-a-risky-experiment-with-our-nations-children.

38. Li, Weilin, et al. "Timing of High-Quality Child Care and Cognitive, Language, and Preacademic Development." *Developmental Psychology*, vol. 49, no. 8, 2013, pp. 1440–1451, https://doi.org/10.1037/a0030613.
39. Statistics Canada. "Parental Leave, 1997 to 2022." June 13, 2023, https://www150.statcan.gc.ca/n1/pub/14-28-0001/2023001/article/00009-eng.htm.
40. Thévenon, Olivier. "Family Policies in OECD Countries: A Comparative Analysis." *Population and Development Review*, vol. 37, no. 1, March 2011, pp. 57–87, https://doi.org/10.1111/j.1728-4457.2011.00390.x.
41. The Link Group and CandL. *CandL Listening Session Analysis: Understanding Barriers and Facilitators to Childcare From the Voices of Parents and Providers Across 33 Counties in North Carolina*. Feb. 2024, https://buildthefoundation.org/wp-content/uploads/2024/02/CandL-Listening-Session-Analysis-Full-Report.pdf.
42. Cohn, D'Vera, et al. "After Decades of Decline, A Rise in Stay-at-Home Mothers." *Pew Research Center*, 8 April 2014, www.pewresearch.org/social-trends/2014/04/08/after-decades-of-decline-a-rise-in-stay-at-home-mothers/.
43. VerBruggen, Robert, and Wang, Wendy. "The Real Housewives of America: Dad's Income and Mom's Work." *Institute for Family Studies*, 23 Jan. 2019, ifstudies.org/blog/the-real-housewives-of-america-dads-income-and-moms-work.
44. Murray, Stephanie H. "If We Value Homemaking, We Should Rethink Welfare Reform." *Public Discourse*, 20 March 2024, www.thepublicdiscourse.com/2024/03/92983/.
45. O'Neal Parker, Lonnae. "Four Years Later, Feminists Split by Michelle Obama's 'Work' as First Lady." *Washington Post*, 18 May 2023, www.washingtonpost.com/lifestyle/style/feminists-split-by-michelle-obamas-work-as-first-lady/2013/01/18/be3d636e-5e5e-11e2-9940-6fc488f3fecd_story.html.
46. Greco, Ivana. "Supporting American Homemakers." American Compass, 2023, americancompass.org/rebuilding-american-capitalism/supportive-communities/supporting-american-homemakers/.
47. Staples, Brent. "Opinion | How the Suffrage Movement Betrayed Black Women." *The New York Times*, 28 July 2018, www.nytimes.com/2018/07/28/opinion/sunday/suffrage-movement-racism-black-women.html.
48. Skocpol, Theda. *Protecting Soldiers and Mothers: The Political Origins of Social Policy in the United States*. Cambridge, MA: Harvard University Press, 1992.
49. Romain, Alana. "Turns Out, Millennial Dads Might Be More Involved in Raising Their Kids than Gen X Dads." *Romper*, 5 April 2018, www.romper.com/p/are-millennial-dads-more-active-in-child-rearing-than-gen-x-dads-there-are-some-important-differences-8692290.
50. Bustillo, Ximena. "With an Eye on Working Families, Democrats Launch the Congressional Dads Caucus." *NPR*, 28 Jan. 2023, www.npr.org/2023/01/28/1151723607/democrats-congressional-dads-caucus.
51. Ohanian, Alexis. "Alexis Ohanian: Paternity Leave Was Crucial after the Birth of My Child, and Every Father Deserves It." *The New York Times*, 15 April 2020, www.nytimes.com/2020/04/15/parenting/alexis-ohanian-paternity-leave.html.
52. Peck, Emily. "At the CEO level, women finally outnumber men named John." *Axios*. 27 April 2023, https://www.axios.com/2023/04/27/women-men-ceo-sp500.
53. Meek, Shantel, et al. *Equity is Quality, Quality is Equity: Operationalizing Equity in Quality Rating and Improvement Systems*. The Children's Equity Project (Arizona State University), June 2022, https://childandfamilysuccess.asu.edu/sites/default/files/2022-06/QRIS-report-062122.pdf.
54. Babbs Hollett, Karen, and Frankenberg, Erica. "A Critical Analysis of Racial Disparities in ECE Subsidy Funding." *Education Policy Analysis Archives*, vol. 30, no. 14, 8 Feb. 2022, https://doi.org/10.14507/epaa.30.7003.
55. Slaughter, Anne-Marie. *Unfinished Business: Women, Men, Work, Family*. New York: Random House, 2015.
56. Michel, Sonya. "Will Federal Child Care Support Vanish Again?" *The American Prospect*, 29 July 2020, prospect.org/health/will-federal-child-care-support-vanish-again/.
57. Cohen, Sally S. *Championing Child Care*. New York: Columbia University Press, Oct. 2001.

Chapter 7

1. Dialogues in Action. "Multnomah County Preschool for All: Pathway to Success" August 2021, https://multco-web7-psh-files-usw2.s3-us-west-2.amazonaws.com/s3fs-public/PFA%20REPORT_0.pdf.
2. Wong, Rose. "Multnomah County Opening Varying Tuition-Free Pre-Ks for 100s of Kids on Its Way toward Preschool for All." *The Oregonian/Oregonlive*, 12 Aug. 2022, www.oregonlive.com/education/2022/08/multnomah-county-opening-varying-tuition-free-pre-ks-for-100s-of-kids-on-its-way-toward-preschool-for-all.html.
3. Schulte, Brigid, and Panfil, Yuliya. "Opinion: The True Victims of the US Eviction Crisis." *CNN*, 14 Feb. 2024, www.cnn.com/2024/02/14/opinions/child-care-crisis-eviction-housing-affordability-panfil-schulte/index.html.
4. Graetz, Nick, et al. "A Comprehensive Demographic Profile of the US Evicted Population." *Proceedings of the National Academy of Sciences of the United States of America*, vol. 120, no. 41, 2 Oct. 2023, https://doi.org/10.1073/pnas.2305860120.
5. Covert, Bryce. "Why Landlords Target Mothers for Eviction." *The New Republic*, 16 March 2021, newrepublic.com/article/161578/landlords-target-mothers-eviction-crisis-covid.
6. Mattingly, Marybeth J., and Wimer, Christopher T. "Child Care Expenses Push Many Families Into Poverty." University of New Hampshire, Carsey School of Public Policy. Spring 2017, https://scholars.unh.edu/cgi/viewcontent.cgi?article=1303&context=carsey.
7. Chen, Stefanos. "Poverty Has Soared in New York, with Children Bearing the Brunt." *The New York Times*, 21 Feb. 2024, www.nytimes.com/2024/02/21/nyregion/nyc-poverty.html.
8. Freeman, Amanda, and Dodson, Lisa. *Getting Me Cheap: How Low-Wage Work Traps Women and Girls in Poverty*. The New Press, 29 Nov. 2022.
9. Barnes, Michelle. "2018 Child Maltreatment Fatality Annual Report." *Colorado Department of Human Services (Division of Quality Assurance & Quality Improvement)*. 2018.
10. Ibid.
11. Michel, Sonya. "Will Federal Child Care Support Vanish Again?" *The American Prospect*, 29 July 2020, prospect.org/health/will-federal-child-care-support-vanish-again/.
12. "Dollar Store." *Maid*, Season 1, Episode 1.
13. Malik, Rasheed. "The Build Back Better Act Substantially Expands Child Care Assistance." *Center for American Progress*, 2 Dec. 2021, https://www.americanprogress.org/article/the-build-back-better-act-substantially-expands-child-care-assistance/.
14. National Women's Law Center. "An Increasing Number of Parents Seek Child Care during Non-Standard Hours." 15 March 2018, https://nwlc.org/an-increasing-number-of-parents-seek-child-care-during-non-standard-hours/.
15. Schilder, Diane, Lou, Cary, and Wagner, Laura. "Child Care Use for Young Children during Nontraditional Hours: Findings from Analysis of the 2019 National Survey of Early Care and Education." *The Urban Institute*, May 2023, https://www.urban.org/research/publication/child-care-use-young-children-during-nontraditional-hours.
16. Savage, Maddy. "Night Nurseries: Sweden's Round-The-Clock Childcare." *BBC News*, 19 March 2013, www.bbc.com/news/magazine-21784716.
17. Haspel, Elliot. "FILM REVIEW: 'Through the Night': An Intimate Portrait of Family Child Care Reveals Deeper Truths about Caregiving." *Early Learning Nation*, 4 March 2021, earlylearningnation.com/2021/03/film-review-through-the-night-an-intimate-portrait-of-family-child-care-reveals-deeper-truths-about-caregiving/.
18. Small, Mario Luis. *Unanticipated Gains: Origins of Network Inequality in Everyday Life*. New York: Oxford University Press, 2010.
19. Princeton University and Columbia University. "About the Future of Families and Child Wellbeing Study." https://ffcws.princeton.edu/about.
20. Claridge, Tristan. "Social Capital And Poverty Alleviation." *Institute for Social Capital*. 19 Jan. 2020, https://www.socialcapitalresearch.com/social-capital-and-poverty-alleviation/.
21. Bruenig, Matt. "Who Are the Poor in 2021 and 2022?" *People's Policy Project*. 18 Sept. 2023, https://www.peoplespolicyproject.org/2023/09/18/who-are-the-poor-in-2021-and-2022/.
22. Kimberlin, Sara, and Berrick, Jill Duerr. "Poor for How Long? Chronic versus Transient Child Poverty in the United States." *Children's Well-Being*, vol. 10, 1 Jan. 2015, pp. 141–158, https://doi.org/10.1007/978-3-319-17506-5_9.

23. Federal Reserve Bank of St. Louis. "Layoffs and Discharges: Total Nonfarm." Time Series (2000–2024), https://fred.stlouisfed.org/series/JTSLDL.
24. American Association of Community Colleges. "DataPoints: Education, Income and Poverty." 26 Oct. 2021, https://www.aacc.nche.edu/2021/10/26/datapoints-education-income-and-poverty/.
25. Williams, Brittani, et al. "For Student Parents, The Biggest Hurdles to A Higher Education are Costs and Finding Child Care." *The Education Trust and Generation Hope.* Aug. 2022, https://edtrust.org/wp-content/uploads/2014/09/For-Student-Parents-The-Biggest-Hurdles-to-a-Higher-Education-Are-Cost-and-Finding-Child-Care-August-2022.pdf.
26. Contreras-Mendez, Susana, and Reichlin Cruse, Lindsey. "Busy With Purpose: Lessons for Education and Policy Leaders from Returning Student Parents." *Institute for Women's Policy Research.* March 2021, https://iwpr.org/wp-content/uploads/2021/03/Busy-With-Purpose-v2b.pdf.
27. Forster, Michael, and Verbist, Gerlinde. "Money or Kindergarten? Distributive Effects of Cash versus In-Kind Family Transfers for Young Children." *OECD Social, Employment and Migration Working Papers,* 11 Sept. 2012, https://doi.org/10.1787/5k92vxbgpmnt-en.
28. Chen, Stefanos. "Poverty Has Soared in New York, with Children Bearing the Brunt." *The New York Times,* 21 Feb. 2024, www.nytimes.com/2024/02/21/nyregion/nyc-poverty.html.
29. Mader, Jackie. "Free Child Care Exists in America—If You Cross Paths with the Right Philanthropist." *The Hechinger Report.* 7 March 2024, https://hechingerreport.org/free-child-care-exists-in-america-if-you-cross-paths-with-the-right-philanthropist/.
30. Barr, Andrew, and Gibbs, Chloe R. "Breaking the Cycle? Intergenerational Effects of an Anti-Poverty Program in Early Childhood." *Journal of Political Economy,* vol. 130, no. 12, 9 May 2022, https://doi.org/10.1086/720764.
31. Herbst, Chris M. "Universal Child Care, Maternal Employment, and Children's Long-Run Outcomes: Evidence from the US Lanham Act of 1940." *Journal of Labor Economics,* vol. 35, no. 2, April 2017, pp. 519–564, https://doi.org/10.1086/689478.
32. Desmond, Matthew. *Poverty, by America.* Crown Publishing Group, 21 March 2023.

Chapter 8

1. Petters, Mike. "Remarks as Prepared, for the Early Childhood Leadership Summit." Early Childhood Leadership Summit, 25 June 2019, New Orleans, LA, https://hunt-institute.org/resources/2019/06/mike-petters-remarks-as-prepared-for-the-early-childhood-leadership-summit/.
2. Morrissey, Taryn. "The Effects of Early Care and Education on Children's Health." *Health Affairs,* 25 April 2019, https://doi.org/10.1377/hpb20190325.519221.
3. Krebs, Ronald R., and Ralston, Robert. "Patriotism or Paychecks: Who Believes What about Why Soldiers Serve." *Armed Forces & Society,* vol. 48, no. 1, 15 April 2020, p. 0095327X2091716, https://doi.org/10.1177/0095327x20917166.
4. U.S. Government Accountability Office. "Military Child Care: DOD Efforts to Provide Affordable, Quality Care for Families." GAO-23-105518, Feb. 2023, https://www.gao.gov/assets/gao-23-105518.pdf.
5. Ibid.
6. Lopez, C. Todd. "Austin Pledges to 'Ease the Load' for Service Members." U.S. Department of Defense News. 22 Sept. 2022, https://www.defense.gov/News/News-Stories/Article/Article/3167740/austin-pledges-to-ease-the-load-for-service-members/.
7. Lohr, Alexandra. "Defense Department Raises Rates in Effort to Hire, Retain, Child Care Workers." *Federal News Network,* 27 Dec. 2022, federalnewsnetwork.com/defense-main/2022/12/defense-department-raises-rates-in-effort-to-hire-retain-child-care-workers/.
8. Serbu, Jared. "Air Force Discovers Higher Salaries Aren't the Only Answer to Its Child Care Shortage." *Federal News Network,* 9 Oct. 2023, federalnewsnetwork.com/federal-report/2023/10/air-force-discovers-higher-salaries-arent-the-only-answer-to-its-child-care-shortage/.
9. Pettypiece, Shannon. "America's Child Care Shortage is Pushing Military Families to a Breaking Point." 27 May 2024, https://www.nbcnews.com/politics/politics-news/americas-child-care-shortage-pushing-military-families-breaking-point-rcna149072.

10. Obis, Anastasia. "DoD Needs Comprehensive Approach to Child Care." *Federal News Network*, 5 Jan. 2024, federalnewsnetwork.com/defense-main/2024/01/dod-needs-comprehensive-approach-to-child-care/.
11. National Academies of Sciences, Engineering, and Medicine. *Transforming the Financing of Early Care and Education*. 2018. The National Academies Press, https://doi.org/10.17226/24984.
12. Nicastro, Luke A. "The U.S. Defense Industrial Base: Background and Issues for Congress." Congressional Research Service, 12 Oct. 2023, https://crsreports.congress.gov/product/pdf/R/R47751.
13. Ibid.
14. Doubleday, Justin. "NSA Getting 'A Lot More Flexible' Under Major Workforce Initiative." Federal News Network. 5 Oct. 2023, https://federalnewsnetwork.com/inside-ic/2023/10/nsa-getting-a-lot-more-flexible-under-major-workforce-initiative/.
15. Jones, Seth G., and Palmer, Alexander. "Rebuilding the Arsenal of Democracy: The U.S. and China Defense Industrial Bases in an Era of Great Power Competition." Center for Strategic & International Studies, March 2024, https://www.csis.org/analysis/china-outpacing-us-defense-industrial-base.
16. Shenker-Osorio, Anat. *Don't Buy It: The Trouble with Talking Nonsense about the Economy*. New York: The Perseus Books Group, 2012.
17. Versteeg, Krista. "It's Time to Talk about Food and Agriculture Security." U.S. Department of Homeland Security, 21 March 2023, https://www.dhs.gov/science-and-technology/news/2023/03/21/its-time-talk-about-food-and-agriculture-security.
18. Haspel, Elliot. "Child Care Down on the Farm." Early Learning Nation. 1 Aug. 2024, https://earlylearningnation.com/2024/08/child-care-on-the-farm/.
19. Mulhollem, Jeff. "Farm Families' Childcare Challenges Impacting Farm Businesses, Research Suggests." Penn State University. 30 July 2024, https://www.psu.edu/news/research/story/farm-families-childcare-challenges-impacting-farm-businesses-research-suggests/.
20. Vespa, Jonathan, et al. "Demographic Turning Points for the United States: Population Projections for 2020 to 2060." U.S. Census Bureau, March 2018 (Rev. Feb. 2020), https://www.census.gov/content/dam/Census/library/publications/2020/demo/p25-1144.pdf.
21. Talavar, Sasha. "Russia's War Is a Failed Answer to Its Demographic Crisis." *Jacobin*, 23 April 2023, jacobin.com/2023/04/russia-ukraine-war-putin-demographic-crisis-social-reproduction-biopolitical-imperialism.
22. Eberstadt, Nicholas, and Abramsky, Evan. "America's Education Crisis Is a National Security Threat." *Foreign Affairs*, 26 Sept. 2022, www.foreignaffairs.com/world/america-education-crisis-national-security-threat.
23. Cuban, Larry, and Tyack, David B. *Tinkering toward Utopia: A Century of Public School Reform*. Cambridge, MA: Harvard University Press, 2009.
24. e.g. Haertel, E. "Reliability and Validity of Inferences About Teacher Based on Student Test Scores." Educational Testing Service, 2013, https://www.ets.org/s/pdf/23497_Angoff%20Report-web.pdf. Goldhaber, D., et. al. "Teacher Effectiveness and the Achievement of Washington Students in Mathematics." Center for Education Data & Research, 2010, http://www.cedr.us/papers/working/CEDR%20WP%202010-6_Teacher%20Effectiveness%20in%20WA%20%2812-7-10%29.pdf.
25. Council for Opportunity in Education. "Estimated Bachelor's Degree Attainment by age 24 for Dependent Family Members by Family Income Quartile: 1970 to 2020." https://coenet.org/indicators-2022-data-and-charts/.
26. Tough, Paul. *The Inequality Machine: How College Divides Us*. Boston: Houghton Mifflin Harcourt, 2019.
27. Peters, Scott. "Providing Child Care for Police Officers Act of 2023." H.R.2722. Introduced 19 April 2023 https://www.congress.gov/bill/118th-congress/house-bill/2722/text.
28. Office of Senator Kirsten Gillibrand. "In Albany, As NY Police Departments Face Unprecedented Staffing Shortages, Senator Gillibrand Announces Bipartisan Bill To Provide $24 Million In Funding For Child Care For The Police Workforce." 10 May 2024, https://www.gillibrand.senate.gov/news/press/release/in-albany-as-ny-police-departments-face-unprecedented-staffing-shortages-senator-gillibrand-announces-bipartisan-bill-to-provide-24-million-in-funding-for-child-care-for-the-police-workforce/.

29. Bishop, Sandra. "High-Quality Early Care & Education is Crime Prevention." Fight Crime: Invest in Kids (Council for a Strong America). April 2022, https://www.strongnation.org/articles/1892-high-quality-early-care-education-is-crime-prevention.
30. Willits, Dale, et al. "Schools, Neighborhood Risk Factors, and Crime." *Crime & Delinquency*, vol. 59, no. 2, 13 Jan. 2013, pp. 292–315, https://doi.org/10.1177/0011128712470991.
31. Ibid.
32. Kirk, David S. "Sampson, Robert J.: Collective Efficacy Theory." *Encyclopedia of Criminological Theory*, 2010, https://doi.org/10.4135/9781412959193.n220.
33. Small, Mario Luis. *Unanticipated Gains: Origins of Network Inequality in Everyday Life*. New York: Oxford University Press, 2010.
34. Klinenberg, Eric. *Palaces for the People: How Social Infrastructure Can Help Fight Inequality, Polarization, and the Decline of Civic Life*. New York: Broadway Books, 2018.
35. Hilber, Christian A. L., and Mayer, Christopher. "Why Do Households without Children Support Local Public Schools? Linking House Price Capitalization to School Spending." *Journal of Urban Economics*, vol. 65, no. 1, Jan. 2009, pp. 74–90, https://doi.org/10.1016/j.jue.2008.09.001.
36. National Center on Early Childhood Quality Assurance (U.S. Administration for Children and Families), Addressing the Decreasing Number of Family Child Care Providers in the United States. May 2020, https://childcareta.acf.hhs.gov/resource/addressing-decreasing-number-family-child-care-providers-united-states.

Chapter 9

1. Abbott, Sam. "The Child Care Economy." Washington Center for Equitable Growth. 15 Sept. 2021, https://equitablegrowth.org/research-paper/the-child-care-economy/.
2. Kashen, Julie, et al. "How States Would Benefit If Congress Truly Invested in Child Care and Pre-K." *The Century Foundation*, 21 March 2022, tcf.org/content/report/how-states-would-benefit-if-congress-truly-invested-in-child-care-and-pre-k/.
3. U.S. Chamber of Commerce Foundation. "Untapped Potential: Economic Impact of Childcare Breakdowns in the U.S." 30 Nov. 2021, www.uschamberfoundation.org/solutions/early-childhood-and-k-12-education/untapped-potential.
4. Cohen, Rachel M. "The Child Care Cliff that Wasn't." *Vox*. 14 May 2024.
5. Cripps, Charlotte. "Muddling: How Ad Hoc Childcare Became the New Normal for Stressed Parents Like Me." *The Independent*, 21 May 2024, https://www.msn.com/en-gb/lifestyle/family-relationships/muddling-how-ad-hoc-childcare-become-the-new-normal-for-stressed-parents-like-me.
6. Nickelsburg, Monica. "Hybrid Revolution Leads to Surge of Working Moms. But Can They Have It All?" *KUOW (NPR)*. 6 March 2024, https://www.kuow.org/stories/hybrid-revolution-leads-to-surge-of-working-moms-but-can-they-have-it-all.
7. Stevens, Katharine B. "Workforce of Today, Workforce of Tomorrow: The Business Case for High-Quality Child Care." *U.S. Chamber of Commerce Foundation*. 21 June 2017.
8. Haspel, Elliot. "Elliot's Provocations: The Minimum Viable Child Care Fallacy—Early Learning Nation." Earlylearningnation.com, 6 July 2023, earlylearningnation.com/2023/07/elliots-provocations-the-minimum-viable-child-care-fallacy/.
9. Haspel, Elliot. "Elliot's Provocations: The Minimum Viable Child Care Fallacy." Early Learning Nation. 6 Jul 2023, https://earlylearningnation.com/2023/07/elliots-provocations-the-minimum-viable-child-care-fallacy/.
10. National Academies of Sciences, Engineering, and Medicine. *Transforming the Financing of Early Care and Education*. 2018. The National Academies Press, https://doi.org/10.17226/24984.
11. Audretsch, David B, et al. *Entrepreneurship and Economic Growth*. New York: Oxford University Press, 2006.
12. Staff writers. "Europe's Technology Startups Are Doing Just Fine." *The Economist*, 7 Dec. 2023, www.economist.com/business/2023/12/07/europes-technology-startups-are-doing-just-fine.
13. Perry, Mark J. "Understanding America's Enormous $20.6T Economy by Comparing US Metro Area GDPs to Entire Countries." *American Enterprise Institute*, 18 Dec. 2019, https://www.aei.org/carpe-diem/understanding-americas-enormous-20-6t-economy-by-comparing-us-metro-area-gdps-to-entire-countries/.

14. Arora, Ashish, et al. "Why the U.S. Innovation Ecosystem Is Slowing Down." *Harvard Business Review*, 26 Nov. 2019, hbr.org/2019/11/why-the-u-s-innovation-ecosystem-is-slowing-down.
15. Kobe, Kathryn, and Schwinn, Richard. "Small Business GDP 1998–2014." *U.S. Small Business Administration*. Dec. 2018, https://advocacy.sba.gov/wp-content/uploads/2018/12/Small-Business-GDP-1998-2014.pdf.
16. Small Business Majority. "Opinion Poll: Small Businesses Support Policy Solutions to Address Our Nation's Childcare Challenges." 9 April 2024, https://smallbusinessmajority.org/sites/default/files/research-reports/small-business-childcare-poll-report.pdf.
17. Carrazana, Chabeli. "Lack of Child Care is Preventing Small Businesses from Growing, Survey Finds." *The 19th*, 20 June 2024, https://19thnews.org/2024/06/small-businesses-struggle-lack-of-child-care-options/.
18. National Women's Business Council. "2022 Annual Report: By The Numbers." 2022, https://www.nwbc.gov/annual-reports/2022/#byTheNumbers.
19. United WE National Commission on Childcare and Women's Entrepreneurship. "The American Economy Depends on Entrepreneurs. Entrepreneurs Depend on Childcare." United WE, June 2024, https://united-we.org/childcare.
20. Haspel, Elliot. "Questioning the Promise of Employer-Sponsored Child Care Benefits." *New America Better Life Lab*, 22 Feb. 2024, https://www.newamerica.org/better-life-lab/reports/questioning-the-promise-of-employer-sponsored-child-care-benefits/.
21. Ibid.
22. Ibid.
23. Haspel, Elliot. "A Tragically American Approach to the Child-Care Crisis." *The Atlantic*, 2 June 2023, https://www.theatlantic.com/family/archive/2023/06/child-care-united-states-employer-based/674269/.
24. Reisman, Barbara, et al. "Child Care: The Bottom Line." *Child Care Action Campaign*. 1988.
25. Jarvik, Elaine. "The Bottom Line for Business: Quality Child Care Makes Sense." *Deseret News*, 15 April 1988.
26. Stevens, Katharine B. "Workforce of Today, Workforce of Tomorrow: The Business Case for High-Quality Child Care." *U.S. Chamber of Commerce Foundation*. 21 June 2017, https://www.uschamberfoundation.org/education/workforce-of-today-workforce-of-tomorrow.
27. Quell, Brit, et al. "Act 76 Leads to Newfound Stability for Child Care Programs and Families." *Rutland Herald*, 3 May 2024, https://www.rutlandherald.com/opinion/commentary/quell-et-all-act-76-leads-to-newfound-stability-for-child-care-programs-and-families/article_f1144760-cf4d-5a0f-8dab-f6a58de5b09c.html.
28. Vermont Senate Committee on Economic Development, Housing, and General Issues. "Hearing on Act 76." 19 Jan. 2023, https://www.youtube.com/watch?v=Bv6adkklVos.
29. Teso, Edoardo. "What Drives U.S. Corporate Elites' Campaign Contribution Behavior?" CEPR Discussion Paper No. DP16966 (SSRN), 1 Jan. 2022, https://ssrn.com/abstract=4026872.
30. Oprysko, Caitlin. "Chamber Launches Ads Targeting Manchin, Hoping to Kill Build Back Better." *Politico*, 16 Dec. 2021, https://www.politico.com/news/2021/12/16/chamber-ad-manchin-build-back-better-525129.
31. Haspel, Elliot. "'The End User Is a Dollar Sign, It's Not a Child': How Private Equity and Shareholders Are Reshaping American Child Care." *Early Learning Nation*, 22 April 2024, https://earlylearningnation.com/2024/04/the-end-user-is-a-dollar-sign-its-not-a-child-how-private-equity-and-shareholders-are-reshaping-american-child-care/.
32. Ibid.
33. Goldstein, Dana. "Can Child Care Be a Big Business? Private Equity Thinks So." *The New York Times*, 16 Dec. 2022, www.nytimes.com/2022/12/16/us/child-care-centers-private-equity.html.
34. Ballou, Brendan. *Plunder: Private Equity's Plan to Pillage America*. PublicAffairs, 2023.
35. Ibid.
36. Haspel, Elliot. "'The End User Is a Dollar Sign, It's Not a Child': How Private Equity and Shareholders Are Reshaping American Child Care." *Early Learning Nation*, 22 April 2024, https://earlylearningnation.com/2024/04/the-end-user-is-a-dollar-sign-its-not-a-child-how-private-equity-and-shareholders-are-reshaping-american-child-care/.
37. Bodick, Nicole. "Blighted Horizons." *The Point Magazine*, 23 May 2024, https://thepointmag.com/examined-life/blighted-horizons/.

38. Lind, Michael. *Hell to Pay: How the Suppression of Wages is Destroying America*. New York: Penguin, 2023.
39. Pressler, Sam. "How Unpredictable Work Strains Family and Community Life: A Q&A with Harvard Sociologist and Shift Project Director, Danny Schneider." Connective Tissue (Substack). 2 May 2024, https://connectivetissue.substack.com/p/how-unpredictable-work-strains-family.
40. Robaton, Anna. "Unpredictable Work Schedule? Help May Be Coming." *CBS News*, 20 Dec. 2016, https://www.cbsnews.com/news/unpredictable-work-schedule-help-may-be-on-the-way/.
41. U.S. Bureau of Labor Statistics. "National Compensation Survey: Employee Benefits in the United States, March 2023," September 2023, https://www.bls.gov/ebs/publications/employee-benefits-in-the-united-states-march-2023.htm.
42. Williamson, Molly Weston. "The State of Paid Family and Medical Leave in the U.S. in 2024." *Center for American Progress*. 17 Jan. 2024, https://www.americanprogress.org/article/the-state-of-paid-family-and-medical-leave-in-the-u-s-in-2024/.
43. Ibid.
44. Balingit, Moriah. "More Republicans Back Spending on Child Care, Saying It's an Economic Issue" *The Associated Press*, 8 Feb. 2024, https://apnews.com/article/daycare-cost-child-care-assistance-0f7943d1b6f55dd4452ffd323e038a4f.

Chapter 10

1. Churchwell, Sarah. "A Brief History of the American Dream." George W. Bush Presidential Center, *The Catalyst*, Winter 2021, www.bushcenter.org/catalyst/state-of-the-american-dream/churchwell-history-of-the-american-dream.
2. VanderWeele, Tyler J. "On the Promotion of Human Flourishing." *Proceedings of the National Academy of Sciences*, vol. 114, no. 31, 1 Aug. 2017, pp. 8148–8156, www.pnas.org/content/114/31/8148#ref-8, https://doi.org/10.1073/pnas.1702996114.
3. Bonicalzi, Sofia, and Patrick Haggard. "From Freedom From to Freedom To: New Perspectives on Intentional Action." *Frontiers in Psychology*, vol. 10, 28 May 2019, https://doi.org/10.3389/fpsyg.2019.01143.
4. Institute for Women's Policy Research and Morning Consult. "Caregiving and Women in the Workforce." March 2024, https://iwpr.org/wp-content/uploads/2024/04/IWPR-MC-Caregiving-Poll-Deck-Mar-24.pdf.
5. Edwards, Kathryn Anne. "The Market Is Dictating How We Raise Our Kids." *Bloomberg*. 28 Aug 2023, https://www.bloomberg.com/opinion/articles/2023-08-28/the-child-care-market-is-dictating-how-we-raise-our-kids.
6. Black, Derek. "The Fundamental Right to Education." *Notre Dame Law Review*, vol. 94, no. 3, 1 Feb. 2019, p. 1059, scholarship.law.nd.edu/ndlr/vol94/iss3/2/.
7. Cohn, Jonathan. *The Ten Year War: Obamacare and the Unfinished Crusade for Universal Coverage*. MacMillan, 2021.
8. Heine, Von Friederike. "Germany Promises Daycare for All." *Der Spiegel International*. 1 Aug. 2013, https://www.spiegel.de/international/germany/law-goes-into-effect-requiring-child-care-for-most-german-children-a-914320.html.
9. Eddy, Melissa. "Germany's Top Court Strikes Down Federal Aid for Home Child Care." *The New York Times*, 21 July 2015, www.nytimes.com/2015/07/22/world/europe/germanys-top-court-strikes-down-federal-aid-for-home-child-care.html.
10. Sandel, Michael J. *The Tyranny of Merit: What's Become of the Common Good?* London: Allen Lane: An Imprint of Penguin Books, 2020.
11. Haspel, Elliot. "'The End User Is a Dollar Sign, It's Not a Child': How Private Equity and Shareholders Are Reshaping American Child Care." *Early Learning Nation*, 22 April 2024, https://earlylearningnation.com/2024/04/the-end-user-is-a-dollar-sign-its-not-a-child-how-private-equity-and-shareholders-are-reshaping-american-child-care/.
12. Haspel, Elliot, and Rosso, Randy. "Where Are Private Equity-Backed Child Care Programs Located?" *Capita*, 23 Oct. 2023, https://www.capita.org/capita-ideas/2023/10/23/where-are-private-equity-backed-child-care-programs-located..
13. Poo, Ai-Jen. *The Age of Dignity: Preparing for the Elder Boom in a Changing America*. The New Press, 2015.

14. Jackson, Tim. "From Davos to Reykjavík: Decoupling Wellbeing from Growth." Speech to the Wellbeing Economy Forum (Reykjavík, Iceland), June 2023, https://cusp.ac.uk/themes/aetw/tj-blog-wef-reykjavik/..
15. Kenway, Emily. *Who Cares: The Hidden Crisis of Caregiving, and How We Solve It.* Seal Press, 2023.
16. Haspel, Elliot. "Elliot's Provocations: The Minimum Viable Child Care Fallacy—Early Learning Nation." Earlylearningnation.com, 6 July 2023, earlylearningnation.com/2023/07/elliots-provocations-the-minimum-viable-child-care-fallacy/.
17. Strauss, Elissa. *When You Care: The Unexpected Magic of Caring for Others.* Gallery Books, 2024.
18. Shams, Shahrzad, et al. "The Cultural Contradictions of Neoliberalism: The Longing for an Alternative Order and the Future of Multiracial Democracy in an Age of Authoritarianism." *The Roosevelt Institute.* 18 April 2024, https://rooseveltinstitute.org/publications/the-cultural-contradictions-of-neoliberalism/..
19. Krznaric, Roman. *The Good Ancestor: How to Think Long-Term in a Short-Term World.* New York: The Experiment, 2020.
20. Weissbourd, Richard, et al. "On Edge: Understanding and Preventing Young Adults' Mental Health Challenges." *Making Caring Common* (Harvard Graduate School of Education), Oct. 2023, https://mcc.gse.harvard.edu/reports/on-edge..

Conclusion

1. Bhargava, Deepak, et al. "The Death of 'Deliverism.'" *Democracy Journal*, 22 June 2023, democracyjournal.org/arguments/the-death-of-deliverism/.
2. Cleveland, Gordon, et al. "What Is 'The Quebec Model' of Early Learning and Child Care?" *Policy Options Politiques (Institute for Research on Public Policy)*, 18 Feb. 2021, https://policyoptions.irpp.org/magazines/february-2021/what-is-the-quebec-model-of-early-learning-and-child-care/.
3. Rosenbaum, Eric. "A 'Deeply Misguided' Political Belief Is Weakening the Economy, Says Secretary of Commerce Gina Raimondo." *CNBC*, 18 April 2024, www.cnbc.com/2024/04/18/the-deeply-misguided-belief-hurting-economy-commerce-sec-raimondo.html.
4. Cassidy, Caroline. "Change is All About the Narrative." *Oxfam.* 15 Dec. 2020, https://views-voices.oxfam.org.uk/2020/12/change-is-all-about-the-narrative/.
5. Moore, Mik, and Sen, Rinku. "Funding Narrative Change." *Convergence Partnership*, Sept. 2022, https://convergencepartnership.org/wp-content/uploads/2022/09/Funding-Narrative-Change.pdf.
6. Shabo, Vicki. "Re-Scripting Gender, Work, Family, and Care: How TV and Film Can Help Create the Gender-Equitable, Caring Country We Need." *New America Better Life Lab.* 9 Sept. 2022, http://newamerica.org/better-life-lab/briefs/re-scripting-gender-work-family-and-care/.
7. Yglesias, Matthew. "The Median Voter is a 50-Something White person Who Didn't Go to College." *Slow Boring* (Substack), 22 Sept. 2021, https://www.slowboring.com/p/the-median-voter-is-a-50-something.
8. Haspel, Elliot. "The Problem With 'Affordable' Child Care." *The Atlantic*, 20 March 2024, https://www.theatlantic.com/family/archive/2024/03/child-care-reform-affordable-free/677802/.
9. Marr, Chuck, et al. "The 2017 Trump Tax Law Was Skewed to the Rich, Expensive, and Failed to Deliver on its Promises." Center for Budget and Policy Priorities. 13 June 2024, https://www.cbpp.org/research/federal-tax/the-2017-trump-tax-law-was-skewed-to-the-rich-expensive-and-failed-to-deliver.
10. Popli, Nik. "Exclusive: Ro Khanna's Bold Proposal to Cap Childcare at $10 a Day for Most Families." *TIME Magazine.* 26 Sept. 2024, https:/time.com/7024525/childcare-congress-bill/.
11. Wadia, Anna Shireen. "Care Is About Democracy—And It Wins at the Ballot Box." *Ms. Magazine.* 13 May 2024, https://msmagazine.com/2024/05/13/childcare-paid-leave-women-voters-2024-elections/.
12. Scott, Tim. "S.3899—Child Care and Development Block Grant Reauthorization Act of 2022." https://www.congress.gov/bill/117th-congress/senate-bill/3899.

Index

For the benefit of digital users, indexed terms that span two pages (e.g., 52–53) may, on occasion, appear on only one of those pages.

A
abortion rates, and childbearing choices, 58–59
Adams, James Truslow, 158
All I Really Need to Know I Learned in Kindergarten (Fulghum), 73–74
Arendt, Hannah, 75
Aries, Emilie, 146
Arnade, Chris, 31
associative life, and benefits of child care for, 30–32
Astuto, Jennifer, 73
au pairs, definition of, 7
Austin, Lloyd, 130

B
Balint, Becca, 70–71
ballot measure, Portland, Oregon, 112–113
Bandelj, Nina, 79
Barr, Andrew, 124–125
Baumol, William, and Baumol Effect, 9–10
Beatty, Barbara, 69
Becker, Gary
    the free-market family, 22
    human capital theory, 79
Becot, Florence, 133–134
Bellah, Robert, 22–23
Berg, Anastasia, 60
Berlin, Isaiah, 160
Bhargava, Deepak, 169
birth rates
    decline of, 60–61
    efforts to increase, 64
    and national security, 134–135
Blackwell, Angela Glover, 31–32
Bodick, Noelle, 152
Body Keeps the Score, The (van der Kolk), 82
Boston Infant School Society, 66–67
Bruenig, Matt, 121

Buchanan, Pat, 17–18
Burke, Edmund, 30
Bustillos, Patricia, 71

C
Cahan, Emily
    infant schools, 67
    nursery schools, 95–96
Calarco, Jessica
    faith communities and child care, 38
    family dynamics, 51
    "motherhood penalty," 99
    stay-at-home parents, 55
camps, summer, 85–87
Carrazana, Chabeli, 41
Challenge of Faith, The (Morgan & Steenland), 38–39
child care
    cases for investment in, 3–4, 11
    definitions of, 6–7
    drive-in daycare, 24–26
    economic argument for, 2–3
    expenses associated with, 8–11, 48–50, 56–61, 65–66, 109
    framework of arguments for, 3–5, 172–173
    as free-market commodity, 21–24
    holistic approach to, 12–13
    parental sacrifices for, 50–53
    private-equity-backed for-profit chains, 151–152
    provided by faith communities, 39–40
    racialized history of, 94–96
    rationale for investment in, 13–14
    settings for, 7–8
    stay-at-home parents, needs of, 53–56, 88–89, 105–107
    values *vs.* policy specifics, 169
Child Care and Development Block Grant Act, 115–116
child-care centers, definition of, 7

child-care policy, challenges to
    implementation, 173–175
child-care programs, as community
    assets, 40–43
childhood
    early childhood development, 78–79
    the "investible child," 78–79
    as modern invention, 77–78
    nurturance in, 82–83
    school readiness, problems with, 79–81
children
    effects on communities, 32
    in farming families, 133–134
    as a luxury good, 56–61
    and poverty, 113–115
    see also parenthood, and status and needs of
        children
Children's Bureau, 19–20
Chronicle of Philanthropy, 37
church attendance, effects of child care
    on, 37–41
civic engagement
    benefits of child care for, 31–32, 70–72
    readiness for, 73–74
climate change, childhood and, 89–91
Clinton, William Jefferson, 1–2
collective efficacy, implications of, 138–139
commodity, child care as a, 18–19
communities, vitality of
    child-care programs as community
        assets, 40–43
    consequences of available child care, 30–32
    departure of families, 32–34
    health and safety, effects of child care
        on, 34–37
    religious affiliations and faith
        communities, 37–40
Comprehensive Child Development Act of
    1971, 17–18, 96
conservatism, and publicly supported child
    care, 21–24
Constance, Paul, 60
Corbin, Ian Marcus, 27–28
Cosslett, Rhiannon Lucy, 43
costs, child-care associated, 8–11
COVID-19 pandemic, labor force in wake
    of, 10–11
"Cultural Contradictions of Neoliberalism,
    The" (Roosevelt Institute), 166
"curb-cut effects," 31–32

D
daycare, drive-in, 24–26
"defense industrial base" (DIB), child care in
    contributing entities, 132–133
definitions, of child care, 6–7
Department of Defense, child care for service
    members, 130–131
Dickens, Molly, 46–48
Dignity (Arnade), 31
Dittmar, Kelly, 70–71
Dodson, Lisa
    child care as welfare, 115–116
    children and poverty, 114
    parental work schedules, 117–118
Doepke, Matthias, 24
domestic labor, worth of unpaid, 55–56
Douglass, Frederick, 93–94
drive-in daycare, 24–26

E
Early Years Climate Action Task Force, 89–90
economic infrastructure, benefits of child care
    for, 141–143, 156–157
    business political muscle,
        leveraging, 150–153
    employers, role of, 147–150
    entrepreneurs and economic
        dynamism, 145–147
    labor force, 141
    maternal labor force, 141–143
    nuances of, 143–144
    paid-leave policies, 155–156
    private-equity-backed for-profit
        chains, 151–152
    scheduling predictability, 155
    workplaces, family-friendly, 153–156
economy, and arguments for child care, 2–3,
    78–79
education
    and civic readiness, 73–74
    higher education and fighting
        poverty, 122–123
    patriotic understanding of, 68–70
Education Trust, 122
Edwards, Kathryn Anne, 161
Eichner, Maxine, 23
employers, role of, 147–150
enslavement, and history of non-kin child
    care, 93–95
entrepreneurs, and economic
    infrastructure, 145–147
equity, gender and racial

Erickson, Jenet, 104
Essential Labor (Garbes), 27–28
Evans, Alice, 101
eviction, risk for children, 113–114
Eviction Lab, Princeton University, 113–114
executive functioning skills, development of, 73–74
expenses, child-care associated, 8–11, 48–50, 56–61, 65–66
    access to subsidies, 109
    as cause of poverty, 113–115
    and college enrollment, 122–123

F
faith communities
    benefits for wider community, 37–40
    child care provided by, 39–40
False Starts (Stockstill), 97–98
families
    child care and dynamics of, 50–53
    farming families, 133–134
families, health and stability of
    childbearing choices, 56–61
    expenses, child-care associated, 8–11, 48–50, 56–61, 65–66
    higher education and, 122–123
    parental mental health, 52
    sacrifices for child care, 50–53
    and stay-at-home parents, 53–56, 88–89, 105–107
    stress, child-care shortage and, 46–48
    supporting and strengthening, 45
family, friends, and neighbor (FFN) caregivers, 7
family child-care homes
    among rural populations, 42
    definition of, 7
family leave, and racial and gender equity, 103–105
farmers, food security and, 133–134
Finland, paid family leave in, 105
Folbre, Nancy, 65–66
food security, as matter of national security, 133–134
Fousekis, Natalie, 16
Fragile Families and Child Wellbeing Study, 119
Fraiberg, Selma, 88
framework, of arguments for child care, 3–5, 172–173
freedom, child care and, 158
    family freedoms, 159–162
    human flourishing, 159
    national purpose, 166–167
    and universal child care, 162–164
    valuing care, 164–166
Freeman, Amanda
    child care as welfare, 115–116
    children and poverty, 114
    parental work schedules, 117–118
Free-Market Family, The (Eichner), 23
Fulghum, Robert, 73–74

G
Garbes, Angela, 27–28
Gardener and the Carpenter, The (Gopnik), 83
gender equity, child care and, 110–111
    access to subsidies, 109
    child care workforce, 101–103
    enslavement, and history of non-kin child care, 93–95
    eviction risk for children, 113–114
    and family leave, 103–105
    opportunities for mothers, child care and, 99–101, 118–120
    racialized history of child care, 94–96
    segregation and child care programs, 96–99
    solidarity among parents, 107–110
    and stay-at-home parents, 105–107
Generation Hope, 122
Germany, right to child care in, 161–162
Getting Me Cheap (Freeman & Dodson), 114
Gibbs, Chloe, 124–125
Gill, Tim, 32
global competitiveness, and national security, 135–137
Gopnik, Alison
    intensive parenting, 84
    nurturance in childhood, 83
Greco, Ivana, 53–55
Greenberg, Erica, 96
Gross Graves, Fatima, 94–95
Guendelsberger, Emily, 50

H
Habits of the Heart (Bellah), 22–23
Hanbury, Harry, 169
Harvard University Human Flourishing Project, 13–14, 159
Head Start
    definition of, 7
    establishment of, 120–121
    intergenerational effects of enrollment, 124–125

and segregation in child care settings, 97–98
health, mental and physical among parents, 52–53
health and safety, effects of child care on, 34–37
Hell to Pay (Lind), 153
Henderson, Rob K., 82
Henley, Skye, 142
Hershey, Pennsylvania, 123–124
Huck's Raft (Mintz), 77–78
human flourishing, 159
Human Flourishing Project, 82, 159
Huntington Ingalls Industries (HII), 127–128
Hutner, Lucy, 46–48

I
"infant school" movement, 66–67
Institute for Family Studies, 106
integral human development, social teaching of, 82
Inwood, Shoshanah, 133–134

J
Jackson, Tim, 164
Jarboe, Jan, 26
Johnson, Glenna B., 16
Johnson, Lyndon, 21, 120–121
Johnson, Ron, 28–29
Johnson, Shavon, 114, 123

K
Kearney, Melissa, 51
Kelley, Florence, 62
Kennedy, Robert F., 13
KinderCare, 24–25, 151
Klinenberg, Eric, social infrastructure, 74, 138–139
Krznaric, Roman, 166

L
labor costs, 8–9
labor force, benefits of child care for, 141–143
Ladies Magazine, 1829 article, 67
Land, Stephanie, 116
Lanham Act
  intergenerational effects of child care centers, 125
  and World War II child-care centers, 15–16
law enforcement, child care and retention of, 34–35
Leffler, Brian, 150
Lelyveld, Joseph, 24–25

Levitsky, Sandra
  collective political action, 27
  history of universal pre-K systems, 69
Lind, Michael, 153
Lochner v. New York (1905), 64
Longman, Phillip, 59
Love, Money & Parenting (Zilibotti & Doepke), 85

M
Macron, Emmanuel, 64
Mader, Jackie
  promise of free child care, 123–124
  school readiness, 81
Maid, Netflix series, 116
Make a Circle, 41
market commodity, child care as a, 18–19
Martinez-Luna, Irisbeth, 112–113
Maternal Stress Project, 46
maternity leave, and racial and gender equity, 103–105
McMillian, Tonia, 101
mental health, declines among parents, 52
Michel, Sonya
  legacy of child care as welfare, 115
  residual welfare state, 110
military service, qualifications for, 128–129
Mintz, Steven
  childhood as modern invention, 77
  enslavement, and history of child care, 95
"Mommy Wars," rise of, 26–29
Monarrez, Tomas, 96
Morgan, Kimberly, 38–39
Motherlands (Ruppanner), 100
mothers, opportunities for, 99–101, 118–120
Mother Untitled organization, 54–55
Muller v. Oregon (1908), 64
Multnomah County, Oregon, child-care ballot measure, 112–113
Murray, Stephanie H.
  child care expenses, 49
  stay-at-home parents, 106

N
nannies, definition of, 7
National Partnership for Women and Families, 103–104
National School Readiness Indicators Initiative, 81
National Women's Law Center, 94–95
neighborhood security, implications of child care, 137–139

neoliberal philosophy, and publicly supported child care, 21–24
Nixon, Richard, 17–18, 21
Noem, Kristi, 28–29
No One Is Coming to Save Us podcast, 50
Novak, Michael, 45
nursery schools, and child care's racialized history, 95–96
nursing professionals, child care and retention of, 35–36

O

Obama, Barack, 1
O'Neal Parker, Lonnae, 107
On the Clock (Guendelsberger), 50
Orellana, Tracey, 123–124
Organization for Economic Co-operation and Development, 123
Origins of Totalitarianism, The (Arendt), 75

P

paid-leave policies, 155–156
Palaces to the People (Klinenberg), 138–139
Panfil, Yuliya, 113–114
parenthood, and status and needs of children, 91–92
  childhood as modern invention, 77–78
  climate change, 89–91
  early childhood development, 78–79
  "good enough" parenting, 87–89
  intensive parenting, 84–85, 87
  nurturance in childhood, 82–83
  parental work schedules, 116–118
  school readiness, 79–81
  stay-at-home parents, 88–89, 105–107
  summer camps, 85–87
parenthood, contributions of, 65–66
parents, as patriots
  case for, 62–64, 75–76
  civic readiness, 73–74
  contributions of parenthood, 65–66
  early child-care efforts, history of, 66–70
  political participation, 70–72
  public education, patriotic understanding of, 68–70
parents, solidarity among
  and child care as free-market commodity, 21–24
  and child care during World War II, 15–17
  and drive-in daycare, 24–26
  "Mommy Wars," rise of, 26–29
  reclaiming parental solidarity, 27–29

and veto of Comprehensive Child Development Act, 18–19
women's groups and, 19–21
parents, valuing stay-at-home, 53–56, 88–89, 105–107
Parker, Qweyonoh, 31
patriotism, parenthood as
  case for, 62–64, 75–76
  civic readiness, 73–74
  contributions of parenthood, 65–66
  early child-care efforts, history of, 66–70
  political participation, 70–72
  public education, patriotic understanding of, 68–70
Perry, Bruce, 82
Petters, Mike, 127–128
physical health, neglect among parents, 53
policy design, 169–172
political muscle, leveraging business, 150–153
political participation, parenthood and, 70–72
poverty, fighting
  child-care ballot measure, 112–113
  children and poverty, 113–115
  higher education and, 122–123
  identifying the poor, 121
  intergenerational effects, 120–122
  intergenerational effects of child care, 124–125
  parental work schedules, 116–118, 155
  and the promise of free child care, 123–125
  role of child care in, 125–126
  social connection, child care as, 118–120
  transient *vs.* chronic poverty, 121
  welfare, child care as, 115–116
Pregnant Then Screwed advocacy group, 58–59
Pre-Kindergarten (Pre-K), definition of, 7
pre-K systems, history of, 68
Prentice, Susan
  child care as free-market commodity, 19
  the "investible child," 79
Primrose, 151
Princeton University, Eviction Lab, 113–114
Protecting Soldiers and Mothers (Skocpol), 63
public schools, enrollment declines in, 33–34
Putnam, Robert, 72

Q

quality, as perceived in child care settings, 109
Quart, Alissa, 66

R

racial equity, child care and, 110–111
  access to subsidies, 109
  child care workforce, 101–103
  enslavement, and history of non-kin care, 93–95
  eviction risk for children, 113–114
  and family leave, 103–105
  opportunities for mothers, child care and, 99–101, 118–120
  racialized history of child care, 94–96
  segregation and child care programs, 96–99
  solidarity among parents, 107–110
  and stay-at-home parents, 105–107
reading practice, and segregation in child care settings, 98
Reagan, Ronald, 23–24
"Rebuilding the Arsenal of Democracy" (Center for Strategic and International Studies), 132
religious affiliation, effects of child care on, 37–41
religious conservatism, and publicly supported child care, 21–24
Roosevelt, Eleanor, 16
Roosevelt, Theodore, 62
Ruck, Martin D., 73
Ruppanner, Leah, 100
rural communities
  closing of child-care centers in, 41–42
  departure of families, 32–33

S

safety and health, effects of child care on, 34–37
Schneider, Danny, 154
school readiness, problems with, 79–81
schools, enrollment declines in, 33–34
Schulte, Brigid, 113–114
security, local and national
  and birth rates, 134–135
  and collective efficacy, 138–139
  "defense industrial base" (DIB), child care in contributing entities, 132–133
  Department of Defense, child care for service members, 130–131
  food security, 133–134
  foundation for, 128–129
  and global competitiveness, 127–128, 135–137
  implications of child care for, 139–140
  neighborhood security, implications of child care, 137–139
self-determination, child care and, 158
  family freedoms, 159–162
  human flourishing, 159
  national purpose, 166–167
  and universal child care, 162–164
  valuing care, 164–166
settings, for child care, 7–8
Shama, Shahrzad, 169
Shenker-Osorio, Anat, 133
Sheppard-Towner Maternity and Infant Protection Act of 1921, 20
Shields, Kiarcia, 113
Skocpol, Theda
  call for "Parents First" movement, 29
  parenthood and political participation, 63–64
Slaughter, Annie-Marie, 109
Small, Mario
  child care and social connection, 118–120
  child care and social infrastructure, 138–139
Smith, Noah, 75
social connection, child care as, 118–120
social infrastructure, universal child care and, 73–74, 137–139
social reform, and child care, 12–13
solidarity, among parents
  and child care as free-market commodity, 21–24
  and child care during World War II, 15–17
  and drive-in daycare, 24–26
  "Mommy Wars," rise of, 26–29
  reclaiming parental solidarity, 27–29
  and veto of Comprehensive Child Development Act, 18–19
  women's groups and, 19–21
Spiegel, Michelle, 79
Steenland, Sally, 38–39
Stevens, Katharine B., 104
Stockstill, Casey
  racialized history of child care, 95
  segregation in child care settings, 97–98
Strauss, Elissa, 165
stress, child-care shortage and, 46–48
subsidies, access to, 109
summer camps, and status and needs of children, 85–87
Sweden, "night nurseries" in, 117

T

Through the Night, documentary, 118, 120
Toderian, Brent, 33
Tragedy of Child Care in America (Zigler), 28
trauma, effects in childhood, 82
Troubled (Henderson), 82
Trump, Donald, 1
Two-Parent Privilege, The (Kearney), 51

U

Unanticipated Gains (Small), 118–120
urban communities, departure of families, 33–34
Urban Institute, 96, 117

V

van der Kolk, Bessel, 82
VanderWeele, Tyler, 82
Vega, Tanzina, 52
Vermont, leveraging business political muscle in, 150–151
VoteMama Foundation, 70–72

W

Waters, Joe, 12, 27–28
wealth penalty, motherhood and the, 52
Weisman, Rachel, 60
welfare, child care as, 115–116
Wessler, Rachel, 74
What Are Children For? (Berg & Weisman), 60
What Happened to You (Perry), 82
When You Care (Strauss), 165
women's groups, and family-policy changes, 19–21
Women's Joint Congressional Committee, 20
workforce, child care, 101–103
Workforce of Today, Workforce of Tomorrow (U.S. Chamber of Commerce), 78–79
workplaces, family-friendly, 153–156
work schedules, parental, 116–118, 155
World War II, child-care centers during, 15–16

Z

Zelizer, Viviana, 77–78
Zigler, Edward, 28
Zilibotti, Fabrizio, 85

www.ingramcontent.com/pod-product-compliance
Ingram Content Group UK Ltd.
Pitfield, Milton Keynes, MK11 3LW, UK
UKHW040209230326
469240UK00004B/8